CANADIAN
FOREIGN POLICY

IN CRITICAL PERSPECTIVE

Edited by

J. MARSHALL BEIER AND LANA WYLIE

OXFORD
UNIVERSITY PRESS

OXFORD
UNIVERSITY PRESS

70 Wynford Drive, Don Mills, Ontario M3C 1J9

www.oupcanada.com

Oxford University Press is a department of the University of Oxford.
It furthers the University's objective of excellence in research, scholarship,
and education by publishing worldwide in

Oxford   New York
Auckland   Cape Town   Dar es Salaam   Hong Kong   Karachi
Kuala Lumpur   Madrid   Melbourne   Mexico City   Nairobi
New Delhi   Shanghai   Taipei   Toronto

With offices in
Argentina   Austria   Brazil   Chile   Czech Republic   France   Greece
Guatemala   Hungary   Italy   Japan   Poland   Portugal   Singapore
South Korea   Switzerland   Thailand   Turkey   Ukraine   Vietnam

Library and Archives Canada Cataloguing in Publication

Canadian foreign policy in critical perspective / J. Marshall
Beier & Lana Wylie, editors.

Includes bibliographical references and index.
ISBN 978-0-19-542888-9

1. Canada—Foreign relations—Textbooks.
I. Beier, J. Marshall, 1966–   II. Wylie, Lana, 1968-

FC242.B435 2009   327.71   C2009-903605-3

Cover image: Liangpv/iStockphoto.com

Oxford University Press is committed to our environment.
This book is printed on Forest Stewardship Council certified paper, harvested from a responsibly managed forest.

Mixed Sources
Product group from well-managed
forests, and other controlled sources
www.fsc.org Cert no. SW-COC-002358
© 1996 Forest Stewardship Council

FSC

Printed and bound in Canada.

1 2 3 4 -- 13 12 11 10

Contents

Part IV: Other Diplomacies

Acknowledgements

Throughout the process of editing this volume, we have accumulated many debts to students, colleagues, friends, and family. It simply is not possible to recognize all the people who played invaluable roles in the success of the project. Though a few bear specific mention, we are forever indebted to all whose everyday contributions influenced our thinking on virtually every aspect of the project, from inception through to publication.

We cannot well enough express our gratitude to Peter Chambers, Katherine Skene, and Richard Tallman from Oxford University Press. Kate played a decisive role in launching the project and we are grateful for her continued support. Peter has been a wonderful developmental editor. He expertly walked the fine line between encouragement and pressure. He kindly endured our struggles with deadlines, realizing the volume faced some unusual challenges, and for that we are ever grateful.

Of course, we thank the many scholars who contributed to this book. We owe a tremendous debt of gratitude to our 13 contributors. Their intellectual contribution was crucial to the success of the volume, not only for their chapters but also for the supportive, collegial, and insightful ways in which they all participated directly in the shaping of the overall project and of our own thinking about what the volume could, should, and ultimately would be. They must also be thanked for their patience with our comments and requests for revisions as well as for their efforts to meet our deadlines.

We would like to recognize the superb intellectual environment provided by the Department of Political Science at McMaster University. In particular, we owe thanks to our International Relations colleagues, Will Coleman, Peter Nyers, Robert O'Brien, Tony Porter, and Richard Stubbs. We have benefited inestimably from their knowledge and inspiration. Likewise, we are grateful for the comments and suggestions received from McMaster University graduate students, who have been interested and generous with their thoughts and insights from the earliest days of the project. Even more numerous, our undergraduate students, through their intellectual curiosities and palpable hunger for critical scholarship on Canadian foreign policy, first made us recognize the need for this volume. The extraordinary insights and enthusiasm of these various colleagues, students, and scholars enrich our lives daily.

Likewise, we are grateful for the comments and suggestions we received when drafts of the various chapters in the volume were presented at academic conferences. In particular, our thanks are owed to the chairs and discussants at those events. We would also like to acknowledge the efforts of four anonymous reviewers for Oxford University Press. The volume is stronger for their comments.

Our thanks must also be expressed to the staff of the Department of Political Science at McMaster University: Gerald Bierling, Manuela Dozzi, Mara Giannotti, Kathleen Hannan, and Rose Mason. We are fortunate to be able to count on their excellent professional support and personal friendship.

Finally, we are forever grateful to our families for their love and support, and for their willingness to give us the time to complete the volume. Special thanks in this regard are owed to Kaelyn Beier, Chloe Hewitt, Duane Hewitt, and Duncan Wylie. We believe in you all and are humbled by your belief in us.

J. Marshall Beier and Lana Wylie
Hamilton, Ontario
April 2009

Contributors

Samantha L. Arnold is Assistant Professor in the Politics Department at the University of Winnipeg. Her research focuses on critical security studies and Canadian foreign policy; currently she is exploring Canadian policy in the Canadian north and in the broader circumpolar context with an emphasis on bilateral Canada–US relations and the role of northern Indigenous peoples. Her work has been published in various edited volumes and journals.

J. Marshall Beier is Associate Professor in the Department of Political Science at McMaster University. His research and teaching interests are in the areas of critical security studies, Canadian foreign policy, and post-colonial and feminist theory. He is the author of *International Relations in Uncommon Places: Indigeneity, Cosmology, and the Limits of International Theory* (2005, 2009), and has an edited volume forthcoming on the international diplomacies of Indigenous peoples. He is a recipient of the Government of Ontario's Leadership in Faculty Teaching (LIFT) Award.

Colleen Bell is an SSHRC Post-Doctoral Fellow in the Department of Politics, University of Bristol (UK). The focus of her work concerns how freedom is shaped by liberal strategies of security. Currently, she is conducting a project exploring the re-emergence of counterinsurgency doctrine as an effort to strategize culture within the schema of war. She is co-editor of an issue in the *Journal of Intervention and Statebuilding* on post-interventionary societies, has published in other academic journals, and is publishing a book on the politics of freedom in Canada's 'War on Terror.'

Ann Denholm Crosby is Associate Professor in the Political Science Department of York University, specializing in issues of Canadian foreign policy, peace research, and global security. She is the author of *Dilemmas in Defence Decision-Making: Constructing Canada's Role in NORAD, 1958–96* (1998), as well as numerous journal articles and chapters in edited volumes.

Kyle Grayson is a Lecturer in International Politics in the School of Geography, Politics, and Sociology at Newcastle University (UK) and co-editor of a new book series on world politics and popular culture. Previously, he was a post-doctoral fellow of the Canadian Consortium on Human Security. His research interests are critical security studies, human security, and the work of Michel Foucault. He is the author of *Chasing Dragons: Security, Identity, and Illicit Drugs in Canada* (2008).

Alison Howell is a Post-Doctoral Fellow in Politics at the University of Manchester, funded by the Social Sciences and Humanities Research Council of Canada. She is currently completing a book titled *Madness in International Relations: Therapeutic Interventions and the Global Governance of Disorder(s)* that considers how mental health policies are deployed in the governance of suspected terrorists, post-conflict populations, and Canadian soldiers. Recent published works have appeared in several journals, and she is presently conducting research on the growth of new mental health policies and practices in Iraq.

David Mutimer is Associate Professor of Political Science and the Deputy Director of the Centre for International and Security Studies at York University. His research considers issues of contemporary international security, and much of his work has focused on nuclear and other weapons proliferation as a reconfigured security concern in the post-Cold War era. More recently he has turned his attention to the politics of the global War on Terror, and of the regional wars around the world presently being fought by Canada and its allies.

Mark Neufeld has been teaching at Trent University since 1991, where he is Associate Professor and Coordinator of the newly established Global Politics Section. He is co-founder, with Andreas Pickel, of Trent's Centre for the Critical Study of Global Power and Politics, and is the author of *The Restructuring of International Relations Theory* (1995). In addition to Canadian foreign policy, his research interests include critical globalization studies and critical International Relations theory. Though his suggestions for possible Canada Heritage Minutes have yet to meet with success, he remains hopeful.

Stéphane Roussel is Associate Professor in the Department of Political Science at the Université du Québec à Montréal (UQAM) and Canada Research Chair in Canadian Foreign and Defence Policy. His published works include *Culture stratégique et politique de defense: l'expérience canadienne* (2007), *Politique internationale et défense au Canada et au Québec* (2007; with Kim Richard Nossal and Stéphane Paquin), and *L'aide canadienne au développement* (2008; with François Audet and Marie-Eve Desrosiers).

Mark B. Salter is Associate Professor at the School of Political Studies, University of Ottawa, and, besides numerous journal articles and an edited volume, is the author of *Rights of Passage: The Passport in International Relations* and *Barbarians and Civilization in International Relations* (also published in Chinese). He has been a consultant on risk management and aviation and border security for Canadian and American governments, as well as for international think-tanks and organizations. In 2007, he was the recipient of the National Capital Educator's Award and the Excellence in Education Prize at the University of Ottawa.

Heather A. Smith is Associate Professor in International Studies at the University of Northern British Columbia. A former Chair of International Studies and former

Acting Director of the UNBC Centre for Teaching, Learning and Technology, Heather is also a 3M National Teaching Fellow. Her primary areas of research are Canadian climate change policy, gender and Canadian foreign policy, and, most recently, Indigenous perspectives on climate change. She has published numerous book chapters and journal articles.

Rebecca Tiessen is Associate Professor in Global Studies and Leadership at the Royal Military College of Canada and Adjunct Professor in Global Development Studies at Queen's University. Her publications include *Everywhere/Nowhere: Gender Mainstreaming in Development Agencies* (2007) and several journal articles and book chapters on gender and Canadian foreign policy. She has carried out research in Malawi, Zimbabwe, Kenya, Sri Lanka, and Indonesia. She is a board member for Partnership Africa Canada and the Canadian Consortium for University Programs in International Development Studies.

Kathryn Trevenen is Assistant Professor in the Institute of Women's Studies and the School of Political Studies at the University of Ottawa. Her teaching and research focus on gendered media representations of war, gendered aspects of political and cultural ideologies, transnational women's issues and rights, the impact of the HIV/AIDS pandemic on women, and LGBTQ human rights and citizenship. Her work has been presented and published in several edited volumes and journals.

Claire Turenne Sjolander is Professor of Political Science at the School of Political Studies, University of Ottawa. From 2000 to 2006, she held a number of administrative positions in the Faculty of Social Sciences, and in 2007–8, she was Distinguished Scholar in Residence at the State University of New York's Centre for the Study of Canada in Plattsburgh. Her most recent volumes include *Feminist Perspectives on Canadian Foreign Policy* (2003; edited with Heather Smith and Deborah Stienstra) and *Gender and Canadian Foreign Policy* (2005; a special issue of *Canadian Foreign Policy* edited with Heather Smith).

Lana Wylie is Assistant Professor in the Department of Political Science at McMaster University and was a post-doctoral fellow at the Institution for Social and Policy Studies at Yale University. Her current research and teaching interests are in International Relations and comparative politics. Her recent publications include *Perceptions of Cuba: Canadian and American Policies in Comparative Perspective* (2010) and *Our Place in the Sun: Canada and Cuba in the Castro Era* (2009; co-edited with Robert Wright).

Dedicated with affection and gratitude to the memory of John Sjolander, husband, musician, pilot, businessman, handyman, reader, humorist, friend, and supporter of all that we do.

Introduction

What's So Critical about Canadian Foreign Policy?

J. Marshall Beier and Lana Wylie

It is perhaps an odd starting point for a book to assert that, had it not been written, few might ever have noticed the omission. And yet, that is precisely how we find ourselves most immediately inclined to introduce what we nevertheless firmly believe to be both a much needed and overdue contribution to the study of Canadian foreign policy. What is so critical about Canadian foreign policy? How we approach that question depends very much on how we happen to read it, on what we think is being asked. How we answer it is also likely to be quite revealing of our own varied starting points, our commitments, convictions, and perspectives. If we take 'critical' to mean 'of vital importance', then our answer must surely be that much is critical about Canadian foreign policy. This is, after all, a realm of politics wherein the stakes are typically very high, not just for Canadians but for others the world over. A country of Canada's means and influence is daily in a position to have some impact on global outcomes in spheres of diplomacy, development, and war. The particular policy positions adopted—or, in the alternative, rejected—may have the potential to influence the global balance of prosperity and want, who will be heard and who will be silenced, who will live and who will die. In this sense, Canadian foreign policy is critical in the extreme.

While recognizing this, the contributors to this volume are also moved by another usage of 'critical'. Here, 'critical' refers to a broad movement in the social sciences arising from a variety of non-traditional perspectives that unites the chapters of this book in challenging dominant ideas about foreign policy, what it is, what it could be, and how best not only to practise but to analyze and study it. As Robert Cox (1986) has famously described them, 'critical' approaches are distinct from traditional ones—what Cox calls 'problem-solving' theories—in that they do not simply take the world as they find it. Rather, they are more concerned with asking how the status quo came to be, how power works through it, who wins and who loses, and whether alternatives are truly unimaginable or have only been made to seem that way by our habits of analysis and by 'common-sense' understandings of the world that might themselves be little more than habits. Critical theories interrogate the status quo as a set of dominant assumptions that may endure as much because they are uncritically accepted as for any other reason. That is to say, the picture we think we have of 'the real world' or 'the way things work' may exert a limiting influence over our ability to imagine alternatives. It might also be self-perpetuating in the sense that when we allow our assumptions to dictate the limits of what we can do, when we accept the status quo and take it as the given frame of reference, our actions are therefore likely to result in the constant remaking of our world within that very set of limits.

By way of example, one of the most rehearsed and most mythologized tropes of Western historical narrative is instructive: as long as Europeans believed the world to be flat, this belief by itself (they otherwise had the necessary skills and technology) prevented them from circumnavigating the globe just as surely as a truly flat world would have done. Thus, their starting assumptions made unthinkable the very thing that would have placed those assumptions in doubt. What is more, the high stakes attached to those assumptions did not encourage risk-taking as long as the prevailing view was that dire consequences awaited those who ventured too far into unknown waters.

Whatever our perspective on the world, our starting conceptual commitments have a similar effect when we study global political interactions. The assumptions that we make about the world, its limits, and its dangers all work to set the limits of what we think plausible as we take on an issue area wherein the stakes can be every bit as daunting as the threat of sailing off the edge of the world. There is an important sense, then, in which our assumptions give us comfort and urge us to approach each new problem in ways that are familiar—even if they have not always fulfilled our best hopes, we still might feel quite reluctant to abandon them so long as we think they might at least forestall our worst fears. With this in mind, could it be that, rather than fashioning our conceptual tools to address the problems of the world, we might sometimes cast the problems of our world in ways that fit the tools to which we have become so accustomed that to do otherwise has become unthinkable? As the psychologist Abraham Maslow (1966: 15–16) observed, 'it is tempting, if the only tool you have is a hammer, to treat everything as if it were a nail.' In this way, the assumptions bound up in our conceptual approaches may direct us to focus on particular things that then come to limit not only the ways in which we are able to understand a problem or opportunity, but also the range of responses we think possible.

This raises a significant challenge to traditional social science and its founding commitment to the disinterested production of objective knowledge. This commitment has been used to call into question the legitimacy of any research and writing that has a conspicuous political project at its heart. Feminists, Marxists, poststructuralists, and others with a self-consciously transformative political agenda have sometimes been regarded with great suspicion for what mainstream theorists have often decried as their lack of objectivity. And this, in turn, has called into question the reliability of the work of such critically-inclined scholars. Perhaps their politics, it is sometimes suggested, is allowed to shape their conclusions. But if our starting assumptions are bound up in the making of the world we see (as much critical work has urged us to accept is the case), then the mainstream social scientist's choice to work according to the dictates of the status quo is quickly revealed to be as political a choice as any other. And with this, the pretension to objectivity becomes a rather less persuasive claim to knowledge that is somehow more certain and reliable. Instead, social science itself becomes recognizable as a political project, not only when it calls for change but also when it settles on things that might not seem particularly contentious (and it is always worth asking why it is that they do not).

As this view has taken hold and spread it has opened spaces that, over the last two decades, have witnessed significant inroads by critical approaches of various sorts into the study of International Relations (IR). Initially, it was very difficult for such approaches to be heard and to be taken seriously by the realist- and liberal-inspired mainstream. Indeed, a substantial literature developed on precisely this issue, epitomized by Richard Ashley and R.B.J. Walker's (1990) exploration of the sources of opposition to what they termed the new 'dissident' voices, among which their own were prominent. As we reach the end of the first decade of the new millennium, however, the critical voices of feminists, Marxists, postcolonialists, poststructuralists, and others have indelibly marked International Relations as a discipline and have moved the limits of what students of global politics now imagine is possible. Traditional approaches have not disappeared, nor should they, but besides the politics of bare state self-interest or co-operation, early interventions by the critical scholars of the 1980s and 1990s have meant that our discussions have come to include more centrally the importance in global politics of such things as gender, class, race, and other sites of power and contestation previously marginalized or left out altogether.

Unfortunately, the sub-field of foreign policy analysis has not been as much touched by these developments. Few critical interventions have been made in the literature on foreign policy, and the exceptions are notable for being just that. Interestingly, the even more specific area of Canadian foreign policy has seen the publication of a collection of important feminist contributions (Turenne Sjolander et al., 2003). Although this suggests an appetite for such work, until now there has not been a more comprehensive collection of critical offerings. As it happens, most critical scholars are drawn to other issues and questions in global politics than the ones on which focused discussions of foreign policy typically turn, and it is for this reason that the omission of this volume, were it not to have been published, might easily have escaped notice. Foreign policy is concerned centrally with the global political practices by and between states. But critical scholars have tended to be less interested in the state as the presumed global political actor par excellence and, in fact, usually work to decentre the state, at least implicitly if not explicitly. As a result, little in the way of critical work has been directly addressed to the foreign policy analysis community.

As this is the case, it might then be appropriate for us to further muddle our opening question by asking, what is so critical (that is, vitally important) about taking Canadian foreign policy in critical perspective? One answer is that a critical viewpoint helps us to address the things that increasingly inform our students' interests. Many of these students no longer accept the objectivist insistence on the separation of scholarship from an engaged politics. Rather, they see scholarship as inherently and necessarily political, but in studying Canadian foreign policy they have found fewer resources with which to press this view and the sorts of transformative agendas it may enable than they have been accustomed to in other areas of study. More broadly, and returning again to the stakes so often involved, it is important that a fuller range of political perspectives be brought to bear in considering Canada's place in the world and what we might hope to make of it. Until now, the imaginable possibilities at play in discussions and debates about Canadian foreign policy have largely been confined to that which sits well with at least the broad strokes of the status quo. This, in turn, has meant that these discussions and debates have been more hospitable to those whose project is in some way to fine-tune the status quo and to make it function better than to those who see it as something to be transformed or transcended altogether. In Cox's view, mainstream problem-solving work evinces a conservative politics in the sense that it 'takes the world as it finds it, with the prevailing social and power relationships and the institutions into which they are organized, as the given framework for action.' He further points out that the 'general aim of problem-solving is to make these relationships and institutions work smoothly by dealing effectively with particular sources of trouble' (Cox, 1986: 208).

When we relate this to the focus of the present volume and recall that states alone practice what we would call 'foreign policy', the implications of ceding this terrain to mainstream problem-solving approaches become apparent. Working with the aim of smoothing the wrinkles and contradictions in foreign policy thus means implicitly accepting these practices of and by states and, at least to some degree, allying oneself with state power in the sense of seeking to make it more workable. To the extent that our focus is limited to these practices by states when we do foreign policy analysis, we also implicitly accept them as the only bona fide diplomacies, or at least the most important ones. For those who are not persuaded of the appropriateness of this, there is a pressing need for critical reflections and rejoinders that invite and perhaps incite broader imaginings of the possible. It is to this that the contributors to this volume have set themselves in the chapters that follow.

Before proceeding, however, an important caveat is very much in order. One of the contributions of critical approaches in the broader discipline of International Relations has been to show that the world is very much messier than the comparatively tidy and parsimonious theories of the mainstream might sometimes make it seem. The coherence and, indeed, the palpably confident claims of much mainstream scholarship in the discipline owe much to this parsimony, which has traditionally been held up as a virtue in theorizing. After all, a central and imperative function of theory has always been presumed to be the simplification of a complex world such that some manageable sense can be made of it and some workable propositions might be made about what to do in it. As far as that goes, it is not particularly contentious. But mainstream theories have also tended to weave this together with a project aiming at the production of objective knowledge, and sometimes claim the fulfillment of this project. As critical theorists have been at pains to point out, however, the need to simplify necessarily leaves out many voices, ideas, interests, and perspectives. This seems very much at odds with the goal of producing objective knowledge since there is no settled objective truth as to whom or what matters and whom or what does not matter, or at least matters less. The choices here are necessarily value-laden ones and must therefore be expressions of a politics and of the circulations of power that allow some voices to rise above and silence others (Der Derian, 1989: 6).

Recognizing this, a volume drawing together a range of scholars committed to various critical perspectives is unavoidably a messy reflection of a world that is much messier still. Readers should not seek to find the same kind of coherence or continuity from chapter to chapter that might shape and guide a collection written from a specific limited perspective, whether realist, liberal, or Marxist, where there is greater consensus about the contours of the world and whom or what in it matters most. Were this volume to have turned exclusively to Marxists, or feminists, or poststructuralists, the reader might expect to find such broad agreement based in shared assumptions about the world, how it is today, and what's wrong (or right) with it. At the same time, it is important to recognize that power also works through this very formula for coherence because it subtly draws authority for each successive voice, and for all in sum, from an aesthetic of consensus that itself functions by placing at least a thread of continuity beyond critical examination. That is, the price of coherence is, of necessity, that some things are simply taken as settled and can therefore tie one chapter to the next thematically in terms of much deeper commitments about our world and whom or what in it matters most.

Without putting too fine a point on it, the problem remains that ours is a messy world, politically and socially, and it defies our attempts to make definitive pronouncements about it. Not least, this defiance comes through the marginalized voices that will inevitably be raised against each and every account—mainstream or critical—we might care to make of it. We must take care, then, that our project is not simply to substitute this or that critical approach for some other (mainstream or critical) that we, for whatever reasons, find wanting or objectionable. In this sense, the continuity and coherence that underwrite the authority of privileged voices are revealed as inseparable from circulations of power. Since the central aim of this volume is to be critical in the sense of disturbing power, privilege, and the pronouncements they might make upon whom or what matters most, one of the most critical (in both senses of the word) moves that can be made is to refuse the temptation to seize authority for critical voices by affecting the aesthetic of the authoritative voice. This aesthetic flows ultimately from a pretension to objectivity that most self-consciously critical theorists would disavow.

Just as the perspectives of the authors that follow are varied, so, too, are the claims they make about whom or what matters. With as broad a rubric as Canadian foreign policy to bind them together (and most venture well beyond the usual boundaries here, too), the result is a volume with an aesthetic that might feel more like a sequence of unsettling turns, drops, and about-faces. This aesthetic, however, should not be characterized superficially as some 'necessary evil' owing only to the choice to range across a wide array of issues, ideas, and perspectives. Like the use of first-person narrative discussed by Heather Smith in her chapter, it is also something much more than a casual disregard for the long-held conventions of academic writing. Rather, it is purposeful and deliberate. It is an aesthetic choice in its own right and one that is very much consistent with the aim of the volume to disturb our comfortable assumptions, to unsettle our pretensions, and to encourage critical thought. If some of the turns taken seem strange or disquieting, they simultaneously urge us to ask why that is: what is it that we think we know about Canadian foreign policy that makes them seem this way and, even more important, why do we think we know the things we do? This is not a book conceived to impart definitive answers about Canadian foreign policy. On the contrary, the intent is to promote the testing of boundaries in a world that is messier than we might wish and that resists the conventions we would seek to impose on it. If it makes us uneasy about Canada's place in such a world and prompts us to ask 'why?' about the things we might otherwise have taken for granted, it will have succeeded on these modest terms.

Part I includes two chapters that examine how we approach the task of making sense of Canadian foreign policy. In Chapter 1, Heather Smith looks at how we 'do' Canadian foreign policy as scholars. She asks us to consider how we have been regulated either as students or as teachers by expectations about what constitutes Canadian foreign policy. Smith challenges us to think critically about how we might have been disciplined. She calls for greater acceptance of diversity in our methods and approaches to doing Canadian foreign policy. In Chapter 2, Samantha Arnold is also investigating how we 'do' Canadian foreign policy. While Smith explores this for students and teachers of Canadian foreign policy, Arnold turns her attention to the ways in which practitioners do Canadian foreign policy. She asks us to question our assumptions about what constitutes public diplomacy. In particular, she wants us to question our understanding of public diplomacy as the 'practice of projecting a ready-made national identity abroad in support of foreign policy goals'. Finding foreign policy to be more complicated and multi-faceted than traditional approaches might sometimes imagine, she argues that public diplomacy is part of the process of constructing the Canadian national identity rather than simply a tool for projecting that identity.

In Part II, Fighting the Global War on Terror, the authors explore the various ways Canada has positioned itself vis-à-vis the US-led 'War on Terror'. In Chapter 3, Ann Denholm Crosby turns a critical eye to Canadian and American co-operation over continental security issues. She explores the implications of the recommendations of binational military studies and warns that the partnership recommended under the guise of continental defence will in fact consolidate the defence, security, and foreign policy interests of Canada and the United States in a manner ensuring the Canadian adoption of the American vision of the world. She calls on us to resist these efforts. To do so, she argues, we must challenge the dominant theoretical discourses on Canada–US defence and security relations. Yet, the reader will notice that it seems as though there is an abrupt turn within the chapter from a focus on the binational report to the praxis of resistance. As readers, we may be made uncomfortable by this unexpected turn, and we may feel even more out of our comfort zone when the chapter evolves from a focus on resistance in terms of the dominant IR theoretical perspectives to a discussion of the possible genetic sources of culture. The author has chosen to disrupt our reading of her chapter in this way. We need to ask ourselves why it is so unsettling to make that turn.

The next two chapters also challenge the dominant discourse of Canadian identity and of Canada's role in the world. In Chapter 4, Claire Turenne Sjolander and Kathryn Trevenen explore how the Canadian state attempts to manage and construct public debate over Canadian foreign policy in wartime. Most particularly, they examine the efforts to depict Canada both as a warrior nation and as a benevolent peacekeeper. In a similar vein, Colleen Bell in Chapter 5 questions Canada's self-image as a force for peace in the world. Bell shows us how Canada's actions in Afghanistan offer little in the way of contributing to greater peace. In fact, she argues, systemic forms of violence can be carried out in the name of peace, and thus not only should we question the military mission but we should also question the developmental practices that are 'too often and too easily aligned with "peace"'.

Turning to the impact of the War on Terror at home, in Chapter 6 Mark Salter shows us how state elites are able to expand their power and restrict public debate about the relevant policies simply by naming a particular issue as a security issue. Calling these elites 'professionals of insecurity', Salter demonstrates that they have created an environment that allows for the greater surveillance of private life. Through an examination of the international agreements on border security, he shows that the Canadian–American border has been delocalized away from the geographical edges of the two states, facilitating the intrusion of foreign policy concerns into domestic policy-making.

Although the remaining chapters turn away from an explicit investigation of the War on Terror, they often address the implications of Canada's role in the post-9/11 world. The chapters in Part III, Security and Self after 9/11, consider some of the 'fallout' and 'fall into' inherent in Canada's foreign policy in a contemporary world where nothing seems certain and the ground we stand on appears always to be shifting. In Chapter 7, Kyle Grayson demonstrates how debates over the relevance and legitimacy of human security actually reveal a host of shared foundations that are not subject to critical scrutiny. He argues that both sides of the debate over human security shared an understanding of Canada's tradition in international affairs, an acceptance of the continuing relevance of state security concerns, and a geopolitical logic focused on containment. He also notes that all sides of the debate made use of the same representations of Canadian identity that involve 'doing good in the world', including 'peacekeeper', 'middle power', and 'international citizen'. David Mutimer, in Chapter 8, also addresses Canadians' desire to see themselves as 'doing good' in the world. Thus, though Mutimer points out that Canada has multiple nuclear identities, such as nuclear salesman and willing participant in nuclear alliances, Canadians prefer to think of themselves as the responsible arms controllers.

In Chapter 9, Alison Howell examines the government's narrative of post-traumatic stress disorder (PTSD) among members of the Canadian Forces. Taking up Heather Smith's call to expand our research methodologies and where we look when we think about Canadian foreign policy, Howell uses a popular painting depicting a soldier suffering from what is now seen as PTSD. In doing so, she addresses the assumption that the condition known as post-traumatic stress disorder is a medical rather than a political problem. Howell argues that the politics of militarization is lost by treating war trauma as a medical problem. In the end, this process reinforces a structure that allows soldiers to be redeployed. Mark Neufeld also addresses an unspoken assumption in Chapter 10. He points out that the assumption that the Pearsonian internationalist tradition is worthy and legitimate serves as a foundation for both sides of the debate about Canada's involvement in the military campaign in Afghanistan. Neufeld challenges that assumption and calls on us to demystify and reject the Pearsonian legacy.

Finally, the four chapters in Part IV, Other Diplomacies, explore issues and topics traditionally excluded from discussions of Canadian foreign policy. In Chapter 11, Rebecca Tiessen explicitly rejects the idea that the state is the necessary starting point of foreign policy analysis. She examines youth internship abroad experiences in the context of Canadian foreign policy and perceptions of 'global citizenship'. She asks how young Canadians abroad comprise part of Canada's foreign policy and international development agendas. Stéphane Roussel, in Chapter 12, looks at the near-total exclusion of French-Canadian scholarship from the English-Canadian literature on Canadian foreign policy, and examines the related exclusion of the question of national unity from Canadian foreign policy scholarship. Roussel speaks to an inward focus we do not see in foreign policy analysis writ large. Like Roussel, Marshall Beier, in Chapter 13, considers what is excluded from discussion. Beier argues that though we still need to talk about state actors in foreign policy analysis, we need to understand that they are not the only actors engaged in diplomacy, and that other ways of understanding diplomacy itself do not find expression in the ways we are accustomed to treating our subject matter. In particular, Beier considers the diplomacies of Indigenous peoples around the drafting of the UN Declaration on the Rights of Indigenous Peoples and asks what is revealed by Canada's recent withdrawal of its support for this historic initiative, both with respect to the practice of Canadian foreign policy and the assumptions we bring to studying it. Finally, in Chapter 14 Lana Wylie concludes the volume with some very personal reflections on what she, as a traditionally trained scholar of Canadian foreign policy, has come to find so critical about critical perspectives.

Together, these varied contributions explore underappreciated aspects and nuances of Canadian foreign policy and seek to situate it in contexts not always well enough considered but in which foreign policy is nevertheless intimately and inextricably entangled. The result is not a volume that aims to provide either a detailed survey of one issue area or a comprehensive survey of many. Others have already done that, and have done it well. It can fairly be said, then, that there is much that has not been addressed herein. But there is also much herein that is not seen elsewhere, and it is in this that the purpose and the contribution of this volume are to be found. The contributors propose different kinds of questions than the ones that may issue first from prevailing 'common senses', and thereby sketch the contours of possibilities we might not have considered. Working from a range of different perspectives, they explore issues whose relevance to Canadian foreign policy might not always be immediately apparent or that challenge us to think differently about that which we might too easily take for granted. In so doing, they complicate our understanding of Canada's conduct and place in the world by challenging our understanding of Canada itself and by including in the world of diplomacy actors, interests, and ways of being that we might too seldom consider. Thus, the authors suggest that a fuller range of options is available to us when we turn to the pressing and often high-stakes issues with which students and practitioners of foreign policy are daily forced to grapple. For these reasons, we believe this text will be welcomed and, we hope, will invite further reflections on Canadian foreign policy from self-consciously critical perspectives.

Part I
Doing Canadian Foreign Policy

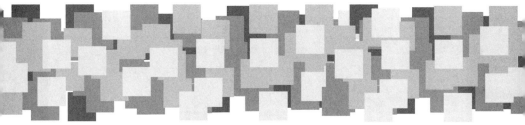

Chapter One

The Disciplining Nature of Canadian Foreign Policy

Heather A. Smith

Yikes! Where to begin? What to say? How to say it? Can I use first person? Will it be logical? Reasonable? What about evidence? How much evidence? Which evidence? What counts as evidence? What about method? Do I need a thesis statement? Who am I writing for? Who's my audience? Where do I begin?

The comments above represent the dialogue between my 'scholarly' training and my critical feminist position, between the 'researcher' and the 'teacher', between the administrator and the educational developer—in brief, my multiple locations, my past and my future. These questions and how they are answered have deep methodological, epistemological, and ontological implications for our and my understanding of Canadian foreign policy.

Writing this chapter has resulted in reflections that have been excessively disruptive. The result is not 'comfort text' (Zalewski, 2006: 47)—either for myself or for you, the reader. If you join me in the voyage that is this chapter, I hope the path is one that challenges you, disquiets you, and encourages reflection on who you are in the 'discipline'. I urge you to find your own answers, because I am disinclined towards authoritative answers. Through text, tone, and style, my intent is to expose the disciplining nature of Canadian foreign policy rather than provide 'concrete answers to concrete questions' (ibid., 60) in a detached, authoritative manner that replicates our disciplinary method, tone, and style.

While pondering the disciplining nature of Canadian foreign policy it struck me that 'disciplining' has a social and political context. As J. Marshall Beier and Samantha Arnold (2005: 43) observe: 'disiplinarity is a practice'. We are disciplined by agencies external to the university and by the culture of the university. Disciplining occurs across disciplines and within disciplines, and is deeply embedded in how we function. We are disciplined in and by our teaching, research, and administration, and the various locations of disciplinary acts reinforce each other.

I must also admit I wonder if sometimes I reinforce the discipline that is so very deeply and structurally embedded in our practices and our institutions. In the end, I am unwilling to give in to the coercive disciplining and choose to be delightfully unruly, and I invite you to join me in mucking about the mess and working together to build our futures.

Explicit Reader Engagement

Central to my work (2003, 2005) and that of other feminist International Relations (IR) scholars (Enloe, 1996; Sylvester, 1996) has been an advocacy of 'everyday practice' and the inclusion of alternative/multiple voices. Combine the theoretical predisposition towards 'everyday practice' with feminist pedagogy and you will understand the desire to engage the reader, early and often.

Engagement is encouraged, in part, through the use of the personal narrative, which establishes a different kind of relationship with the reader than if one engaged in a formal detached style of writing. Engagement is also encouraged by authenticating the voice of the reader in some way (Doty, 2001). The experience of the reader is significant and noteworthy. To engage you, the reader, recognizes you read with particular insights that can enhance the work. You, as reader, then, are part of the everyday practice. Finally, engaging you, whether you are a student or a colleague, provides you with an opportunity for reflection, and that is when our learning is most transformative.

So here is the task: the topic of the chapter is the 'disciplining' nature of the discipline. What does this mean to you? Have you had an experience where you have been told the how and what of Canadian foreign policy in such a way that if you felt you dissented there were negative implications? How did this make you feel?

What are your answers? Keep these answers in mind as you read this chapter. Return to your answers at the end of the chapter and consider the relevance of your reflections to the topic at hand. My sense is that so many of us have had these kinds of experiences that volumes could be written if we told our stories.

These stories—our personal stories—matter. For me to expose my experience with disciplining runs the risk of attempting to universalize my experience and that is not the intent. My story is not authoritative and I suspect there are a host of untold, almost secret, experiences that are similar. Yet, we are too often rendered mute by experiences labelled 'personal' or 'anecdotal'. Some of our experiences we hold tightly because we deem them dangerous to our own place in the field. Yet, we need to acknowledge and speak to those experiences. So, reader, use this place and time to begin to acknowledge your experiences.

While on the point of experiences, it seems worthwhile to provide some of my background. Having a glimpse at my background provides some understanding as to how I view Canadian foreign policy. It provides some context for what follows.

A Bit about Me

I was trained traditionally in the study of Canadian foreign policy. I had some exposure to feminist and critical theory but it was not the focus of my doctoral work. It's safe to say that I moved from working from a mainstream liberal perspective to critical feminism after completing my Ph.D. The shift has multiple sources.

In the latter part of my doctoral studies I was inspired by my officemate, David Black, to give Robert Cox a second look. Another friend introduced me to feminist IR theorizing. I also found myself in a position where as a 'woman' I was to teach the feminist courses and I was lucky to have feminist colleagues who provided me with support to design course outlines. I was also introduced to colleagues such as Claire Turenne Sjolander and Deborah Stienstra, who would become guides, mentors, thoughtful critics, and friends on the path to the present day, where I would categorize myself as a critical feminist. I also need to acknowledge the host of positive experiences and engaged discussions with scholars I will shortly label 'mainstream'. They read my work, engaged me in thoughtful discussions and through their practice, and modelled a pluralist approach to the discipline. We didn't always agree but that's OK. Conversations, space to express my ideas, and often thoughtful challenges to explain myself were central to all of this.

Critical feminist academic/professor/student/scholar is where I position myself within the field. It is also worth noting that over the last several years I've undertaken a heavy administrative load, having been a chair, a dean, and an acting director of the University of Northern British Columbia Centre for Teaching, Learning and Technology. In the midst of this I won a 3M National Teaching Fellowship in 2006. I have worn many hats over the last several years and those experiences shape my understanding of 'disciplining'.

Defining the Discipline

If there is one part of this chapter that makes me the most uneasy, it is this one. I'm uneasy because to define the discipline requires that I adopt some tone of authority and engage in the categorization of others in ways that are akin to pigeon-holing.[1] Given the diversity of approaches and content areas in the study of Canadian foreign policy, I will undoubtedly do a disservice to that diversity through labelling, and for that I do apologize. Nonetheless, I will dive into the deep end, caveats and all.

What Is a Discipline?

In his assessment of International Relations as a discipline, Chris Brown has suggested we need to move beyond the understanding of a discipline as simply a degree subject and proposes that 'we look to a discipline as having its own characteristic focus distinct from other branches of learning, its own methods, modes of training and habits of thought . . . to be adept in a discipline means to practice a specific trade' (Brown, 2007: 347). The value of Brown's definition is that disciplines are not simply about content but also about teaching students and conducting research. Ken Booth (2007) and Kim Nossal (2006) add to this the sense that our disciplines do not exist in a vacuum and we need to remember the context of working in and for universities, funded by provinces and granting councils, supported by and engaged with industry, and so forth. This understanding informs my discussion below.

Is Canadian Foreign Policy a Discipline?

So, is Canadian foreign policy (CFP) a discipline? I would be hard-pressed to make the argument that CFP is a discipline. It is an area of study that is a branch of International Relations and, hence, political studies, but not itself a discipline.

However, I do not have to argue that Canadian foreign policy is a discipline to argue that it is marked by particular types of content and influenced by modes of training and habits of thought (Nossal, 2000). The content has a canon, and the modes and habits also function as implicit rules and regulations that discipline when breached. With this in mind, we can turn our attention to a description of the content, theory, and modes of training as traditionally understood.

According to Kim Nossal (1997: 4), author of the most commonly used text in field, foreign policy 'is concerned with explaining the behavior of those who have the capability to exercise supreme political authority over a given set of issue areas, for a given people in a given territory.'

Content commonly found in mainstream texts on Canadian foreign policy includes:

- the role and status debate;
- the Golden Era;
- the role and impact of the provinces, Parliament, prime ministers, and society, as well as Canada–US relations;
- the evolution of defence and security policy;
- trade policy;
- multilateralism and Canada's various interactions with a host of international organizations;
- human rights;
- peacekeeping;
- development assistance;
- Canadian interaction with other states.

And the list goes on (Nossal, 1997; Cooper, 1997). The traditional literature includes a variety of scholars working from positivist-influenced theories and epistemologies. Some scholars have been labelled or have self-identified as realist or some variation thereof, such as Kim Nossal or Denis Stairs, and some are defined as liberal, such as Stéphane Roussel. Some authors, such as Tom Keating, are influenced by the English School, while others, such as John Kirton, have drawn off from a combination of American schools of thought. So there is a broad scope of literature under the umbrella term 'traditional Canadian foreign policy'.

This literature, while diverse in its theoretical orientation, is nonetheless marked by a shared commitment to a problem-solving approach to Canadian foreign policy. Problem-solving theory, as described by Robert Cox (1996: 88), 'takes the world as it finds it, with the prevailing social and power relationships and institutions into which they are organized, as the given framework for action.' Cox (ibid., 88–90) further notes that problem-solving theory assumes it is possible to identify laws and regularities, is ahistorical, claims to be value-free, and serves the interests of those within a given order by not explicitly questioning that order.

In terms of the description of 'modes of training', this area is even more slippery than the areas of content and theoretical predispositions. When I think of modes of training, I think of the hidden elements of our training in terms of 'how to be a professor'. What is a professor of Canadian foreign policy? Based on my experience, our professional code is one that prizes research: peer-reviewed publications in the form of journal articles or university press books. Single authorship is prized and grants are deemed a reflection of one's standing in the discipline. Teaching—well, in my day little attention was paid to training us as teachers and so the message you get is that this isn't what the discipline is about (and if you think of prizes granted at the Canadian Political Science Association, it is worth noting, as of 2009, there is one prize for teaching but several for research).

Most of the teaching I was exposed to was 'stand and deliver'. Beyond that, I was taught to write formally, gather evidence, and design a thesis statement and was exposed to giving presentations. I recall my supervisor giving me tips on how to present (which I still use), but there was no training on giving a good presentation and no preparation for the forum (and I use that specifically in the lions vs Christians kind of way) that is conference presentation. As for administration, I learned that through observation and a lot of trial and error. And what prepared me best for administration, especially at the senior levels, was an understanding of realism.

In contrast to the traditional content, theoretical predispositions, and modes of training, there are those who have engaged Canadian foreign policy from a post-positivist or critical perspective, including critical theorists, feminists (at least some), post-colonial theorists, and postmodernists. Again drawing from Cox (ibid., 87), these theorists share an understanding that 'there is . . . no such thing as theory in itself, divorced from a standpoint in time and space', or as Steve Smith (2004: 503) writes: 'there is no view from nowhere.' Critical theory 'stands apart from the prevailing order of the world and asks how that order came about. Critical theory . . . does not take institutions and social and power relations for granted but calls them into question' (Cox, 1996: 89). We question institutions and social and power relations, and acknowledge that 'theory is always for someone and for some purpose' (ibid., 87).

Those engaged in critical projects make 'a normative choice in favor of a social and political order different from the prevailing order' (ibid., 90), and are skeptical of the hegemonic vision of what constitutes appropriate theorizing in Canadian foreign policy. Critical theory, as characterized by Steve Smith (2004: 507), does not cloak itself in the language of 'legitimate social science' and 'objectivity' as a means by which to avoid 'normative or moral stances', and we are willing to 'question all social and political boundaries and all systems of inclusion and exclusion' (Linklater, 1996: 286).

Just as 'mainstream' scholars address a wide range of content areas, so, too, do critical and feminist scholars. In the Turenne Sjolander, Smith, and Stienstra (2003) volume, *Feminist Perspectives on Canadian Foreign Policy*, content areas covered include trade, internationalism, human rights, refugees, sex trafficking, peacekeeping, human security, and sustainable development. In contrast to Nossal's understanding, many of the chapters refer to voices that would not be considered authoritative, and there is also a chapter in the volume on teaching, which to my knowledge is the first of its kind in a 'scholarly' volume on Canadian foreign policy. Other areas that have been examined from critical perspectives include Indigenous peoples (Beier, 2007), hegemony and the middle-power myth (Neufeld, 2007), and Canada's relations with various world regions (Black, 2007). Of course, as with the discussion of content areas covered by mainstream scholars, this brief list cannot capture the depth and breadth of analysis taking place under the umbrella of critical scholarship (as is clear from this volume).

Is there a disciplinary way of teaching? There are content expectations, but what about style, or are content expectations also about style? This question is hard to answer. While the stand-and-deliver model of teaching was the way I was taught, the growing requirements for teaching dossiers, the growth of teaching informed by the scholarship of teaching, and the increased focus on student learning outcomes may translate into a change of teaching style. This merits further consideration.[2]

Feeling Disciplined?

So what does it mean to be disciplined? Let's turn to dictionary.com for some insight on the definition. This may seem an unlikely source to some who are skeptical of the value of such a site—they may wonder if it's up to appropriate academic standards and may encourage students to use a 'real' dictionary and suggest that my use of this website is setting poor standards. At the end of the day this comes down to the question of 'whose knowledge?', and using a site such as dictionary.com thrusts us right into the debate between sites of knowledge (literally and figuratively) and sources of knowledge that confound us in the classroom full of millennial students and challenge us across perspectives. Rest assured, the definition below from dictionary.com actually comes from the *Random House Unabridged Dictionary*.

So, according to dictionary.com, a 'discipline' can be an area of study, but more interesting for our purposes is the notion that it means 'training to act in accordance with rules; drill: *military discipline*; activity, exercise, or a regimen that develops or improves a skill; training; . . . punishment inflicted by way of correction and training; the rigor or training effect of experience, adversity, etc; . . . behavior in accord with rules of conduct; behavior and order maintained by training and control; . . . a set or system of rules and regulations; an instrument of punishment, esp. a whip or scourge, used in the practice of self-mortification or as an instrument of chastisement in certain religious communities; . . . a branch of instruction or learning; . . . to punish or penalize in order to train and control; correct; chastise; from Latin *disciplina,* from *discipulus, pupil,* see disciple'(*Random House Unabridged Dictionary,* 2006). These definitions are in accordance with my meaning—a sense of being trained to act in accordance with sometimes unwritten rules, designed to keep you in order; indeed, sometimes you feel controlled, and there is often concern for the implications of dissent. You somehow feel that you will be excommunicated.[3]

As argued above, discipline comes from a variety of sites and in a variety of forms. In the interest of staying orderly, let's deal with each of these in turn.

Disciplining by Agencies External to the University

Perhaps the best example I have of being disciplined by agencies external to the university is found in the introduction to Turenne Sjolander, Smith, and Stienstra (2003: xii), where we tell the story of having received a grant from the Canadian Centre for Foreign Policy Development (which we greatly appreciated) but then were chastised by Foreign Affairs staff for our work. Our approach to gender and Canadian foreign policy garnered some hostility. Ultimately, however, the volume was published. There may also be instances that readers have experienced with other granting agencies and funding partners that are not public, or cannot be made public, that speak to this kind of disciplining.

Disciplining Nature of University Culture

Kim Nossal's address as president of the Canadian Political Science Association in 2006 eloquently assesses the disciplining nature of university culture. Nossal does not use the language of discipline; rather, he refers to the '*cult of research intensivity*' (Nossal, 2006: 378). Nossal qualifies the use of the term 'cult' with reference to its Latin meaning of worship when he states: 'Use of this word is intended to convey the degree to which research intensivity is regarded . . . with a kind of reverential enthusiasm for the benefits that embracing research intensivity brings.' Then he discusses the tension between teaching and research and appears to lament the pressure to shift away from teaching in favour of research. He notes, for example, that we have course buyouts for research and administration, and teaching-only positions are routinely regarded as somehow lesser than research-focused positions. He also challenges the assumption that one cannot be both an excellent researcher and teacher and speaks to commodification of the university, where research now becomes knowledge production.

Ken Booth (2007: 362) has made similar observations of the British academy, noting the 'growing corporate involvement/intrusion . . . into university life' and 'our increasingly professionalised, commodified and bureaucratised lives'. Booth goes a bit further than Nossal, in terms of the connections he makes to the state and the state of the world in which we live, when he writes: 'the threat is of a future in which universities, and departments of international studies, would exist in a world increasingly dominated by states whose political culture has become hyper-nationalistic, militaristic and authoritarian' (ibid., 363). We are asked by Booth to consider if we would and will stand up to these trends and he warns us all to 'not be smug' (ibid.).

Booth and Nossal remind us that we must be mindful that CFP and IR do not exist in a vacuum. Giving real-life examples to support the disciplining nature of the university culture is far too easy for any of us. Have you ever been told you spend too much time doing research and should focus more on your teaching? The reverse is more likely. Have you ever sat in budget meetings where the language was cleansed to avoid discussion of people? Have you ever dealt with staff units that must find external funding to support their core functions? What are the names on your buildings? Is a 3M award as prestigious as an SSHRC grant?

And so the message I received and continue to receive is that the university is a place of competition and bottom lines where knowledge products are valued over committed teaching and 'impractical research'. It is in such a setting that our disciplines exist.

Disciplining across Disciplines and Disciplinary Niches

For anyone who has engaged in interdisciplinary work, you will know that there remains resistance to interdisciplinarity, and those brave enough to follow this path will encounter criticism. The criticism often comes in the form of peer reviews suggesting the writer has a lack of knowledge of the field in which she or he dares to traverse. These disciplinary trespassers, however, are sometimes critiqued for their use of particular kinds of evidence. For example, in my case, I write on climate change, and one of the first pieces I wrote was rejected by a reviewer who didn't like that I used statements by the Prime Minister to back up my argument. The reviewer said, 'I don't care if this is the Prime Minister of Canada, he's wrong.' Yet, the point of the evidence wasn't whether or not the Prime Minister was scientifically accurate; the point was that the Prime Minister had made a public commitment that merited consideration.

I've also recently begun publishing in the area of teaching Canadian foreign policy—what some would call the scholarship of teaching and learning. The difficulty has been that I've been criticized for not including enough on the scholarship of teaching and learning, for either including too much Canadian foreign policy (read: content) or not enough Canadian foreign policy content, and for saying too much about the scholarship of teaching and learning. Hmm . . . makes you wonder, doesn't it? I feel like I'm in some disciplinary pincher move with both areas telling me not to integrate the literatures and both looking for the dominance of content or theory of their own type, rather than providing for openings in discussion.

While I am on the point of disciplining between disciplines and teaching, let me note that as a faculty developer, who does presentations on student engagement in the classroom, or learning objectives, I've run into disciplines' sense of how they train their scholars. As a social scientist, I am regularly told that the strategies I suggest won't work for someone who teaches the sciences. It's almost like a double trespass: talking about teaching is assumed by many, ipso facto, to be a failure to privilege research, and daring to suggest there might be some common features in terms of teaching and research, at the same time, is beyond the pale.

Disciplining within Disciplines

Of all the areas of 'discipline', that of disciplining within the disciplines is the type with which we most commonly identify. A wide range of disciplining falls under this category.

There are, for example, the often quiet whispers from folks who say 'are you sure you want to be known as a feminist?' (read: is this really a wise move?). One of my favourite stories about such a whisper occurred when someone told me at a book fair that doing feminist research is something I should keep as a sideline because it won't get me anywhere.

There are also the accusations of bias in my work that I always find amusing because, given my starting point, I'm pretty much convinced that we are all biased. To accuse another of bias requires that the accuser has some sort of foundation by which to make that claim. All of our theorizing comes from somewhere. This argument doesn't always go over well with editors, and thus there is a cost in terms of what could have been a good solid publication and, indeed, perhaps my reputation as a 'scholar'.

Some accusations or assumptions of bias find their way into the blind peer review process, too. Mark Neufeld (1999a) wrote in a footnote to his contribution to a round table on Canadian foreign policy about a piece that was rejected and ultimately published in *Studies in Political Economy*.[4]

One type of disciplining I've also experienced is public chastisement. I was told my work was silly—at a conference. I just shrugged my shoulders, thinking a reaction wasn't merited. Of course, I am an associate professor, and so whether this person thought my work was silly was not of immediate importance. If I was a graduate student or a beginning assistant professor, my response may have been entirely different.

Disciplining comes through textbooks and course outlines. Textbooks reinforce the subject and method of Canadian foreign policy, and the canon includes too few examples of critical and feminist work. The recent reader by Duane Bratt and Chris Kukucha (2007: 5–6) does include a range of authors, but those engaged from critical perspectives are referred to as using 'non-traditional' approaches, which is kind of an odd label. As Claire Turenne Sjolander (2007: 104) shows, the dominant text adopted in Canadian foreign policy classes remains Nossal. It is 'the Bible'. The second most popular text is Keating, with the work of Denis Stairs, John Kirton, Andrew Cooper, and Don Munton figuring prominently (ibid.). She doesn't mention the extent to which critical or feminist work is used in the courses, but in conversation has indicated that alternative approaches did not figure prominently in Canadian foreign policy course outlines.[5] How we shape our course outlines is a disciplining practice and those outlines send signals to students about what is authoritative and valued. The boundaries of the field are defined in 13 weeks.

How we teach also matters. My teaching is now very different from what it was in the past and is informed by more self-selected, but not required, training. I've heard that some who are more research-oriented find my passion for teaching weird and unorthodox, but I believe the classroom is a sacred space. And as an administrator tasked with promoting teaching and learning excellence, I can guarantee that my view is not universally shared.

But I Wonder . . .

Throughout this chapter I have described my experience with the different sites of disciplining, but I begin to wonder if I, too, engage in disciplining of sorts. I know in my teaching, research, and administration I've made judgements based on my standards. Think about it: Do you have standards for what is considered 'good' research? Have you ever reviewed an article and rejected it? Have you ever graded a paper? Have you reviewed an sshrc proposal and rejected or supported it? Have you designed a course outline? Have you ever excluded someone from a conference because you didn't like their work? Have you delivered a paper in the traditional stand-and-deliver way, thus reinforcing standard practice? Have you written formally? Worried about evidence?

I think it's safe to say that many who call themselves critical theorists have engaged in scholarly activity and have acted in ways that reinforce the 'standards' of scholarship as we know it. Yet, I have a feeling that our engagement in scholarship isn't the same as engaging in disciplining acts that reinforce the status quo of Canadian foreign policy.

I've had papers rejected by obviously well-read reviewers who required more work on my part, and they were right. I've also had work rejected because I didn't fit with someone's sense of the canon or because they felt that feminist work was silly. Disciplining is subtle (sometimes). Not meeting standards for originality or content or writing has a different feel from that of being excommunicated for heretical writing.

Some Concluding Thoughts

When I spend too much time pondering disciplining it makes me think it might just be easier to give in and give up. I know there are some who will seek to dismiss this piece as nothing but the equivalent of a personal diary entry—the vain ramblings of a navel-gazing scholar. It will be criticized for a lack of data or for not being broadly generalizable. Part of me says the point wasn't to be generalizable. Why would I ask people to reflect on their personal experience, reject my claims as an authoritative voice, and dispense with standard operating procedures if I wanted it to be generalizable? There is, however, that other part of me, the part that will point to the work cited in this chapter—the comments made by Mark Neufeld, the experience faced by Claire Turenne Sjolander, Deborah Stienstra, myself, and indeed all the authors of the feminist foreign policy volume, and the work of J. Ann Tickner (1997), Roxanne Doty (2001), and Marysia Zalewski (2006) that speak to disciplining. How many cases are enough for it to become generalizable? Oh, the disciplining: counting cases to make my experience valid. If I give in to these disciplining structures, I allow myself to be silenced. I am unwilling to be afraid.

We know there have been openings and a slow accumulation of scholarship informed by post-positivist approaches. The work of Robert Cox, Cynthia Enloe, David Black, Claire Turenne Sjolander, Deborah Stienstra, Steve Smith, Roxanne Doty, Marysia Zalewski, and a host others has shown me that there are different routes for critical scholars and we can be part of creating those alternative routes for each other.

The future I seek is one where we expand our research methodologies to be more inclusive: consider the use of narrative, ethnography, and photos as an expression of alternative views and voices. It is a future that includes more diversity of content matter in Canadian foreign policy. Much more work can be done on indigeneity, race, faith, myth, identity, and teaching and learning in Canadian foreign policy, to name only a few areas. We need to question 'the ideas that made us and the theories that constructed through time a world that does not work for most people on earth' (Booth, 2007: 365).

At the same time, I think we need to take seriously our experiences of having been disciplined and encourage theoretical pluralism, not closure. This isn't about overthrowing the canon, but rather engaging across perspectives while simultaneously mapping our own future. As noted earlier in this chapter, I greatly value the insights gained from my mentors and colleagues who work from different perspectives—they have made me a better scholar/teacher/person as they have modelled scholarly excellence, a willingness to engage with my ideas, and a graciousness that only rarely can be found in a textbook or journal article. We cannot lose sight of the fact that our Canadian foreign policy community is made up of people and not simply publication records or theoretical perspectives.

As teachers and scholars we can support our undergraduate students, graduate students, and colleagues to feel welcome to explore their ideas in an opening, thoughtful environment. Let's engage in authentic conversations, transformative reflection, and open discussion about who we are and what we want our collective future to be in the study and practice of Canadian foreign policy.

Notes

1. This is not a new issue. See, for example, Nossal (1999).
2. I would like to thank Kim Richard Nossal for prompting further thought on this point.

3.   The link to the word 'disciple' is most intriguing and worth considering further.
4.   See Neufeld (1999a: 8). It is worth noting that the same article Neufeld refers to is included in the Bratt and Kukucha collection.
5.   Personal conversation with Claire Turenne Sjolander, November 2007.

Chapter Two

Home and Away
Public Diplomacy and the Canadian Self

Samantha L. Arnold

Introduction

Although it wasn't until 1965 that the term 'public diplomacy' was coined by American diplomat Edmund Gullion in an effort to protect America's international information programs from the 'taint' of any association with 'propaganda' (Cowan and Cull, 2008: 6), states have long been in the business of attempting to influence public opinion in other states to advance their own interests. As an instrument of statecraft that predates the current term used to describe it, the importance of public diplomacy through such conduits as cultural events, international expositions, and academic exchanges has been well appreciated by diplomats and other foreign policy practitioners. However, as a field of study, public diplomacy, until quite recently, has received little systematic scholarly attention—Kristin Lord (2005: 1) suggests that policy-makers listening for insights from the academy on this subject 'could hear a pin drop'. This is perhaps an overstatement, but not by much. As Bruce Gregory (2008: 275) points out, although there are literatures with clear relevance to the study of public diplomacy (among which he includes propaganda studies, public opinion research, media studies, political communication studies, cultural anthropology, identity theory, and governance studies), their potential contribution to knowledge about public diplomacy as a field of study has been largely unintentional. However, this inattention is beginning to change. It is beyond the scope of this chapter to determine whether there is a direct link between the recent attention to public diplomacy as a field of study and the post-9/11 'battle for hearts and minds', but it is clear from the proliferation of academic work on public diplomacy in the past several years that many agree with former US Secretary of State Condoleezza Rice's assertion that 'the time has come to look anew at our institutions of public diplomacy' (US Department of State, 2005).

Notwithstanding the many definitional debates that can be traced through the growing literature on public diplomacy, or the inconsistency with which public diplomacy is distinguished (or not) from concepts/practices such as propaganda, public affairs, and cultural diplomacy, it is widely understood that public diplomacy is a foreign policy practice that, according to one oft-cited definition, refers to 'a government's process of communicating with foreign publics in an attempt to bring about understanding for its nation's ideas and ideals, its institutions and culture, as well as its national goals and current policies' (Tuch, 1990: 3). This chapter offers a reformulation of public diplomacy that breaks with this image of public diplomacy as the practice of projecting a ready-made national identity abroad in support of foreign policy goals. This view, I argue, turns on and repro-duces a fundamental assumption typically informing the study and practice of foreign policy—that the internal and external realms, the 'home' and the 'away', exist prior to and independently of the 'bridging function' generally attributed to foreign policy. Contra this understanding of what foreign policy does, I argue that foreign policy works in important ways to *create* the sphere of 'the foreign'—and thus also 'the domestic'—that is generally presumed by foreign policy analysis. Moreover, I argue that public diplomacy isn't best thought of as a *tool* of foreign policy, but rather in and of itself as foreign policy; understood as such, public diplomacy is thereby implicated in the process of creating the very national identity that it is otherwise seen as projecting.

If public diplomacy can be seen as working, in part, to constitute the domestic even while it projects a national image abroad, then the importance of focusing on the 'home' when studying foreign policy cannot be denied. That said, it has long been noted that the domestic realm provides an important context for the development and practice of foreign policy. Yet, the domestic sphere tends overwhelmingly to be positioned as an important 'determinant' of, 'constraint' on, or 'source' of foreign policy by working to 'set parameters' or by providing the range of 'dominant ideas' that shape foreign policy. Understood thus, it is not surprising to see that scholars of foreign policy are increasingly attentive to the importance and implications of the apparent move towards 'democratized' or 'responsive' foreign policy-making (see, among others, Ayres, 2006; Bátora, 2006; Black and Smith, 1993). Without denying that important insights into the foreign policy process are generated by such accounts, I argue here that a key implication of rethinking public diplomacy is that the domestic sphere isn't simply a *context* that somehow influences foreign policy; rather, it is an important *site* of foreign policy itself. Thus, an important implication is that public diplomacy includes a range of domestic practices— 'public affairs'—that the great majority of scholars explicitly position as necessary to, but distinct from and, indeed, prior to, public diplomacy. In other words, a core assertion in this chapter, illustrated with reference to Canadian foreign policy in the circumpolar context, is that foreign policy cannot be defined in terms of its audience or target, but rather by the way it operates.

At issue, then, is not simply a reframing of public diplomacy but, more funda-mentally, a rethinking of foreign policy itself. What might it mean to speak of foreign policy if its practices can be seen as constituting rather than merely reflecting the very conditions that make it possible to speak of 'foreign' policy in the first place? It is to this issue that I turn first, drawing on insights from the literature on post-structuralism and International Relations that point to the possibility of rereading foreign policy as a performative practice that works to constitute the spheres of 'domestic' and 'foreign' it otherwise seems to take as given. Reframed in these terms, the study of foreign policy draws our attention to sites that are not normally considered by students and practitioners.

This understanding of foreign policy, as noted above, invites us to reconsider the way that the relationship between 'home' and 'away' has been imagined in conceptual terms by the great majority of foreign policy scholars and practitioners. More than this, however, a performative approach to foreign policy decentres 'policy' itself, if policy is understood as emanating from the familiar list of those government actors formally authorized to 'do' foreign policy. While policy understood in these terms remains important to the study of foreign policy re-thought, foreign policy as a performance understands that an audience forms an integral part of a successful performance. Taken together with the importance of the 'home', this approach to foreign policy necessitates the inclusion of domestic audiences as much as foreign audiences in the study of foreign policy. And, to extend the metaphor further, if we acknowledge that audiences are never passive recipients of a performance but are instead active participants in a shared discursive context that makes the performance meaningful (and that they work, through their reactions, to reproduce or destabilize), then foreign policy as understood in this chapter ultimately requires us to rethink even who it is that 'does' foreign policy.

Away?

As Richard Ashley (1987: 51) argued more than 20 years ago, '[f]oreign policy . . . is not so much behavior across boundaries. It is instead a specific sort of boundary-producing political performance.' However, it remains the case that foreign policy is widely understood instead as *bridging* distinct and pre-given spheres of 'domestic' and 'foreign', and it is certainly this image that frames public diplomacy as an instrumental process of reflecting or projecting the values, interests, and goals of an assumed and more or less stable 'domestic' or national sphere. Thus, the first step in a reformulation of public diplomacy is to consider what happens when we disturb this foundational assumption.

In this context, David Campbell's contribution to a revision of foreign policy along these lines is well known. In his *Writing Security* (1998 [1992]), Campbell argues that identity is constituted through difference, and difference through identity. Put differently, we define ourselves as much through what or who we are not as through what or who we are. But how do we recognize difference? Are there objectively given and knowable markers or traits that map out the boundary between Self and Other? For Campbell, the answer is 'no', because Self and Other are discursively constituted. A post-structural perspective entails taking seriously the idea that there is 'nothing outside of discourse', and while some take this as a denial of the objective world, it really means simply that nothing, including the objectively existing world, is apprehended by us except through interpretation. Interpretation, of course, occurs within a framework of meaning that defines things and the relationships between things. What this means is that we know things about the world, about ourselves, only through discourse. In this sense, discourse is constitutive of our world.

In light of this, Ashley (1987: 53) asks, '[w]hy not understand foreign policy as a specific sort of interpretative performance?' How might 'foreign policy' look different if we understand it not simply as 'behaviour across boundaries' but rather as a discursive undertaking that inscribes those very boundaries? This suggests that while foreign policy appears to be an expression of pre-given difference, of relating to the world 'outside' the state, as a discursive strategy it more fundamentally works in a productive way to create the very difference (the 'outside') it presumes—after all, what can 'foreign policy' mean without a pre-given 'foreign?' If discourse is understood as a structure of meanings that defines things and the relationships between things, 'foreign policy' presupposes and thus discursively produces the insides and outsides upon which it is predicated, and only within this discourse does it make sense to speak of or practice 'foreign' policy. Understood in these terms, foreign policy isn't a projection of the 'inside'; rather, it is one of the ways in which the inside is produced and affirmed. As Lene Hansen (2006: 26) puts it, 'identities are produced, and reproduced, through foreign policy discourse, and there is thus no identity existing prior to and independently of foreign policy.'

To suggest that foreign policy is a 'specific sort of performance' that operates to create insides and outsides begs the question of how this works. As Ashley (1987: 53) stresses, as a performance, foreign policy depends on its ability to 'elicit recognition as a warranted, valid, and indeed naturally appropriate way of seeing, saying, and making the world'. Put differently, foreign policy draws its authority and significance from prevailing discursive structures. In this context, Roxanne Doty (1993) advances what she describes as a 'discursive practices approach' to understanding the relationship between foreign policy and the discursive resources that naturalize it. According to Doty, this approach takes seriously the discursive construction of reality, whereby the meanings deployed through foreign policy discourses are part of a broader social intertext. Foreign policy is recognized as valid, to return to Ashley's point, because policy-makers are able to 'draw upon socially available cognitive resources, recognized precedents and shared symbolic materials' (Ashley, 1987: 53) that make foreign policy make sense. As Doty (1993: 305) puts it, '[t]he reception as meaningful of statements revolving around policy situations depends on how well they fit into the general system of representation of a given society.' At the same time, expressed as authoritative claims to know (Hansen, 2006: 8), foreign policy statements become implicated in the ritual reproduction of the very order from which they derive their authority.

For this reason, Campbell (1998: 68–9) suggests that we need to differentiate between two ways of understanding foreign policy. The first he calls 'foreign policy', which refers to 'all practices of differentiation or modes of exclusion . . . that constitute their objects as "foreign" in the process of dealing with them'; 'foreign policy', then, constitutes the 'conventional matrix of interpretations' (ibid., 69) within which specific decisions or events become meaningful. The second way of understanding foreign policy is described by Campbell as Foreign Policy, which corresponds to the practices, policies, and decisions to which the field traditionally attributes the bridging function between domestic and foreign. Says Campbell, 'Foreign Policy serves to *reproduce* the constitution of identity made possible by "foreign policy" and to *contain* challenges to the identity that results' (ibid.). Situated within a broader system of representation, foreign policy analysis therefore goes beyond 'the actual making of specific decisions [or] the analysis of temporally and spatially bounded "events"' (Doty, 1993: 303) that we can describe, following Campbell, as Foreign Policy. Equally relevant to the study of foreign policy is 'foreign policy', the matrix of interpretations that marks off and naturalizes the Self in opposition to perceived difference, and gives meaning to Foreign Policy.

Home and Away?

All of this has implications for thinking about public diplomacy. I suggested at the outset that public diplomacy isn't best thought of as a *tool* of foreign policy, but rather as foreign policy per se; I suggested, further, that public diplomacy is thus implicated in the process of *creating* the national identity that it is otherwise seen as projecting. Drawing on Campbell, let me now restate this intention with the benefit of his distinction between 'foreign policy' and Foreign Policy: what I will argue below is that while public diplomacy is typically understood as a Foreign Policy tool, it may more productively be appreciated as an identity practice that contributes to the 'conventional matrix of interpretations' constituted by 'foreign policy'.

Although not identical in conceptual terms, the basic idea informing public diplomacy can be captured with reference to the growing literature on 'place' or 'nation branding' (Anholt, 2006; Van Ham, 2001, 2002, 2008). In other words, whatever else it may be, public diplomacy is broadly seen as a state-directed and purposeful mechanism for the cultivation of a favourable 'national brand' in the minds of foreign publics through activities—cultural diplomacy, educational exchanges, international expos, and so on—designed to highlight national virtues and values. Taken as such, an important assumption informing the notion of public diplomacy is that there is a coherent 'product' being 'marketed' internationally. Put differently, if public diplomacy is understood as a tool involving the instrumental projection of national identities abroad, the underlying implication is that there is, in fact, such a national identity ready and available for projection. The business of constructing a national identity in the first place is by this account no more necessary to the study of public diplomacy than, to paraphrase Alexander Wendt (1994: 385), a theory of society needs to explain the existence of people. This is entirely in keeping with an understanding of foreign policy as 'behaviour across boundaries', that is, as Foreign Policy.

Is this a fair characterization? Without question, as traditionally understood, public diplomacy is simply the process of 'selling' whatever policies a government has developed; Simon Anholt (2006: 274) captures this in his recounting of a Cold War exchange in which a public diplomacy officer is told, 'Look, you just forget about policy, that's not your business; we'll make the policy and then you can put it on your damn radio.' Certainly, the scope of public diplomacy has shifted away from this overtly propagandizing function since the Cold War. As Anholt notes, public diplomacy considerations are now playing a role in the development of policy, and public diplomacy is increasingly to be understood as an instrument of policy. And yet, the primary function of public diplomacy continues to be to act as a soft-power resource in the pursuit of an externally oriented Foreign Policy agenda.

More recently, however, a growing academic literature on public diplomacy has taken as its starting point the assertion that the line between 'domestic' and 'international' has broken down in the face of globalization, and thus the separation between domestic and foreign policy is harder to maintain both conceptually and in practice. According to this 'new public diplomacy' approach, advances in communications technology and processes of globalization more generally have produced 'porous borders', an increased ability of people and NGOs to communicate and network, a proliferation of media, the transnationalization of political issues, and growing expectations of increased transparency and public participation in policy-making, all of which have changed the way that public diplomacy is conducted, and by whom. (With specific reference to Canadian public diplomacy, see Bátora, 2005, 2006; Copeland, 2004, 2005; Potter, 2002–3; Vickers, 2004.)

For all of these reasons, as Rhiannon Vickers (2004: 185) points out, there is an 'increased acceptance by governments that citizens have a role to play in diplomacy', and thus a hallmark of the new public diplomacy is the necessary engagement of domestic actors, practically and conceptually, in the foreign policy process. This approach highlights the *inseparability* of domestic and international policy issues, and appears to create space for an appreciation of foreign policy practices as having a domestic function. On the surface, this seems potentially compatible with the reformulation of foreign policy I have suggested above. However, the domestic sphere operates in a very limited way in the new public diplomacy, because this approach remains predicated on an understanding of foreign policy that preserves the idea of the domestic sphere as ontologically prior to the foreign. In other words, the new public diplomacy maintains the image of public diplomacy, new or otherwise, as an exercise in identity projection, and thus remains wedded to Foreign Policy.

As a way to explore this, consider Jozef Bátora's assertion that public diplomacy has a 'two-dimensional character bridging the traditional divide between home and abroad' (Bátora, 2005: 1). On the one hand, the characterization of public diplomacy as two-dimensional is a promising innovation that potentially breaks with the image of public diplomacy as an exclusively externally oriented undertaking. Clearly, though, Bátora does not connect this two-dimensionality to any sense that home and abroad are mutually constituted. For Bátora, the two-dimensionality of public diplomacy derives instead from the necessity on the part of the state to tap into 'the positive images and values associated with domestic non-state actors' so as to enable their deployment abroad. As he puts it, '[a]ssociation of non-state actors with the state is the primary means through which the state can harness the image and value resources of non-state actors. In this way, the state's ability to capture the mind space of foreign audiences is enhanced' (ibid., 4). Thus, the emphasis in Bátora's formulation is on appreciating how public diplomacy, as an undertaking intended to influence foreign audiences, depends on the state's ability to mobilize important domestic resources.

This is a common theme in the new public diplomacy literature, with the emphasis placed on the ways in which foreign policies draw to varying degrees on domestic constituencies. In this context, scholars (and practitioners) of the new public diplomacy emphasize the vital importance of securing 'buy-in' from domestic stakeholders as a way of establishing the legitimacy of a particular foreign policy agenda, or as a way of mobilizing their active participation as agents of public diplomacy in support of a foreign policy agenda (see, e.g., Bátora, 2006; Copeland, 2005; Nimijean, 2006, Vickers, 2004).

It is obvious that a government concerned with its own political survival would seek domestic legitimacy for its foreign policy agenda. However, scholars of the new public diplomacy, appreciative of the changing realities that impact the traditional conduct of diplomacy, understand the significance of domestic legitimacy differently. For them, domestic legitimacy is less about the political survival of government and more about the ability of government to convincingly market itself abroad. People now have the ability to communicate easily and directly with citizens of other states—in practical terms, this means that governments no longer have a monopoly on international communications, nor do they have any meaningful control over what messages are being conveyed to foreign publics. As Vickers (2004: 185) points out, powerful information and communications technologies require the state to be attentive to the 'opportunities for many-to-many communications rather than traditional hierarchical, linear, one-to-many communications'. The ability of the state to effectively market its national brand, then, will depend heavily on whether its message is contradicted or echoed by its own citizens. Returning to Bátora's argument, the attractiveness of the values and ideas represented by a state to its own citizens is thus 'an essential pre-condition for a successful public diplomacy' because only in this way will they 'gladly associate their actions abroad with their state and hence promote its soft power' (Bátora, 2005: 3).

Drawing on this theme in the new public diplomacy literature, it can be said that public diplomacy involves an interesting two-way quality. On the one hand, the potential impact of domestic constituencies on the success of the state's efforts to represent itself abroad in particular ways is well appreciated by scholars of the new public diplomacy. For this reason, states must seek 'buy-in' from stakeholders at home in support of the national image being deployed abroad. On the other hand, there is a sense in which the success of the state's public diplomacy activities abroad depends on the degree to which the brand being projected corresponds to the 'values and images' that the domestic constituencies already have about 'home'. In this way, it may appear that a coherent sense of national self—the home—is both a prerequisite and an outcome of successful public diplomacy to the extent that the values and ideas that define the self are simultaneously 'tapped into' and reinforced as the state works to project a national brand abroad. Understood in these terms, public diplomacy is potentially consistent with the idea of 'foreign policy' outlined above insofar as there is space for thinking about public diplomacy both as a Foreign Policy tool intended to project a national brand abroad and as a 'foreign policy' practice that works to reproduce the system of representation within which that Foreign Policy makes sense.

That said, there is a problem. This potential thinking space is foreclosed by the explicit insistence among virtually all scholars of the new public diplomacy that the domestically oriented processes of securing legitimacy and buy-in are vital prerequisites of successful public diplomacy, but are at the same time distinct from it. These processes are typically characterized instead as 'public affairs' or 'public outreach'.

What is the rationale for analytically separating public affairs from public diplomacy? The issue for scholars of the new public diplomacy seems ultimately to come down to the question of audience. Public diplomacy, for them, makes use of domestic resources, and may even be determined by domestic considerations, but ultimately it is defined in terms of its audience—it is about the attempt to cultivate a favourable national brand among *foreign* audiences. When states target their own domestic audience, this is by definition not foreign policy but domestic policy, even while that domestic policy may act in the service of a foreign agenda. Of course, this distinction only holds true if we limit our understanding of foreign policy to Foreign Policy.

Consider, for example, Daryl Copeland's discussion of the new public diplomacy, or what he calls simply the new diplomacy. Copeland acknowledges that international branding strategies must make sense to Canadians, and for this reason he says that domestic constituencies play an important role in shaping these strategies. However, he specifically differentiates the new diplomacy from public affairs in terms of the intended audiences of these practices; while the new diplomacy is about 'explaining Canada to the world', public affairs is about 'explaining the world to Canada' (Copeland, 2005: 751). Similarly, Evan Potter distinguishes between public diplomacy and public affairs in terms of audience; he suggests that while the activities and techniques of public affairs might be the same as those used in public diplomacy initiatives, public affairs activities are directed at domestic constituencies to 'help them interpret the outside world from a national perspective and to raise awareness of their country's international role' (Potter, 2002–3: 47). Potter is critical of the tendency of Canada's Department of Foreign Affairs and International Trade (DFAIT) to identify consultation and communication programs aimed at domestic audiences as public diplomacy in its official documents. These activities, says Potter, reflect domestic imperatives rather than international ones—they highlight DFAIT's contribution to national priorities, and they 'use Canada's international activities to highlight and promote Canada's success as a unified nation *to Canadians*' (ibid., 48; my emphasis). In this way, Potter acknowledges that Canada's role in the world is an important resource in the cultivation of a Canadian identity in the minds of Canadians, but this, for Potter, is not foreign policy in and of itself.

Public diplomacy understood in these terms is thus conceptually truncated; only intentional and instrumental communication strategies directed towards foreign audiences are considered to be public diplomacy, and public diplomacy is thereby restricted to the realm of Foreign Policy. Ideas and values operating in the domestic sphere are relevant resources of public diplomacy as Foreign Policy, and can be accessed through a range of consultative activities (on these in the Canadian context, see Bátora, 2005, 2006; Vickers, 2004). According to this view, however, no space exists for questioning how those ideas and values are themselves constituted and affirmed through the practice of public diplomacy. Instead, from a Foreign Policy perspective, the existence of these ideas and values is presupposed, and while it is possible to consider how they are drawn into the Foreign Policy process via public consultation, the parsing off of domestically oriented strategies as 'public affairs' from public diplomacy leaves no possibility of considering how Foreign Policy and 'foreign policy' are mutually constitutive. It is public affairs, as Potter notes, that works to 'interpret the outside world from a national perspective', and it is this that brings us back to the operation of 'foreign policy'. If public affairs are ultimately about explaining the world to Canada, then a 'conventional matrix of interpretations' is what makes such explanations make sense. And indeed, it is precisely this matrix that Potter's analysis links to public affairs in his appreciation of how public affairs work to promote national identity—that is, a sense of 'home' as distinct from 'away'.

What all of this means is that if public diplomacy is ultimately about cultivating a favourable national brand, there can be little justification for a conceptual distinction between public diplomacy and public affairs on the grounds that one of these practices targets foreign audiences and the other targets domestic audiences. True, as a tool of Foreign Policy, the question of audience becomes relevant—although domestic constituents are relevant to Foreign Policy insofar as they contribute to policy legitimacy or development in various ways, they are not themselves understood to be the targets of Foreign Policy. However, if we are prepared to think about foreign policy as 'foreign policy', that is, as being about the constitution of 'home' and 'away' through shared notions of difference and the self that make particular policies make sense, then the 'home' is every bit as relevant as a *site* of foreign policy as the 'away'. In this sense, then, the state's efforts to secure 'buy-in' at home are part and parcel of 'foreign policy'. If audience is no longer a meaningful basis for differentiating between public diplomacy and public affairs, then public diplomacy can be defined instead in terms of how it operates to produce a national brand—whether at home or away.

Home?

I have suggested in this chapter that public diplomacy is a 'foreign policy' practice that operates in important ways to contribute to the interpretive framework that makes particular actions, decisions, or events make sense. It is 'foreign policy', I have argued, that helps to constitute the 'domestic' against which any sense of Foreign Policy can be established, maintained, and made to make sense—and vice versa! That said, it is vital to stress that nothing in what I have argued should be taken to mean that 'foreign policy' and Foreign Policy understandings of public diplomacy are mutually incompatible. Rather, it is important to take seriously the ways in which 'foreign policy' and Foreign Policy work to affirm each other; Foreign Policy is an effect of 'foreign policy' even while it authoritatively re-inscribes 'foreign policy'. For this reason, as suggested above, public diplomacy can be reframed as a practice that operates to produce a national brand, irrespective of audience. Branding occurs both at home and away, through the mutually constitutive practices of 'foreign policy' and Foreign Policy.

In light of this argument, what can be said about the practice of Canadian public diplomacy? This is a question that warrants a more sustained response than is possible in this chapter; that said, I would like briefly to highlight certain features of Canada's branding strategy in the circumpolar context as a first step towards exploring how public diplomacy contributes to Canada's Foreign Policy and 'foreign' policy.

As many observers have pointed out, the circumpolar region has taken on a new significance in the post-Cold War context. Challenges posed to the environment and northern communities by climate change and economic activity are a growing concern, while the hunt for oil and mineral resources is potentially fuelling a renewal of geopolitical tensions in the region as states jockey for exclusive economic rights over resources on, over, and under the continental shelf. Amid concern that the Arctic is becoming a militarized zone, the international reaction to the planting of a Russian flag on the sea bed at the North Pole and the Canadian reaction to the planting of a Danish flag on Hans Island provide an indication of how easily international conflict in the region might erupt. For these reasons, Canada shares with the other Arctic states an interest in actively cultivating robust multilateral structures of governance in the circumpolar world in order to facilitate the management of the considerable ecological, economic, and geopolitical concerns in the region.

Without question, Canada has made important contributions to the development of norms, principles, and structures of Arctic governance, not the least of which was this country's work in establishing the Arctic Council (Keskitalo, 2004; Nord, 2006). Importantly, Canada's posture in the circumpolar region is informed by the claim that Canada enjoys a natural leadership role in the region by virtue of being a 'northern nation'. The idea of Canadian nordicity is both familiar and powerful; it is in many ways understood to be a defining feature of Canada's national identity. At the same, however, it is fundamentally an 'empty' or 'floating' signifier that is defined discursively rather than with reference to an objectively knowable 'northernness' (see, e.g., Grace, 2001; Hamelin, 1978; Heininen and Nicol, 2007; Keskitalo, 2004; West, 1991). What this suggests is that Canada's 'northernness' is something that is produced, rather than given. In keeping with the argument developed in this chapter, public diplomacy plays a key role in simultaneously projecting and constituting a Canadian national brand based on Canadian nordicity both at home and away.

Thinking about Foreign Policy in this context, the Canadian government has undertaken a range of initiatives—easily recognized as public diplomacy, traditionally defined—intended to communicate Canada's 'northernness' to an international audience in the circumpolar world. Perhaps the most notorious example, given what many saw as an excessively hefty price tag at over $5 million, was the 2003 circumpolar tour conducted by Governor General Adrienne Clarkson to promote 'a modern image of the Canadian North' in Russia, Iceland, and Finland. This tour was explicitly linked to, and was intended to support, the Northern Dimension of Canada's Foreign Policy initiated in June 2000 (DFAIT, 2000). More in line with practices associated with the new public diplomacy, the government also has actively drawn on domestic actors in support of its messaging to foreign publics. Just one example in this context has been the enlisting of Canadian Inuit in the government's campaign to counteract economically costly opposition to the annual seal hunt (Saunders, 2007: A1). The delegation, which included Inuit Tapiriit Kanatami president Mary Simon, participated in a DFAIT-sponsored series of meetings with European government officials intended to offer an Inuit perspective. Interestingly, one participant indicated that she was tired of Europeans dictating how she should live her life (CBC News, 2007).

This latter example is particularly interesting because it points to an important theme in Canada's northern foreign policy. As I have argued elsewhere (Arnold, 2008), Canadian nordicity is increasingly becoming linked through Canada's Foreign Policy to what is described as a 'partnership' with Canada's northern Indigenous peoples. In 1998, DFAIT produced a consultation paper entitled 'Towards a Northern Foreign Policy for Canada' in which Lloyd Axworthy suggested that Canada is beginning a new relationship with Indigenous peoples based on what he described as 'a spirit of partnership'. This represents, he said, 'a renewal of relations between northern and southern Canada. They also reflect a greater focus in the north itself on self-reliance and sustainable development. Together, they indicate the need to harness all available means, including foreign policy, to the achievement of the full array of Canadian domestic, and especially northern, interests.' A key feature of this strategy was the view that northern Indigenous peoples must be able to actively participate in decision-making both at the domestic level and on the international stage. A great deal of Canada's credibility as a circumpolar leader rests on the extent to which Canada lives up to its side of this partnership.

From a 'foreign policy' perspective, this notion of 'partnership' serves an important function at home and works discursively to create Indigenous northerners as stakeholders in Canada's northern policies at both the domestic and international levels. Moreover, it works to provide content to the free-floating idea of Canada as a northern nation. 'Northernness' has become linked to the engagement of northern Indigenous peoples in the full range of economic, social, and political decisions at issue in the North. At the same time, this is further linked in official and unofficial statements on the northern dimension to an enduring theme in Canadian politics—that of national unity (see, e.g., DFAIT, 1998b; Fraser and Harker, 1994–5; Standing Committee on Foreign Affairs and International Trade, 1997). The common theme is that national unity depends critically on a northern identity that is not merely symbolic or geographical, but rather is predicated on the participation of northern Indigenous peoples as full partners in the Canadian state.

Of particular interest to me as an issue for further exploration is how public diplomacy on the domestic side works to engage northerners in this image of Canada, and there are certainly interesting questions to be asked about how this brand is constituted in the south as well. In this context, the government has engaged in a range of domestically oriented strategies designed to cultivate domestic 'buy-in' for the northern foreign policy agenda, and further to provide credibility to Canada's claim to involve northern peoples in decision-making. These would include the formalized process of extensive consultation in northern communities leading up to the 2000 DFAIT document on northern foreign policy (DFAIT, 2000; see especially Standing Committee on Foreign Affairs and International Trade, 1997), and the series of tours undertaken by Canadian officials in the North. While Prime Minister Stephen Harper's trips north in the past few years come easily to mind, visits by Governor General Adrienne Clarkson to northern communities were also highly publicized in local media as important gestures of unity and partnership. Less conventionally, DFAIT has partnered with Indian and Northern Affairs Canada to produce the 'North³' website targeting northern youth.

As laid out in this chapter, public diplomacy certainly includes those externally oriented practices designed to tell the world that Canada, as a northern nation committed to a 'spirit of partnership' with northern Indigenous peoples, is justified in seeking—and deserving—a leadership role in the circumpolar world. At the same time, it also includes those domestically oriented practices that work to tell us what it means to be Canadian, and in this context, operate performatively to constitute a 'matrix of interpretation' according to which Canadian Foreign Policy claims in the North make sense.[1] Either way, the key is that public diplomacy must be seen as part and parcel of the way that 'foreign policy' and Foreign Policy actually work to enact discourses of sameness and difference, and thereby constitute both 'home' and 'away'.

Note

1. While the formal framework of Canadian foreign policy in the North remains largely unchanged from that of the previous government, it is clear that a militarized northern discourse is emerging under Prime Minister Stephen Harper. In the midst of ongoing concerns about Canadian sovereignty, Canadian nordicity seems increasingly to be mobilized in support of the 'defence of the North', and it is interesting to consider how Canadian public diplomacy under Harper's government might be constituting and drawing upon a competing northern 'foreign policy' in which a more militarized Foreign Policy in the North makes sense.

Part II
Fighting the Global War on Terror

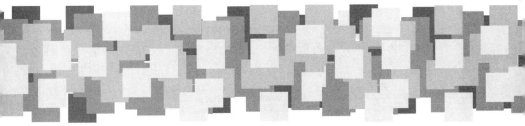

Chapter Three

Canada–US Defence Relations

Weapons of Mass Control and a Praxis of Mass Resistance

Ann Denholm Crosby

In their post-9/11 efforts to address continental defence and security issues, the governments of Canada and the United States established the Bi-National Planning Group to study and recommend 'the way forward' in terms of enhancing military co-operation between the two countries. For this purpose, continental security was defined as involving co-ordinated efforts to 'prevent attacks within the United States and/or Canada, reduce vulnerability to terrorism and minimize the damage and recover from attacks that could occur', while continental defence involved 'protection of Canadian or United States sovereignty, territory, domestic population, and critical infrastructure against external threats and aggression or other threats as directed by the President and/or Prime Minister' (Bi-National Planning Group, 2006: 2).

To achieve these goals, the Planning Group's *Final Report*, issued in March 2006, recommended the creation of a Canada–United States Comprehensive Defense and Security Agreement designed to 'bring unity of effort and direction to each of the defence, security and foreign policy organizations' of the two countries, and more specifically, 'to achieve the level (although not necessarily the form) of cooperation that now exists in NORAD in all other domains' (ibid., 1).

Since 9/11, the Canadian government has undertaken major initiatives both to secure the country against terrorist activities and to demonstrate to the US that Canada is a conscientious security neighbour. These initiatives include adopting anti-terrorist legislation, instituting 'Smart Border' policies and practices, tightening its immigration and refugee policies, establishing the Department of Public Safety and Emergency Preparedness Canada, and restructuring the Canadian military command system. Still, although the national security documents of both countries cite terrorism as the primary threat to the continent and its population, there are some clear distinctions between Canadian and American defence, security, and foreign policy interests in this regard, the three policy areas of interest to the Bi-National Planning Group.

In terms of global security, Canada refused to formally participate in the US-led Iraq war, and indeed, Canadian security is not understood to depend on either Canadian or US capabilities or willingness to undertake unilateral and pre-emptive strikes against possible enemies elsewhere. With regard to the two countries' activities in Afghanistan, Canada does not support the US practice of 'rendition', of transferring detainees for confinement to countries that condone the use of torture. The two countries also differ on a range of related security and foreign policy issues involving human rights, the rule of law, and the role of multilateralism in global security pursuits (Whitaker, 2004). With regard to continental defence, the US national missile defence program (NMD) includes plans for placing weapons in space. Canada has a policy of non-participation in NMD and a long-standing position against the weaponization of space.[1] In terms of domestic security, the Canadian government has not expressed an inclination to adopt the invasive surveillance and curtailment of rights practices afforded the US government by its Patriot Act.

In the context of these differences, the recommendations of the *Final Report* produced by the Bi-National Planning Group are problematic, and particularly so in that NORAD is cited as the model for the level of co-operation being pursued. NORAD, the North American Aerospace Defence Command, is the most institutionally developed form of Canada–US military co-operation. Since its inception as a joint air defence command in 1958, defence analysts and successive Canadian governments have consistently argued that the joint military command affords Canada a level of defence and security it could not enjoy on the basis of its own resources alone, while a seat at the continental planning table provides the government access to US intelligence and continental defence planning, as well as the opportunity to influence the latter in accordance with distinctively Canadian interests.

Just as consistently, however, Canadian defence, security, and foreign policy interests have been compromised through this venue. Cases in point include accepting a nuclear weapons role for Canadian air defence forces in 1963; the deletion, in 1981, of a clause that Canada had inserted in the NORAD agreement in 1968 establishing a non-participation position for Canada in US missile defence initiatives;[2] and agreeing to the testing of US cruise missiles in Canada's North beginning in 1984 and ending in 1994. Each of these cases involved reversals of previously held Canadian disarmament, arms control, and/or diplomatic policy positions. Each of these cases also reflected the recommendations of continental defence programs developed by joint Canadian–US military study groups working to US exigencies (Denholm Crosby, 1998).

Similarly, the Bi-National Planning Group consisted of Canadian and US military personnel. It also included, however, representatives of 15 companies that contract to the US government. Three contractors in particular participated in producing the *Final Report*: Northrop Grumman, the third largest contractor for the US military and specialists in the research and development of missile defence and space weapon technologies; SAIC, the ninth largest defence contractor in the US working with the Department of Defense, the intelligence community, and the National Security Agency; and Booz Allen Hamilton, a large contractor in surveillance technologies to the US Department of Homeland Security. There were no Canadian political representatives at the Bi-National table to influence planning according to distinctive Canadian defence, security, and foreign policy interests. Indeed, the only Canadian non-military person to be involved, and not for the duration, was a public affairs officer with the Department of National Defence.[3]

Following the *Report*'s release, the Conservative Minister of National Defence at the time, Gordon O'Connor, announced that although the Planning Group's term had expired, its functions would be integrated 'into a number of other bodies, such as the Permanent Joint Board on Defence, Canada Command, the US Northern Command, the Military Cooperative Committee, and of course, the new enhanced NORAD' (Canada, *Hansard*, 2006). The 'enhancement' of NORAD was a reference to the partially rewritten NORAD agreement, renewed in 2006 as a permanent agreement no longer subject to periodic renewals. Hence, very real efforts are afoot in both Canada and the US to integrate and institutionalize Canadian and US defence, security, and foreign policies, and every indication is that this will be done in accordance with US interests, supported, of course, by those interests within Canada that favour policy integration.

The purpose of this chapter is twofold. First, I explore the Bi-National *Report*'s recommendations in the context of contemporary US security interests, both global and continental. Indeed, the two cannot be separated. The military systems the US has erected, and is continuing to build, to defend the continent are the same systems upon which the US depends to project its military power worldwide, thus allowing the US and its allies to define the security environments of non-Western peoples in accordance with US interests, both political and economic. As such, they can be understood as systems of mass control, and the destruction they can produce in pursuit of US and allied interests is manifest in the rubble of Iraq and Afghanistan. Enhancing any kind of military co-operation that legitimates these systems, it will be argued, diminishes rather than increases both continental and global security.

The second focus of this chapter relates to resistance against these systems and the military initiatives they facilitate. Two levels of resistance will be considered. The first level is empirical and involves resisting the recommendations of the Bi-National *Report* to harmonize Canada–US defence, security, and foreign policy interests. The second level is perspectival and involves resisting the world views in which contemporary US-led Western security practices are rooted. For students of foreign policy, this means resisting the theoretical perspectives in which those world views are embedded. Key to this resistance is the understanding that the dominant International Relations (IR) theoretical perspectives, realism and neo-liberalism, are culturally specific narratives about deeply rooted Western practices and knowledges rather than generic theories involving exogenously given universals. As such, they provide rationales for the reproduction of Western relations of social, economic, and political power on a global basis. As will be discussed, these relations of power *inherently* produce vast insecurities for vast numbers of peoples. Formulas for addressing these insecurities, then, do not, and cannot, reside in the theories that support their reproduction.

Therefore, the final section of the chapter discusses a possible praxis of resistance that involves a search for theoretical grounds upon which to imagine, and act in the interest of, processes that might produce alternative global security futures. This includes the ability to recognize, as R.B.J. Walker writes, 'the multiple journeys' already being undertaken in this regard (Walker, 2002: 18). In these journeys—indicated but only briefly discussed due to space constraints—maps may be found for resisting efforts, such as those embodied in the recommendations of the Bi-National Planning Group, to reinforce the security of the West through processes that create insecurity for the rest of the world.

This chapter, then, is an invitation to consider how the theories—realist, neo-liberal, or critical—we use to make sense of Canadian foreign policy are themselves political discourses that function in support of particular political agendas. Indeed, the choices we make about which theories to use are themselves political choices.

US Post-Cold War Security Interests

The US post-9/11 national security strategy of pre-emption and unilateralism, of 'taking the fight to the enemy', has depended on an integrated defence system of global proportions, developed and deployed under the auspices of the Missile Defense Agency. The organization's mandate, since its inception in 1991 (then called the Ballistic Missile Defense Organization), has been to 'Develop and field an integrated Ballistic Missile Defense System (BMD) capable of providing a layered defense for the homeland and its deployed forces, friends, and allies against ballistic missiles of all ranges in all phases of flight' (Missile Defense Agency website). Accomplishing this is the work of three integrated missile defence programs (Baucom, 2000; Cirincione, 2005; Denholm Crosby, 1998).

The Global Warning Program consists of a layering of land, sea, air, and space-based radars, sensors, and communication technologies designed to provide the US military with global surveillance, warning, communication, and battle management tools. These technologies support the work of the second program, Theatre Missile Defense, which allows the US military to address the use of short- and medium-range missiles in regional conflicts. These two programs have been central to the management of the US war on terror in Iraq and Afghanistan and now also support US defence and security interests in the North American 'theatre'.

Throughout the 1990s, the funding for research and development was focused on these two components of the program. By 2000, and particularly after 9/11, attention turned to the National Missile Defense program designed to close the gap in the global system through its capacity to address an accidental, or hostile, launch of a limited number of long-range missiles aimed at the US by intercepting and destroying the missiles in mid-course either in space or at high altitudes. In support of all three programs are long-range plans to develop a range of space-based weapons, including space-based interceptors for which the US hopes to deploy a test bed by 2012 (Regehr, 2004a: 1). Representatives of the defence industry corporations heavily committed to the research and development of missile defence technologies, including space-based technologies, were members of the Bi-National Planning Group.

It is not possible to separate continental defence from the larger global defence system in which it is embedded, and it is in this context that the *Report*'s recommendation that NORAD be the model, if not the form, of continental defence, security, and foreign policy co-ordination is not incidental. NORAD has proven to be an effective forum for co-ordinating Canadian and US policies in the past, although 'co-ordination' has generally meant compromising distinctive Canadian interests and/or policies. That process of compromise is continuing within the Command.

The NORAD Connection

In February 2005, the Liberal government announced that Canada would not participate in the US National Missile Defense (NMD) program. In May 2006, following a lengthy discussion in the House of Commons in which all parties expressed their support for Canada's position of non-participation, Parliament voted to renew the NORAD agreement (Canada, *Hansard*, 2006). The overwhelming support for both renewing the NORAD agreement and non-participation in NMD gave the appearance that NORAD activities and missile defence are two separate issues.

The US global missile defence system, however, depends significantly on NORAD technologies and functions, and the NORAD agreement was rewritten in 1996 to allow for Canada's formal participation in missile defence in the future (Canada, Treaty Series, 1996). In the meantime, the rewritten agreement mandated Canadian NORAD military personnel at NORAD headquarters to work within other US commands in the Cheyenne Mountain Operations Centre in Colorado to perform NORAD duties and to support the missions of those American commands in the process. When the US military command system was reorganized in 2002, this clause mandated Canadian NORAD military personnel to work within and support the missions of the three commands working out of Cheyenne Mountain Operations Centre: the US Strategic Command, a command with a global mandate including missile defence; NORTHCOM, responsible for continental defence, including missile defence operations; and the US Air Force Space Command. Indeed, during the Iraq War, an initiative in which Canada chose not to participate, NORAD surveillance, warning, and conflict management information was transferred instantaneously to the US Central Command (CENTCOM), the operational command responsible for the war (Regehr, 2004b: 5).

In August 2004, the NORAD agreement was amended to allow NORAD's aerospace warning capabilities to be used 'in support of the designated commands responsible for missile defence of North America' (Canada, Treaty Series, 2004). Anticipating such an agreement, Ernie Regehr argued that it would situate Canadian NORAD military personnel as active participants in continental missile defence activities (Regehr, 2004b: 1). Despite the government's announcement in 2005 that Canada would not participate in the US missile defence program, the 2006 NORAD renewal agreement actually increased the level of Canadian military participation (Canada, Treaty Series, 2006). The 2004 amendment was replaced with a clause allowing for NORAD's warning capabilities to be used in support of US missile defence activities in general, not just North American missile defence. As well, the clause in the previous agreement mandating Canadian military personnel assigned to NORAD to work within other US commands to perform NORAD duties was modified to allow those personnel to perform NORAD support functions for *non*-NORAD activities within those other commands and, in the process, to support the missions of those US commands as appropriate. In these ways, NORAD is fully integrated into the US military command system and its global operations. To this extent, too, it becomes apparent that the recommendations of the Bi-National Planning Group reflected the policy interests of both governments.

Given US efforts to weaponize space and Canada's long-standing position against such activities, compromising its policy positions stands as an ongoing phenomenon of Canada's NORAD membership. Joel Sokolsky's suggestion that in the interests of co-operation with the US, 'Canada must simply put aside its arms control difficulties regarding the possible weaponization of space' (Sokolsky, 2005: 322), indicates that a discourse of compromise is already being mounted in the public realm. For the Canadian government, however, an abiding concern, expressed frequently during the House debate on the renewal, is to keep the seat at the table. The contradiction between maintaining that seat while also maintaining a position of non-participation in missile defence is managed in large part by perpetuating the myth that NORAD and global missile defence are discrete programs. Such is not the case, and both are rooted in a particular understanding of what constitutes global security.

The Operative Western Perspective on Global Security

Sokolsky writes from the dominant security perspective of the West in which the global missile defence systems, NORAD, and the *Report* of the Bi-National Planning Group are embedded. In this perspective, the security of the continent, and indeed the West, is understood to ultimately reside in the projection of US military power. As Sokolsky puts it, in seeking to sustain 'its dominant military position in the world, the United States makes possible the stable international environment that all but eliminates any major challenge to the security of the West' (ibid., 313). What constitutes a 'stable international environment' in this perspective is the global exercise of capitalist market relations and of the form, if not the substance, of liberal democratic politics (see Neufeld, 1999b: 97–119). Promoting the twin forces of neo-liberal politics and capitalist markets on a global basis is a primary goal of both Canadian and US national security documents, and underwriting the promotion of both with the exercise of military power is one of the foundational assumptions of the Bi-National *Report* (Bi-National Planning Group, 2006: 2, 3, 6).

In this context, the projection of US military power is understood as both benevolent and benign in that it is designed to 'stabilize' recalcitrant regions of the world so that Western economic and political forces can bring all peoples, as expressed in Canada's penultimate foreign policy statement, into 'the virtuous circle of rising prosperity' (Canada, 2005b: 2). The 'virtue' of this 'circle', however, is not self-evident to all peoples for, as Thomas Friedman argues, 'the hidden hand of the market will never work without a hidden fist' (Friedman, 1999: 96). According to the Bi-National *Report*, that 'hidden fist' is itself financed by the global market. 'Free access to global markets', the *Report* argues, 'serves as the guarantor of the resources necessary to our strong national defenses' (Bi-National Planning Group, 2006: 2).

The virtuousness of this perspective and the practices it supports, however, are not self-evident to all peoples, as critical security theorists have demonstrated and as Lloyd Axworthy acknowledged when he was Canada's Foreign Affairs Minister, because there is a 'dark underside' to the twin forces of political and economic globalization (Axworthy, 1999). These forces are responsible for, and/or exacerbate, environmental degradation, resource depletion, and an inequitable distribution of the world's natural, manufactured, and social resources. The result is relative and/or abject poverty among growing numbers of the world's peoples. In turn, these conditions are breeding grounds for a host of other insecurities, including malnutrition, disease, human rights abuses, population movements, crime, violent conflicts, and support for terrorist activities. These conditions are the inevitable product of market forces that depend on competition for profits and growth, and on political systems to discipline populations to market exigencies.

Since the security of the West, then, is reliant on forces that create insecurity in the lives of vast numbers of people elsewhere, it is little wonder that force is required to promote these conditions and to control the peoples that suffer from their effects. In this context, the global weapons system that supports the projection of US power worldwide can be understood as a weapons system of mass control. What is not clear in this perspective, however, is how, in a world of growing populations, diminishing resources, and increasing environmental degradation, the use of force, either direct or structural, can sustain the security of 15 per cent of the world's population that lives in Western industrial states at the expense of the other 85 per cent. In other words, using force to promote these conditions is a precarious security practice for the West. Yet, that is precisely the context within which the Bi-National *Report* is set.

Resisting the Recommendations of the Bi-National Planning Group

At the level of the Canadian state, the *discourse* of resistance involves resisting the myths that support the recommendations of the Bi-National Planning Group's

Report and the arguments of those who support enhanced Canada–US military and foreign policy co-operation. This includes recognizing that the *Report* is embedded in US post-Cold War global security interests and pursuits as much as it is a particular response to 9/11. In this context, the *Report* seeks to co-ordinate Canadian and US defence, security, and foreign policy interests.

Resistance also involves resisting the popular notion that NORAD is a benign, passive, joint continental defence institution that affords Canada 'cheap defence' and a meaningful seat at the continental defence planning table. This includes recognizing that NORAD is intimately and actively involved in the operations of the US global missile defence system, a system that constrains the ability of non-Western peoples to define for themselves what constitutes their security and to pursue that within a non-coercive environment that enables negotiation and co-operation.

In terms of exercising influence at the continental defence planning table, Canada has always been more influenced than influential at that table. In the post-9/11 environment, pundits of Canadian–American defence relations argue that the possibility of exercising influence has become even more elusive (Sokolsky, 2005: 315; Sands, 2006). At the same time, it is argued that Canada's geopolitical integrity within the international community depends on deeper military co-operation with American global security initiatives and interests.[4] Since the 'international community' to which they refer consists primarily of the US and Britain, this, too, is a myth to be resisted.

At the same state level, the *practice* of resistance involves withdrawing from NORAD. As a Canadian military command, NORAD necessarily reflects Canadian foreign policy interests. Remaining a member of NORAD in the context of its role in shaping global security environments to US-led Western interests sends a clear signal that Canada is a willing partner in these initiatives when, as discussed, there are some clear policy distinctions between the two countries in this regard. This is not to argue that Canada abandon its role in continental defence, but it is to argue that such can be accomplished through protocols and agreements, formulated through a political, rather than a military, process, and related to specific continental defence and/or security activities (Regehr, 2006: 4–5), but as unrelated as possible to initiatives associated with the US global projection of power and control.

However, addressing the concerns specific to resisting the recommendations of the Bi-National *Report* provides very little resistance to its foundational world view, which is also the essential world view of American-led Western efforts to project power and influence globally. Embedded in this world view are the realist and neo-liberal theoretical assumptions about the exogenously given nature of states and markets, and corresponding understandings of self-interest, competitiveness, and aggressive individualism as a priori characteristics of human nature. Resisting this world view involves resisting the universalizing assumptions of these dominant theoretical perspectives in International Relations theory.

Resisting Theory

Central to resisting dominant IR theoretical perspectives is the understanding that both realism and neo-liberalism are theories in only a very limited sense. How well these perspectives explain or fail to explain what they purport to is not the issue here. Rather, it is to argue that both realism and neo-liberalism are concerned with explaining only one particular set of culturally specific knowledges and practices associated with states and capitalist markets as historically specific forms of political, economic, and social relations.

The claims these theories make about states and markets reflecting external, objective laws that govern social, political, and economic organization can only be made from inside those theoretical constructs themselves. Outside those constructs, there are no objective measures by which one set of economic, political, and social practices and one particular way of viewing the world can be judged as quintessentially reflecting external natural laws, and therefore as superior to all other practices and views. Yet, the promotion by the West of capitalist economic relations and neo-liberal political practices on a global scale reflects exactly that calculation, and that calculation, in turn, justifies the use of force, both structural and direct, in imposing these relations on all peoples. Since there are as many different ways of organizing political, social, and economic relations as there are, and have been, peoples with different cultural formations, realism and neo-liberalism can only be understood as narratives—and partial narratives at that—about the discourses and practices associated with states and markets as particular ways of organizing human activity.

As a host of critical IR theorists have argued (Miller, 1990; Biersteker and Weber, 1996; Rosenberg, 1994; Ruggie, 1993),[5] the state as a particular form of political organization with a formal separation of public and private powers masking mutually supportive informal relationships, which involves the political management of public spaces and the private management of economic spaces, emerged from a set of specific conditions over the course of several hundred years in premodern Europe. The key conditions include the crumbling of a relatively stable feudal system due to wars, famine, and disease that decimated the European population, beginning in the mid-fourteenth century with the plague, which decimated one-third to one-half of the population. The subsequent rebuilding of European societies took place as the use of trade routes to the Near and Far East became more regularized and as products from Africa (including people) and the newly discovered Americas were becoming readily available. This constituted an environment of potential wealth and opportunity for the growing ranks of European merchants and entrepreneurs, the growth of both ranks being facilitated by the collapse of the feudal order and its system of ascription.

The 1648 Treaties of Westphalia formalized the sets of emerging liberal political and capitalist market relations by defining states as discrete, unitary, self-interested structures, each responsible for defining and maintaining its domestic public order and reliant on self-help to defend territory and promote interests. It was the *choice* of the signatories to keep the political spaces between states unordered, or anarchical, and to legitimize the use of force by states to defend their territories and interests. It was also a choice to leave economic actors unconstrained by formal political controls, either domestically or internationally. Thus, the treaties formalized a particular set of political, economic, and social relations among Westphalian peoples that were carried by the institution of the state. Practising these new forms of economic and political relations involved practising specific sets of competitive, aggressive, self-interested, and self-reliant behaviours, which were quintessentially functional for the emerging practice of liberal political and capitalist economic relations, as well as for the exercise of the strongly hierarchical power relations embedded in both.[6]

At the same time, vast changes taking place in the realm of ideas provided social empowerment to the emerging political and economic relations of capitalist production. As Max Weber argued, the Protestant Reformation's efforts to separate church and state reinforced emerging practices of locating authority territorially, while the Protestant ethic, which held that working hard in support of the 'common good' was in itself a moral activity, translated into a social understanding that a division of labour, such as that supporting the emerging capitalist relations of production, promoted the common good. Therefore, working within and reproducing the ranks of wage labour were considered acts of piety (Weber, 1958: 155–83).

Further, a revolution in scientific thinking produced a general societal understanding that life on earth, both physical and social, was governed by a set of God-given laws that were discoverable through scientific observation (Davies, 1997: 507–10). By living in accordance with these laws, both the individual and society were perfectible. As well as complementing the Protestant ethic of grace through hard work, the scientific revolution gave rise to the notion of a progressive evolution in human society of which European society was at the pinnacle. Thus, the scientific revolution and the Protestant ethic both reinforced the ideas and practices of self-reliant individualism that were being honed by the emerging relations of liberal politics and capitalist markets.

The Renaissance in art and literature (ibid., 471–82) also played a significant role in the development of new social epistemes that supported the pursuit, experience, and expression of individualism. Humanism, an intellectual movement 'marked by a fundamental shift from the theocratic or God-centered world view of the Middle Ages to the anthropocentric or man-centered view of the Renaissance' (ibid., 479), paved the way for artists to work with the depiction of human expressions and single-perspective representations of nature. Literary works began to use the vernacular and 'I-centred' perspectives. Intellectual/political writers of the era, including Machiavelli, Bodin, Grotius, Hobbes, and, somewhat later, Locke, focused in various ways on the meanings of fixing secularized rule territorially and the implications for a 'civil' society of sovereign individuals.

In short, the twin structures of states and capitalist markets arose out of historically specific political and economic conditions, and the emergence of both structures was reinforced by an array of developing scientific, artistic, and religious practices and knowledge that included ideas about human nature and social evolution. As such, states and markets are historically and culturally specific constructs. Over the last 400-plus years, states and markets have successfully globalized, not because they are the embodiment of natural, objective laws governing social organization and human nature, but because they are deeply rooted in the relations and practices upon which the accumulation of wealth and power depends, including ideas about the appropriateness of using force in the pursuit of self-interest and of situating other peoples as subservient to the forces of wealth and power accumulation.

To be sure, aspects of Western culture exist in other cultures to greater and lesser degrees, but at no other time or place in the history of human organization has this particular constellation of social, political, and economic practices emerged in a sustained fashion. Yet it is these specific cultural constructs that are represented as universals by both liberalism and realism. And it is these claims to universality that continue to support Western efforts to export Western forms of political, social, and economic relations and practices to non-Western peoples, the contemporary effort being reinforced by the US weapons system of mass control.

The problem is, how is it possible to attempt to think about, or imagine, alternate global security environments without grounding that thinking in Eurocentric, or any other cultural-centric theoretical discourses? And since praxis involves acting in theoretically grounded ways, how can one act in ways that might foster those futures without acting on the basis of culturally specific knowledges and values? In her book, *in search of human nature*, mary e. clark (*sic*), a geneticist by profession, provides some interesting points of departure in these regards.

A Praxis of Resistance

Based on Darwin's theory of evolution, clark develops two arguments that have direct bearing on our ability to escape the cultural boundaries of traditional IR theories. First, in terms of our understanding of human nature, she argues that although the popular interpretation of the Darwinian 'survival of the fittest' thesis is that inter- and intra-species competition for survival established individualistic, self-centred, competitive, and aggressive behaviours as being of primary adaptive significance for the evolution of *Homo sapiens*, Darwin himself never made this argument (clark, 2002: 68–70). Rather, he argued that 'survival of the fittest' involved a selection for those behaviours that allowed for survival in specific environments.

Clark's alternate Darwinian 'story' is that *Homo erectus*, our most immediate ancestor, survived two glacial periods and migrated beyond Africa before *Homo sapiens* first appeared in Africa about 250,000 years ago.[7] *Homo sapiens* then migrated successfully to Europe, Asia, the Americas, and Australia, surviving two more glacial periods and the eruption of Mount Toba, which darkened the earth for some 17 years. Given that adaptation to severe fluctuations in climate required innovation for survival, including the ability to migrate and to readapt to new environments, clark concludes that there was a selection '*against* rigid genetic control over behavior and *for* indeterminacy and flexibility. . . . [Q]uick learning, problem-solving and the creative sharing of knowledge', she argues, 'superseded all other adaptive qualities' (ibid., 99). In other words, she is arguing that there was genetic selection for behavioural *capacities* rather than for specific behaviours.

Further, she argues that, for two reasons, the survival of the species depended more on a selection for pro-social capacities than on a selection for the relatively anti-social behaviours of self-centred individualism, competition, and aggression. First, during the long evolutionary period of *Homo sapiens*, the adult brain of successive hominid species increased in size, and for birthing purposes infants were born increasingly immature in terms of both their brain size and its development. Consequently, infants of the species were dependent on adult care and protection for long periods of time. Successful reproduction of the population, then, required the group to protect offspring from disease, exposure, and predation. Hence, clark argues that capacities for flexibility, co-operation, and caring that promoted group survival would have been strongly selected for, and that, indeed, selection was based on group, rather than individual, survival.

Second, clark argues that the successful evolution of *Homo sapiens* depended on a group capacity for developing and co-ordinating multiple intelligences used for innovation, problem-solving, and communication. These activities required the evolving brain to develop capacities for learning and remembering and to conceptualize and communicate in spatial, temporal, and symbolic terms. In short, survival depended on the group's ability to develop a capacity for culture. Clark argues that the development of these capacities was group dependent and, indeed, 'that a large brain co-evolved with an increasingly interdependent social life' (ibid., 124).

Hence, in terms of human nature and according to clark, the successful evolution of *Homo sapiens* was about a selection for pro-social *capacities*, and the flexibility to exercise them in various ways depending on the survival needs of the group in a plethora of ecological and social environments that favoured the survival of the group, rather than a selection for specific kinds of individual human behaviours that either favoured the survival of the individual over the group or constrained the flexibility of the group. The extent to which individualistic, self-centred, competitive, and aggressive behaviours were functional for group survival is the extent to which they, too, were selected for the survival of the species. Rather than establishing a rigid blueprint for these behaviours, however, evolution selected for a *capacity* for these behaviours. The extent to which they do, or do not, define a social order is a specific cultural phenomenon.

During the long transition period from feudalism to modernity in Europe, emerging Western cultural practices *did* increasingly select for these behaviours, establishing strongly hierarchical sets of economic, political, and social relations which became, over time, embedded in structures of power (Rosenberg, 1994: 46–58). Not all cultures, across time and space, however, have been thusly organized and so it is not possible to argue that Western cultural knowledges and practices, including Western forms of power relations, represent exogenously given universals. In this way, the postmodern theoretical assumption, rooted largely in the writings of Foucault, that power is everywhere, and that all relations are power relations, is emptied of its universalist meaning. To assume such a universalism is to speak for other cultures on the basis of Western knowledges and practices. In the same way, theoretical constructions of human nature, in terms of specific behaviours that universally shape social organization, are also meaningless. Hence, two constraints on our ability to imagine alternate security futures are removed.

Clark has a second argument that also opens space for thinking about alternate security futures, and this argument does contain universals. She proposes that, although no universals characterize human nature in terms of specific behaviours, there are universals in terms of social needs (clark, 2002: 229–62), and that these social needs are as important for the survival of both the individual and the group as the basic physical and material requirements for sustaining life.

The primary social need is the need for meaning. The social cohesion required for the successful emergence of the species involved a sustained degree of organization and structuring of various relationships. That is, it required a social order that allowed for predictable results from organized group life. Central to the organization of a social order is a meaning system—there have to be collectively understood reasons for doing certain things and doing them in particular ways. Indeed, the human brain stores and retrieves information on the basis of meanings.

As an increasingly successful species in the Darwinian sense of success, the size of coherent groups of *Homo sapiens* increased and their group survival activities became more complex and more dependent on specialized knowledges, the coordination of these knowledges for collective quotidian living, and the teaching of these knowledges for future survival success. Language provided an efficient medium for this work as it allowed for the development of shared meanings about a division of labour, about reproduction, about norms, rules, and values adopted for group cohesiveness; about histories, origins, and futures, and about the unexplainable. In other words, language allowed for the development of culture. As clark writes, 'Culture is created through communication' and comprises 'the set of stable consensual frames in a social system' (ibid., 230).

Indeed, clark's argument is that the success of *Homo sapiens* as a species is because adaptation increasingly selected for *cultural groups*, those with complex societal organization, language skills, and meaning systems. Further, adaptation also increasingly selected for the ability of these groups to intermingle and interbreed, 'giving rise to functional communities of genetically highly diverse individuals able to live in large cohesive groups'. Once *Homo sapiens* was firmly established as a species and living in relatively large and relatively cohesive groups throughout the world, clark suggests that 'the last 10,000 years of human history . . . [is] a history of meaning systems' (ibid., 125). It is, therefore, a history of different ways of being human, but the universal is the need for meaning.

With regard to thinking about alternate security futures, the corollary to this argument is that because identities, both group and individual, are forged within meaning systems and because meaning systems are essential to the survival of both the group and the individual, then both meaning systems and identities are security issues of prime importance in exactly the same way that basic physical and material survival needs are security issues. Because meaning systems differ, this means that securing difference is a basic security issue. Meaning systems are of course flexible, and securing difference does not mean freezing it in place. It does mean, however, establishing the conditions whereby different peoples are able to meet their basic physical, material, and social needs differently, including during periods of socially consensual cultural transition.

Based on the above, there are perhaps some useful tools for thinking about alternative security orders. It seems the imagination need not be constrained by theoretically or culturally based ideas about universals in terms of either specific human behaviours or types of social formations. Human nature, according to this perspective, is characterized by capacities, rather than specific behaviours, and by flexibility in the exercise of those capabilities, while social orders are contingent entities.

There *are* universals, however, involving the physical, material, and social needs for survival. Focusing on these minimal but universal human needs provides a basis for thinking about alternative security futures. Because these needs are met differently by different societies, or cultures, the imagination need not be constrained by the specifics of meeting these needs. Rather, thought is required about the kinds of global relations that might allow for securing different ways of meeting universally held basic human needs—physical, material, and social. This involves thinking about the possible spaces in which 'differences' might meet with equal integrity to negotiate the fulfillment of common human needs differently.

The 'practice' part of praxis involves acting in these spaces and with these insights, and here, as R.B.J. Walker points out, civil society is already involved in 'multiple journeys' to alternative security futures (Walker, 2002: 18). Many of these journeys involve advocacy efforts aimed at reforming rather than transforming the global structures of Western power relations (Keck and Sikkink, 1998). Many of these journeys, however, involve efforts that carry the potential to create new kinds of political communities that operate outside, above, and below the state, rooted in a global consciousness that is the product of ongoing processes of cross-cultural mediations of meanings and practices. As such, they may themselves represent, in nascent form, the future they are attempting to build.

Ronnie Lipshutz explores this dynamic in regard to environmentalism (Lipshutz, 1997; Lipshutz and Mayer, 1996), while both David McNally and Naomi Klein recognize the dynamic within the anti-globalist movement (McNally, 2002; Klein, 2000). And it is not the case that these 'journeys' are all dominated by Western activists or Western values and goals. Indeed, on the basis of his discussion of a number of non-Western anti-globalist resistances since 2000, McNally concludes that the anti-globalist movement is a 'truly popular' movement in which 'the oppressed of the South, as it is often described, are playing a leading role' (McNally, 2002: 26). In terms of cross-cultural activism within the movement, McNally argues that anti-globalist organizations and networks are significantly shaped by processes of plural and participatory democratic practices, and these practices do not reflect only Western understandings of participatory democracy. Communal decision-making processes of non-Western peoples reflecting non-Western ways of knowing and doing are often the models for these practices.

Although it would be hugely remiss to underestimate the ability of the forces of the status quo to resist such movements, it is just as remiss to dismiss them as mere noise on the margins. To do so both reinforces the status quo and limits, to Western ways of knowing and doing, the ability to imagine, and to act in the interest of building, alternative security futures.

Resisting the still evolving global systems of control now in use by the US as the leader of Western peoples and states requires short-term problem-solving activities such as those suggested above with regard to the recommendations of the *Report* of the Bi-National Planning Group and Canada's membership in NORAD. More importantly, however, resistance requires resisting the theoretical perspectives in which these systems of control are embedded. After all, these perspectives limit our ability to imagine alternative global security futures, to recognize where they might be in the process of nascent construction, and to act in ways that might foster that construction.

Notes

1. This is evidenced in consistent policy statements and speeches since the 1960s and in Canada's efforts in the United Nations' Permanent Conference on Disarmament to establish a treaty on the Prevention of an Arms Race in Outer Space.

2. The public controversy in this instance did not emerge until the mid-1980s when the removal of the clause first became public knowledge, at the same time as the Reagan administration invited Canada to participate in its Strategic Defense Initiative (SDI).

3. The *Final Report* contains a list of the present and past members of the Bi-National Planning Group, including the defence production industries represented.

4. See any of the 12 articles in Segal (2005).

5. For a comprehensive social, political, and economic history, see Davies (1997).

6. Peterson (1992) explores the origins of the hierarchical relations of power as functional for the accumulation of wealth and power, and as the bases for Western gendering.

7. Clark (2002: 98–125); unless referenced otherwise, and apart from quotations, the following arguments are contained in these pages.

Chapter Four

Constructing Canadian Foreign Policy

Myths of Good International Citizens, Protectors, and the War in Afghanistan

Claire Turenne Sjolander and Kathryn Trevenen

We are not daunted by shadows because we carry the light that defines them—the light of freedom and democracy, of human rights and the rule of law.... Our role in Afghanistan is Canada at its best and the Canadian people are proud to stand with you. (Prime Minister Stephen Harper, quoted in Blanchfield, 2007: A3)

Canada has a noble tradition of helping the world's needy. There are few countries more needy than Afghanistan. . . . Afghans cannot rebuild their society unless they can be confident their efforts won't be wrecked by terrorists and insurgents. Canadian forces are helping give them the security they need. The forces are also playing humanitarian roles, delivering aid supplies, medical treatment, and other services. Because of international help, Afghans can now vote freely in elections, send their children to school, and go about their daily lives. Women are regaining some of the rights erased by the fanatical Taliban regime. As Mr. Harper put it, these are things worth standing up for. What Canada is doing in Afghanistan is 'in the very best of the traditions of this country ... stepping up to the plate, and doing good when good is required.' (*Globe and Mail*, 2006: A16)

Nowhere is Canada making a difference more clearly than in Afghanistan. Canada has joined the United Nations-sanctioned mission in Afghanistan because it is noble and necessary. Canadians understand that development and security go hand in hand. Without security, there can be no humanitarian aid, no reconstruction and no democratic development. Progress will be slow, but our efforts are bearing fruit. There is no better measure of this progress than the four million Afghan boys and two million girls who can dream of a better future because they now go to school. . . . Like the North Star, Canada has been a guide to other nations; through difficult times, Canada has shone as an example of what a people joined in common purpose can achieve. (Canada, 2007)

Portrayals of Canadian soldiers who 'carry the light' of freedom and democracy, who fund and build schools for orphans, and who do 'good when good is required' play a central role in defining the Canadian imaginary. These portrayals respond to the idea that Canada is a morally virtuous international actor, that it protects the rights of women and children at home and abroad, and that Canadian forces have a disinterested and 'noble tradition of helping the world's needy'. As Canadians, we are used to thinking of our armed forces as primarily concerned with the work of peacekeeping and, in so doing, as representing the best of what Canada has to offer to the world.[1] In these national narratives, Canada indeed imagines itself as a 'north star' guiding other nations.

In this chapter, we argue that the Conservative government's representations of the war in Afghanistan during its first two years in office depend on and continually reiterate two main national narratives: the first portrays Canada as a 'good international citizen', a noble and disinterested multilateral international actor; the second depicts Canada as 'protector' of the weak. We examine how these narratives evoke a moral position based in Canada's perceived tradition of upholding ideals of equality, multiculturalism, and human rights at home, and how they function by mobilizing powerful stories of gender and nation. In portraying Canada as a good international citizen, government speeches have largely focused on the development work that the Canadian troops have been doing in Afghanistan (such as reconstruction projects, including building schools), and on the humanitarian reasons for intervening—reasons often supported by pointing to the situation confronting women and children. These representations blur the realities of Canada's involvement in Afghanistan and function to limit debate about the justifications and ongoing feasibility of the mission. The narrative of Canada as the moral protector of the 'weak' functions in a similar way to police the parameters of debate. As protector of Afghan civilians (notably women and children), and as combat soldiers (who are really peacekeepers), the image of the Canadian military—and thereby of the Canadian state—as protector becomes one against which political opposition is difficult to articulate.

This chapter examines the narratives used by the Conservative government through an analysis of government speeches in 2006 and 2007 discussing the Afghanistan mission. While Canada's intervention in Afghanistan hardly ended in 2007, and as of the early summer of 2009 is committed to continue until 2011, the 2006–7 period provides a useful examination of a particular period in Canada's

Afghan war. While Canada first intervened in the conflict in Afghanistan in the weeks following the events of 11 September 2001, it was not until early 2006 that Canadian forces found themselves directly involved in a sustained and costly combat mission, no matter what Canadians believed about the nature of that mission. In early March 2006, for example, Strategic Counsel, a market research firm, conducted the first of a series of surveys on Canadians' opinions towards the Afghanistan mission. This poll revealed that Canadians were overwhelmingly likely to identify peacekeeping rather than combat as the primary role of Canadian troops in Afghanistan (with 70 per cent of Canadians, and 76 per cent of Quebecers, identifying peacekeeping as the primary focus of the mission) (Strategic Counsel, 2006: 21).[2] The reality on the ground in Kandahar had begun to suggest otherwise, however. From the initial deployments of 2001–2 until the move to Kandahar in late 2005, eight Canadian soldiers had been killed in Afghanistan: four in April 2002 as a result of a 'friendly fire' incident at the hands of a US fighter jet; two in October 2003 when their vehicle hit a roadside bomb outside Kabul; one in January 2004 as a result of a suicide bomber; and the eighth in November 2005, the victim of a traffic accident outside Kandahar. By contrast, 36 Canadian soldiers and one Canadian diplomat were killed in Afghanistan in 2006, and a further 30 perished in 2007. By mid-June 2009, 120 Canadian troops had lost their lives in Afghanistan. Of those killed in 2006 and 2007, only five died as a result of friendly fire or other accidents—the others perished in combat.[3] This number of fallen Canadian troops represented the largest death toll for Canada's military since the Korean War—and the numbers were diligently reported to a public long unaccustomed to news of death from the front.

The return of Canadian troops to the southern province of Kandahar, beginning in late 2005, clearly heralded the start of the most dangerous phase in Canada's military operations in Afghanistan. By early 2006, Taliban insurgents were beginning to mount major offensives against NATO troops, with Kandahar province—and thereby Canadian soldiers—as one of the primary targets for such action. In early 2006, as well, a new minority Conservative government led by Stephen Harper had come to power in Ottawa—a coincidence with respect to developments in Afghanistan that nonetheless permits the marking of a departure from the previous phases of the mission.

That the deployment of Canadian troops back to southern Afghanistan coincides both with a significant increase in fatal attacks *and* a change in government in Ottawa provides reason enough for a particular focus on this phase of Canada's Afghan mission. One additional factor motivates our interest in the period after 2005, however. The year 2006 marks the start of the period during which Canadian public opinion became increasingly aware—and increasingly critical—of Canada's involvement in Afghanistan. While the souring of Canadian opinion on the mission is at least in part related to the increase in battle fatalities, the growing negative assessment of the war became, in and of itself, a source of pressure on the Canadian government—and a factor increasingly important to the framing of the discourses on the war presented by that government.

A total of 66 speeches on the topic of Canada's involvement in Afghanistan were collected for the period between 31 January 2006 and 31 December 2007. The speeches retained for analysis were those of official representatives of Canada's Conservative government: Prime Minister Stephen Harper, Defence Ministers Gordon O'Connor and Peter MacKay, Foreign Affairs Ministers Peter MacKay and Maxime Bernier, as well as Ministers of International Co-operation Josée Verner and Beverley Oda. In addition, the speeches of senior public officials acting on behalf of Canadian ministers of the Crown (speaking in their absence) were included. While the media coverage of these speeches, as well as of comments made by government officials to the press, is crucial to examine in the construction of Canada's foreign policy in a time of war, such a systematic assessment is not attempted in this chapter. Rather, the messaging provided by those speaking in the name of the Canadian government is the focus of this analysis, for this messaging allows us to assess the extent to which the main narratives of Canadian foreign policy are deployed and reiterated by the government itself.

Canada as the Good International Citizen

In order to understand the construction and functioning of the good international citizen/peacekeeper narrative, we first need to examine the context in which it operates. During the first days of the Harper administration, the government painted Canada's security interests starkly against the image of the terrorist attacks of 11 September 2001. As the Minister of National Defence, Gordon O'Connor, had argued in his first speech in February 2006, Canada's 'mission to Afghanistan is in our national interest. On September 11th 2001, terrorists attacked North America and Canadians were killed. Let me be clear: when terrorists attack Canadians, Canada will defend itself. That's why we're in Afghanistan' (O'Connor, 2006a). The continental context (as well as Canada's partnership with the United States) was emphasized. By 2007, however, reference to 9/11 begins to fade from the government's speeches, replaced by an emphasis on the multilateral institutions to which Canada belongs. Softer and more altruistic messages become the norm in response to an increasingly skeptical Canadian public. A 2007 Strategic Counsel report obtained by the *Globe and Mail* emphasized the importance of so doing, recommending that the Canadian government place the emphasis on "'rebuilding,'" "enhancing the lives of women and children,'" and "peacekeeping'" in communicating with the Canadian public in order to change negative perceptions of the Afghan mission (Freeman, 2007: A1).[4]

The softening of the government rhetoric through minimal reference to 9/11 allowed government officials to emphasize more altruistic motivations for the Canadian involvement in Afghanistan. This should not be interpreted to mean that the Harper government has argued for an exclusively 'altruistic' explanation of our role in Afghanistan, however. Rather, the government has made a strong link between Canada's security interests and the broader goals of helping Afghans, as a February 2007 speech by the Prime Minister illustrates:

Canada's involvement and sacrifices in Afghanistan serve our national interests and values on several levels. It's not just about foreign aid, though that's part of it. It's not just about doing our duty with the United Nations and our NATO allies, though that too is part of it. And it's not just about living up to our beliefs in freedom, democracy, human rights and the rule of law, though that most certainly is part of it too.

But as Chris Alexander [deputy special representative of the United Nations Secretary-General for Afghanistan and former Canadian Ambassador to Afghanistan] has frequently pointed out, global security hinges on success in Afghanistan. If we fail in Afghanistan, if that country relapses into anarchy and once again becomes a haven for extremists and terrorists, the world will be manifestly more dangerous. Afghanistan is the front line of the international security challenge of the modern, post-Cold War world. We must build a successful alternative there in order to defeat extremism and terrorism everywhere. (Canada, Office of the Prime Minister, 2007)

Harper begins by recalling the selfless motives behind intervention: foreign aid, duty to the values and goals of the UN and NATO, defending Canada's belief in freedom, democracy, human rights, and the rule of law, but the Prime Minister also links the Afghan mission to Canada's security interests—Afghanistan is the 'front line' for contemporary security challenges, and these are as relevant to Canada as they are to any other member of the international community of states. By connecting Canada's security interests, at least as constructed by the Conservative government, to the more altruistic goals of freedom, democracy, and aid, Harper has effectively covered all bases. Under this formulation, even Canada's 'national interests' are morally defensible—they are about making the world a less dangerous place. By arguing that 'we must build a successful alternative there in order to defeat extremism and terrorism everywhere', Harper appears to address both disinterested and interested motivations—Canada wants to help others at the same time as it strives to keep itself safe. This formulation, however, offers a simplistic view of Canada's so-called 'self-interest' and functions to limit true debate on the justifications for intervention in Afghanistan.

The disinterested motivations alluded to in even Harper's self-interested speeches point to the first narrative that the government has drawn on to explain and justify the Afghan mission. This narrative mobilizes conceptions of Canada's role as an enlightened middle power, concerned with multilateralism and peacekeeping. It portrays Canada as a good international citizen, more concerned with helping others than with advancing its own self-interest. Central to this narrative is the image of the Canadian peacekeeper.

As Sandra Whitworth has argued, this image of Canada as peacekeeper is a central myth in the Canadian imaginary. In this myth, 'Canada is an altruistic and benign middle power, acting with a kind of moral purity not normally exhibited by contemporary states' (Whitworth, 2003: 76). Although Canadians are now in Kandahar in a combat mission that evolved out of the American invasion in 2001, the government continues to capitalize on the public perception that the

Canadian military is first and foremost a peacekeeping force, acting under the auspices of the United Nations. This perception has meant that as the Canadian participation in Afghanistan evolved from Kabul to Kandahar, public debate has not seemed to fully acknowledge that the Afghanistan mission is part of a war, not a result of an established consensus to create a peacekeeping force. In particular, many government speeches highlight the argument that Canada is in Afghanistan at the invitation of the democratically elected Afghan government. While this was true in 2007, it was certainly not the case in 2001 when the invasion took place; framing speeches around the Afghan government's request presents the mission in Afghanistan as if it is similar to other 'muscular peacekeeping' missions that begin with a clear invitation from the government.

This construction of Canada as a good international citizen, a peacekeeper (even if self-interested), is not neutral, however. Central to this myth of Canada as a peacekeeping 'good citizen' is a portrait of Afghanistan as backward, uncivilized, and helpless in the face of internal strife. Following Sherene Razack, we question the racial logic that informs narratives depicting peacekeepers as subduing unruly and savage Third World people. In *Dark Threats and White Knights*, speaking to the US intervention in Afghanistan and Iraq, Razack contends that:

> embedded deep within the conceptual foundations of the Bush admin-istration's notion of a life-and-death struggle against the 'axis of evil' is a thoroughly racial logic. Disciplining, instructing, and keeping in line Third World peoples who irrationally hate and wish to destroy their saviours derives from the idea that Northern peoples inhabit civilized lands while the South, in Chinua Achebe's words, 'is a metaphysical battlefield devoid of all recog-nizable humanity into which the wandering European enters at his peril.' . . . [C]olour-line thinking was certainly in evidence in the American invasions of both Afghanistan . . . and Iraq . . . , invasions justified on the ground that it was necessary to drop thousands of bombs on Afghanis and Iraqis in order to save them from the excesses of their own society. . . . Oil, the free market, and the historical support the United States has given to the Taliban and to Saddam Hussein, among other despotic regimes, all disappear under 'smart' bombs. Once the smoke clears, peacekeepers walk in. (Razack, 2004: 7–8)

The Canadian government draws on this same racial logic to stifle debate on the Afghan mission. Government speeches foreclose any notion that non-military methods could have led to a democratic Afghanistan (or that negotiating peace with the Taliban and rival factions should—or even could—be the primary goal of foreign intervention), and always imply that ousting the Taliban was first and foremost a humanitarian project—one that nonetheless could employ any means necessary. Throughout the operation of the narrative of Canada as a good interna-tional citizen, Canada's motives remain unquestioned and unquestionable.

Although the Prime Minister and other ministers refer to Canada's undefined 'security interests' throughout their speeches in 2006 and 2007, Canada's role as good international citizen gets the most detailed elaboration. The Ministers of Defence and Foreign Affairs stick to three key messages throughout their speeches on Afghanistan. The first is that Canada is participating in an international coalition in Afghanistan. Maxime Bernier, Minister of Foreign Affairs, explains that 'Canada currently has troops in Afghanistan because it made a commitment to the international community. We are there under a UN mandate. We are there at the invitation of a democratically elected Afghan government, with 36 other countries, including Australia, the Netherlands, Germany, Italy, France and the United Kingdom' (Bernier, 2007). The second message is that the Afghan people themselves support the mission and have requested Canadian help. Bernier argues that 'Canadian soldiers, diplomats and humanitarian workers are in Afghanistan to defend the universal values of respect for basic human rights, as enunciated by the Afghans themselves in their constitution' (ibid.). Finally, Bernier drives home the point that, at its foundation, the Afghan mission is about helping Afghans:

> our mission in Afghanistan is about helping people rebuild their lives after years of oppression. It is about ensuring they have the resources to realize their aspirations. It is a stabilization mission. A development mission. It is our most important mission—a mission that promotes freedom, democracy, human rights and the rule of law. (Ibid.)

The Minister of National Defence, Peter MacKay, reiterates the connections between stabilization, development, and the work that the Canadian military is doing. In an address titled 'The Hard Questions', MacKay explains:

> Security enables good governance and development, and good governance and development reinforce security. The three are indivisible. The Canadian Forces are fighting with other countries in Afghanistan to allow for permanent and self-sustaining development. We are seeing developmental progress that reinforces our security successes. Here again, the military is just one part of a team working in Afghanistan. (MacKay, 2007e)

He asserts the same connections in an earlier speech, arguing that 'the Afghanistan Compact outlines a three-pronged approach to stabilizing Afghanistan: security, governance and development—three fronts closely intertwined and mutually reinforcing. Governance and development are dependent on security, but security cannot be maintained without governance and development' (MacKay, 2007d).

In all of Harper, Bernier, and MacKay's statements above, military intervention—'security'—is inextricably linked to development and good governance, conveying the message that Western military intervention is the only way that Afghanistan can create a democratic government. MacKay makes this logic clear in an address in March of 2007. He maintains that:

> only if there is security in Afghanistan can development workers and humanitarian assistance specialists get on with their tasks of helping Afghans through

economic development, education and reconstruction projects. Only if there is security can the fledgling steps in democratic governance and the rule of law be consolidated and extended. And only if there is security, can human rights in Afghanistan be grounded and protected in law and enforced in public. (MacKay, 2007a)

Here, history and context are both erased—Afghanistan is portrayed as a country that can only be 'tamed' by a strong Canadian military effort and no mention is made of the long history of foreign military and colonial intervention that shaped contemporary Afghanistan's many conflicts and divisions.

The Canadian government also frequently refers to the professionalism and skill of its military. In the same speech, MacKay stated that, 'thanks to the skills, professionalism and courage of our soldiers, the nascent peace stretching over most of the country has now been extended to large parts of Kandahar province' (ibid.). Again, MacKay makes the links between security and development: 'we are now consolidating those security gains and using this opportunity to increase our focus on bettering the lives of civilians, pushing ahead with reconstruction projects, building schools, encouraging small businesses and implementing governance programs' (ibid.). The narrative of Canada as good citizen depends on the assumption that Canadians are better equipped than Afghans—equipped not only with material resources like military hardware and development dollars but also with *moral* resources such as courage and professionalism.

Importantly, in the representation of the Canadian military as good international citizen in Afghanistan, the *actual* tasks performed by the military are less important than the public perception of the 'appropriate role' of that military. It is not necessary for Canadian policy-makers to actually use the word 'peacekeeping' in defining the nature of Canada's mission in Afghanistan, nor does the 'selling of the mission' depend on the explicit use of such a phrase. What is important is the place of peacekeeping in the Canadian imaginary; as Whitworth noted earlier, and as Lane Anker has argued: '"Peacekeeping" represents a defining aspect of Canadian identity, reflecting fundamental values, beliefs and interests. . . . Public support for a strong Canadian role internationally is largely rooted in our proud history of peacekeeping. In fact, many Canadians regard peacekeeping as the most positive contribution that Canada makes to the world' (Anker, 2005: 23).[5] The image of Canada as a good international citizen, through its narrative focus on building schools, on democratic governance, on humanitarian assistance, on the rule of law, and on the promotion of individual freedom, reinforces a perception among Canadians that its military engages in tasks that are peaceful, or that 'make' peace. This morally unquestionable position combines with a portrait of Canada as a protector of the weak to render Afghanistan as an abstract and ahistorical canvas on which to write the story of Canada's national virtues.

Canada as Protector

While the narrative of Canada as the 'good international citizen' depends on many national myths relating to Canada's perceived historical role as middle power, peacekeeper, and moral conscience, it also works in harmony with the second narrative frequently mobilized by the government relating to Canada's role as 'protector'. This narrative of Canada as protector of the weak complements the narrative of Canada as a moral citizen by creating a model of the stern but righteous father who must protect his family. Here, Afghan women and children, in particular, become the object of Canada's concern.

Canada's paternal role involves both the soldiers and the government that directs them. In a speech to the troops in Kandahar in May 2007, Harper tells the military:

> Because of you, the people of Afghanistan have seen the institution of democratic elections, the stirring of human rights and freedoms for women, the construction of schools, healthcare facilities and the basic infrastructure of a functional economy. Still, you know that your work is not complete. You know that we cannot just put down our arms and hope for peace. You know that we can't set arbitrary deadlines and simply wish for the best. And you must also know that your hard work is making a real difference to real people and their families. (Harper, 2007b)

Foreign Affairs Minister Peter MacKay echoes these sentiments: 'perhaps the single most noticeable difference in that country is that women are now not only permitted to start and operate a business, but they can also vote, they can sit along male counterparts in government, they can simply walk the streets unharassed—activities that were unheard of under the brutal Taliban regime' (MacKay, 2007b).

In almost all of the speeches delivered by the Prime Minister, the Defence Ministers, and the Foreign Affairs Ministers in 2006 and 2007, women's rights, schools, and health care are evoked as primary concerns for the military mission. Like the comments linking security to development, these speeches argue that the oppression of women and children is a primary reason for Canada's presence in Afghanistan. First, Canada's military will liberate Afghan women from the oppression of the Taliban, and then they will deliver the necessary development aid required to put girls in schools and women in government. In 2007, many government ministers pointed to progress for women in Afghanistan as proof of Canada's beneficial role in the country. Returning to his 'Hard Questions' address, we find Peter MacKay arguing that:

> we are supporting women who, under the Taliban regime, were forbidden to go to school, to work or to vote. Their voices were silenced, and to drive home that point, they were beaten for unimaginable things, such as for wearing shoes that made noise on the pavement as they walked. We are building a future for children, so that they can all be educated, have access to medical

care, and have the freedom to grow up in a climate of security and hope rather than in fear. (MacKay, 2007e)

Josée Verner, Minister of International Co-operation, was particularly positive about the mission's impact on women. Her speaking notes for a breakfast during International Development Week in 2007 reflect this optimism:

> women in Afghanistan suffered terribly under the Taliban regime. Previously, they were teachers, doctors, journalists, and homemakers. Then, overnight, they lost the right, not only to practice their profession, but also to leave their homes. Girls did not go to school. Now, things are gradually changing. With Canada's support, Afghanistan adopted a new constitution that recognizes equality between women and men. As a result, in recent elections, 25 per cent of the seats in Parliament were filled by women. We are working with the Government of Afghanistan, our Canadian partners, and civil society on several fronts, to ensure that women and girls in Afghanistan are actively involved in rebuilding their country. (Verner, 2007)

Verner's speaking notes reveal two interesting claims. The first is that women in Afghanistan lost their rights 'overnight' under the Taliban regime. While no one would challenge the claim that the Taliban ruthlessly targeted women and radically restricted their basic rights and safety, this attack on women did not happen overnight, nor did it entirely originate with the Taliban. As organizations such as the Revolutionary Association of Women of Afghanistan, Human Rights Watch, and Amnesty International have all documented, widespread abuse and oppression of women took place under different warlords and regional govern-ments in Afghanistan before the Taliban, and continues today (Human Rights Watch, 2002). The claim that women suddenly lost their rights dehistoricizes women's situations in Afghanistan and makes them an object of rescue. As a homogeneous group of suffering women, Afghan women become an unques-tionable reason for intervention and Canada as protector becomes particularly suited to the task. As other scholars have argued, this justification for the war in Afghanistan begs the question of why the international community didn't inter-vene to help Afghan women before the 9/11 attacks (see, e.g., Rawi, 2006). It also highlights the strategic importance of the 'rescuing women' argument, an argument that doesn't seem to be helping the thousands of women in Darfur who are currently being killed and raped.

Chandra Mohanty's discussion of Western feminism's colonizing impulse and ethnocentric universality identifies three principles often assumed in feminist work on women in the Third World and here reflected in the Canadian govern-ment's portrait of Afghan women. The principles are, first:

> the assumption of women as an already constituted, coherent group with identical interests and desires, regardless of class, ethnic or racial location, or contradictions that implies a notion of gender or sexual difference or even

patriarchy which can be applied universally and cross-culturally. The second analytical presupposition is evident on the methodological level, in the uncritical way 'proof' of universality and cross-cultural validity are provided. The third is a more specifically political presupposition underlying the methodologies and the analytic strategies, i.e., the model of power and struggle they imply and suggest. (Mohanty, 1997: 175–6; also see Mohanty, 1991)

These analytic strategies construct a uniform representation of an average Third World woman who 'leads an essentially truncated life based on her feminine gender (read: sexually constrained) and her being "Third World" (read: ignorant, poor, uneducated, tradition-bound, domestic, family-oriented, victimized etc.)' (ibid., 176). They also constitute the counter-image of the independent, educated, and empowered Western woman.

Mohanty's analysis of the colonizing impulse in some Western work on the 'Third World woman' is important in the context of the war in Afghanistan because it reveals the homogenizing effects the government narratives have. Instead of recognizing the heterogeneity of subjects it reports on, Canadian government representations erase the complexity, flexibility, and moments of agency found in Afghan women's experiences. Mohanty explains that by using 'Third World women' as a stable category of analysis, some Western accounts 'assume an ahistorical, universal unity between women based on a generalized notion of their subordination'(ibid., 182). This perspective on subordination means not only that the Canadian government fails to recognize the agency of Afghan women, it also gives them a reason to step in and 'save' them from oppressive cultures. As Gayatri Spivak further argues, it is through this produced imbalance in power and agency that 'imperialism's (or globalization's) image as the establisher of the good society is marked by the espousal of the woman as *object* of protection from her own kind' (Spivak, 1999: 291).

The importance of critically assessing representations of Third World women in the West lies in part in the portrayal of women as the helpless, passive, or innocent casualties of patriarchal cultural traditions, religions, or governments. Portraits of Afghan women during the war against the Taliban regime disclose the dangers in such a narrow representation. During the war, Afghan women have often been portrayed by Western media and governments as part of the reason for armed intervention—they had to be saved from the brutal oppression of the Taliban. Again, that the Taliban enacted policies violently repressing women's rights, education, and activities is not in contention. But by evoking the 'innocent' female victims of the Taliban as a reason to intervene *after* 9/11, the coalition perpetuated the practice of using the category 'women' as part of a self-serving foreign policy. Representing any group of women as a coherent category carries this danger. Although appeals to 'women's rights' or 'Afghan women's suffering' are understandable at times (when trying to mobilize money, media attention, or government resources, for example), they can inadvertently abet counter-attempts by the Taliban to generate an equally general category of the opposite sort. By mobilizing and exploiting the image of Afghan women as helpless victims of their religion, country, or culture,

Western coalition governments simultaneously increased the stakes of attempts to control Afghan women and regulate their activities. It is thus necessary to question and complicate the coherence of these categories by attending to complex realities that exceed the generality invoked, while simultaneously working to build effective alliances. To complicate these categories we not only need to attend to the history and heterogeneity of Afghan women's experiences, but we also need to disrupt the power of the narrative of Canada as 'protector' of the weak.

Limiting Debate: The Impact of Narratives

Demonstrating that the government uses particular narratives to sell the war in Afghanistan seems like a fairly obvious point to make. Of course the government tries to spin its policy, and of course wars will be portrayed in ways that make the 'home nation' look just and righteous. In this case, however, these narratives not only offer a justification for the mission in Afghanistan, they also try to eliminate debate about the mission by mobilizing moral arguments. By evoking an image of Canada as a just international citizen with a particular moral compass and as a protector of women and children, the government implies that any critic of the mission is therefore content to sacrifice democracy and let women suffer. The narratives forestall discussion of Canada's strategic alliance and shared interests with the US, the complex history of conflict in Afghanistan, the role that Canadian-made armaments play in conflicts around the globe, and the many times when Canada and the international community have ignored (and continue to ignore) the widespread oppression faced by women.

In the context of this moral outrage, critics of the war become the 'real' enemy. In his 'Hard Questions' speech Peter MacKay makes this link clear:

> Canada understands that there are real risks involved in helping the Afghan people achieve these gains. Without a doubt, we will continue to stand by our brave Canadian soldiers and our fallen heroes. We believe that each and every soldier serving in Afghanistan is leaving a proud legacy, and we honour their commitment.
>
> However, what we face is the Taliban still working to generate doubt and fear. They would like nothing better than Canada and other NATO countries to withdraw from Afghanistan. They know that the Canadian court of public opinion has tremendous influence. They are very aware of our domestic discussions on this issue, and they will try to exploit our debate for military gain.
>
> They can't beat us on the battlefield. That is the only way this cunning adversary can win. This is the enemy that our brave men and women in uniform face. (MacKay, 2007e)

Public debate, in this passage, becomes the ally of the Taliban and the enemy of Canada's commitment, soldiers, and legacy. Under these conditions, any questions about the war are framed as a betrayal of Canada's national character.

By mobilizing ahistorical moral outrage to justify the mission in Afghanistan, the government also ignores criticisms from NGOs, government agencies, and the military itself regarding the dangers of having soldiers trying to deliver development aid as they are fighting a war. The contradictions (both theoretical and practical) between the narrative of Canada as good international citizen and protector and the realities of combat are covered over by this layer of moral outrage and certainty. In this way, the deaths of Canadian soldiers (and never the deaths of Afghans) become the ongoing justification for continuing the mission. The narratives of the good international citizen, committed to multilateralism and peacekeeping, and of Canada as protector of the weak combine to foreclose the public space for debate on the purposes and legitimacy of Canada's intervention in Afghanistan. As the *Calgary Herald* insisted two days following the death of Captain Nichola Goddard in Afghanistan:

> Those who complain of the meaninglessness of a soldier's death do not grasp how utterly vain such a death would be if Canada abruptly left Afghanistan because of it and the seeds of democracy languished, unwatered, in the volatile climate there. We will pay a far greater tribute to Goddard and to the other Canadian soldiers who have lost their lives there if we finish what they started. (*Calgary Herald*, 2006: A30)

The lessons of the 2006–7 period of Canada's military intervention are simple: the government's deployment of the narratives of good international citizen and protector of the weak framed Canada's intervention in Afghanistan in such a way that it became nearly impossible to reach any other conclusion than that of the *Calgary Herald* editorialist—and democratic debate in Canada became all the poorer for it.

Since 2007, of course, the circumstances in Afghanistan have not improved, and the Harper government has repeatedly reiterated its intention to withdraw (at least militarily) by 2011. The Prime Minister has even gone on record to state that the war in Afghanistan is now unwinnable (CNN, 2009). Despite these apparent changes in the government's orientation towards the war, the justification for Canada's presence continues to be articulated around the mythologies of Canada as good international citizen and protector. Opposition to the war is muted. The window on public debate over the mission in Afghanistan opened a crack, however, with the news in early April 2009 that the Afghan government was prepared to adopt a law effectively sanctioning marital rape. 'Canada continues to call on the Afghan government, in the strongest of terms, to honour its human rights treaty obligations under international law, including respect for the equality of women before the law', Prime Minister Harper responded. 'We cannot state strongly enough our concern for the rights of women in Afghanistan' (Canada, Office of the Prime Minister, 2009). If the prosecution of the war leads to outcomes that clearly undermine Canada's good international citizen and protector roles, is Canada's participation in the war politically sustainable?

Notes

1.   As an article posted on the Department of National Defence website notes, despite the evolution of the role the Canadian Forces have been called upon to perform, Canadians overwhelmingly cite peacekeeping as a key contribution of Canadian foreign policy. As the article points out, this is in part a reflection of the lack of understanding of the actual tasks performed by the Canadian Forces: 'Notwithstanding this lack of awareness of operations, when asked what the most positive contribution that Canada as a country makes to the world, "peacekeeping" remains the most frequent selection. Almost nine in ten Canadians, in fact, report that "promoting world peace" is the most important foreign policy objective for Canada' (Anker, 2005: 27).

2.   The poll question read: 'What do Canadians perceive to be the purpose of our troops in Afghanistan—peacekeeping or combat?' The survey of 1,000 Canadians was conducted between 9–12 March 2006, with an overall margin of error of 3.1 per cent.

3.   It should be noted that many Canadian deaths in Afghanistan have occurred as a result of improvised explosive devices (IEDs). These are reported as such rather than as combat deaths (deaths as a result of a military offensive or enemy attack) by the Canadian military. Having said this, the Canadian military does classify the vast majority of Canadian deaths in Afghanistan as combat-related, on the assumption that IEDs are not traditionally found in non-combat zones.

4.   The 16 July 2007 Strategic Counsel poll revealed that 81 per cent of Canadians, including 79 per cent of Quebecers, felt that the possible negative impact on the rights of women and children needed to be taken into consideration when considering if Canadians should stay in Afghanistan beyond 2009 (see Strategic Counsel, 2007: 16).

5.   Despite the key role peacekeeping plays in defining the Canadian imaginary, it is important to note that by 2006, for example, Canada ranked fifty-fifth out of 108 as a UN peacekeeping country based on its commitment of equipment and military personnel (United Nations Association in Canada, 2007).

Chapter Five

Fighting the War and Winning the Peace

Three Critiques of the War in Afghanistan

Colleen Bell

In February of 2002 Canada sent troops to Afghanistan as part of the US's Operation Enduring Freedom, the first offensive in the US-led 'War on Terror', or what is now, many years later, referred to as the 'long war'. By 2003 Canada's mission was broadened under NATO's International Security Assistance Force (ISAF), involving the continued presence of more than 2,000 Canadian soldiers stationed mainly in southern Afghanistan's Kandahar province and, to a lesser degree, in the capital city of Kabul.

Canada's deployment to Afghanistan has been the subject of continued debate and at times confusion over the direction of Canadian foreign policy. For instance, in the beginning years of the mission many people, including media venues such as the CBC (2004), were comforted by the mistaken impression that Canada was on a peacekeeping operation in Afghanistan. To be sure, Canada has been courted as a global 'peacekeeper', an international deal broker among groups and nations engaged in conflict. It thus came as a shock to many when media reports surfaced that the Canadian Forces were engaged in offensive operations in Afghanistan's southern region of Kandahar. Canada, it became increasingly clear, is engaged in full frontal combat, a design of intervention that falls far outside the realm of providing impartial, non-offensive support for a peace process. But the point here is not just that Canada was never on a peacekeeping mission in Afghanistan. Rather, the confusion over the nature of the mission speaks to a deeper debate over Canada's active participation in US-led counter-terrorism operations and what this means for Canada's self-image as a force for peace in the world. If Canada is not engaged in a traditional peacekeeping mission, if there is, as the Department of National Defence claims, 'no peace to keep', then the question in the minds of many is how, or perhaps whether, Canada is upholding its self-image as a force for global peace? How, in short, is Canada working for peace?

In attempting to answer this question we need to examine the debate that cropped up where the controversy over peacekeeping left off. That is, the question of how Canada is promoting peace is very much tied to a more recent debate over the effectiveness and importance of reconstruction and aid efforts in comparison to the military effort. For many, the legitimacy of the intervention depends not simply on defeating the Taliban, but on creating peace through aid and development in Afghanistan. This chapter navigates through some of the assumptions that inform the debate over the relationship between military action and development. It is first argued that development and reconstruction efforts are overly simplified as presenting the peaceful and non-controversial aspect of the mission in Afghanistan. I suggest that the utter inadequacy of these efforts to date and the way in which development and aid efforts are being shaped provide some important clues about the political, and indeed violent, utility of humanitarian objectives used by Canada and other intervening NATO countries. In particular, the 'whole-of-government' approach that Canada is deploying in Afghanistan, which binds development to security, is not simply a design for peace, but is itself a strategy of war. Next, I explore the purported claim of the Canadian government that Canada has intervened in Afghanistan to 'assist' and 'help' the people escape poverty, violence, and corruption. The mission, I argue, is much more an expression of Canada's national security agenda, especially as it is defined by defence professionals and business elites, which is then crudely mapped onto Afghanistan. In doing so, the mission infantilizes Afghans and equates the country with terrorism, thereby moving human suffering and oppression into the realm of risk and threat. The final section analyzes how Canada's foreign policy practices present the nation as an innocent responder to insecurity and underdevelopment in Afghanistan. Yet there are important ways in which these very practices elide how Canada (in addition to much of the West) is deeply implicated in the creation of instability and poverty in Afghanistan, both historically and currently.

Sticks and Carrots: Aid as a Strategy of War

While much discussion of Canada's deployment has been focused on the work of the armed forces to quash the Taliban, the mission is also much more than a classical military undertaking. This is because the problem, as coalition nations see it, is not simply with active Taliban insurgents and an Al-Qaeda network in hiding, but that Afghanistan is itself a 'terrorist haven'. It is, in other words, hospitable to the organization of terrorist networks and affords them the capacity to act with impunity. The question of Afghanistan's future, a future that the US and other NATO powers have claimed a central role in shaping, is thus a question of underdevelopment and political organization as much as it is a question of military prowess. The social, political, and economic climate requires transformation so that, according to popular parlance, the 'roots' of terrorism are addressed.

For Canada, in addition to military defeat of the Taliban, actually securing Afghanistan is critically tied to certain kinds of development and governance reform. In policy documents this three-part concern is expressed as the 'whole-of-government' strategy. The origin of this approach of Canada's current Conservative government lies with the former Liberal government's '3D'—defence, diplomacy, development—approach, which was articulated in the 2005 *International Policy Statement*. The 3D or whole-of-government approach is meant to improve coherence and avoid duplication among aid and non-aid programs and policies as a means of overcoming conflict and increasing stability (Canada, 2005c: 10). It represents the view that military and non-military activities are interdependent foreign policy objectives. As one defence analyst noted, 'without security, development cannot happen, and without development, lasting security cannot be sustained' (Peabody, 2005: 4). Along these lines, the whole-of-government strategy is designed to facilitate and improve the co-ordination of different areas of action, producing 'discrete yet synchronized operations across the full spectrum of conflict' (Howard, 2006).

This framework of synchronization and interdependence, as it informs Canada's ongoing Afghanistan deployment, is outlined in an important pamphlet entitled *Canadians Making a Difference in the World: Afghanistan*. As it states:

> Afghanistan is facing numerous challenges, including security sector reform, reducing narcotics production and trafficking, promoting human rights and gender equality, good governance and economic reconstruction. These are mutually reinforcing and must be addressed simultaneously...Meeting these challenges involves an integrated and coordinated approach. In leveraging resources and expertise across all levels of government, along with complementary engagement of military and Canadian civilians, Canada plays an active role in assisting the Afghan authorities and Afghan people in stabilizing the country, strengthening governance and reducing poverty. (Canada, 2006: 2)

What is articulated by the push towards integration and co-ordination across levels of government is that war fighting and peace work ought to be simultaneous, and that they are mutually indispensable components of Canadian interventionism. One concrete example of this integration is the introduction of Provincial Reconstruction Teams (PRTs) in Afghanistan. While they vary in size and composition depending on command structure, local circumstance, and the availability of civilian agencies, they do retain a number of general characteristics that encapsulate this view.

As integrated civil military operations, PRTs are semi-mobile project groups designed to extend the authority and governance of the central government, rebuild Afghanistan, and provide needed services to the population (DND, 2007). They purport to provide humanitarian assistance by working in partnership with the

Afghanistan government, the UN, donor nations, and NGOs. Currently, 24 PRTs are scattered throughout Afghanistan, the majority of which fall under US command while others are carried out under ISAF command (US Department of State, 2006). The US Department of Defense refers to PRTs as 'small military teams' and distinctly not experienced developmental agencies or reconstruction teams. The function of PRTs, it is noted, is to 'reach into remote communities and serve as the "eyes and ears" on the ground, and simultaneously provide a deterrence presence and a tangible oversight of central government programs' (US Department of Defense, 2004). Canada's PRT in Kandahar, which is comprised of 330 personnel, performs precisely this function by bringing together personnel from the Canadian Forces, Foreign Affairs and International Trade, the Canadian International Development Agency (CIDA), and civilian police under the jurisdiction of the Royal Canadian Mounted Police (RCMP). It encapsulates, in micro form, the actual deployment of the whole-of-government approach in Afghanistan, drawing governance and reconstruction activities into the war effort.

While PRTs have been praised within defence circles, Canada's mission in general has come under sustained criticism for overemphasizing military operations and drastically underfunding aid and reconstruction efforts. Some have charged that this imbalance amounts to 90 per cent of total spending on military efforts in Afghanistan and only 10 per cent on development (Senlis Council, 2006a: xii; Laxer, 2007). As early as 2003, the non-governmental organizations Care International and the Centre on International Cooperation chastised donor governments for meeting less that half of Afghanistan's reconstruction needs and for pledging to provide only a quarter of its needs for aid and reconstruction for future years (Care International, 2003). This same criticism was echoed several years later in a Senlis Council report that made a series of recommendations to an independent panel headed by John Manley to assess Canada's future in Afghanistan. In addition to noting Canada's failure to produce tangible development and reconstruction in Afghanistan, the report states that 'as a beneficiary of international aid, Afghanistan receives the lowest amount of reconstruction financing compared to all other post-conflict nations' (Senlis Council, 2007: 9; Smith, 2007). The result, according to some researchers, has been a marked deterioration of support for NATO troops and the Karzai government (Senlis Council, 2006b; Loyn, 2007). In southern districts where Canadian Forces and its PRTs operate there has been a clear 'lack of visible results' and aid has utterly failed to reach people at all (MacDonald, 2007). With purposeful bombing of villages and the withholding of aid and food, reports Senlis Council researcher Norine MacDonald, 'the level of human suffering in the region has in fact increased as a direct consequence of the military campaigns conducted by our Canadian soldiers and their colleagues in addition to the political neglect of the civilian population' (ibid., 9). While it is increasingly common to note that security and development are interdependent objectives, resources for war, so it would appear, far outweigh those for aid and reconstruction.

In response to the humanitarian situation in Afghanistan some have argued that the problem was not only insufficient aid levels, but that delivery was proving difficult due to the conflict. Originally, however, the integrated approach of combining military and civilian operations was criticized for militarizing aid under the pretense that development work is inconsistent with military conflict and cannot be effectively carried out by the same people, at the same time, in the same place (Jaimet, 2006). Yet, in the face of stark failures by the Canadian International Development Agency (CIDA) to have any kind of visible impact on the humanitarian situation in Afghanistan and for allegedly relying on appalling employment practices, including the use of child labour in reconstruction projects, a growing contingent of commentators have argued that the military is better suited than CIDA to effectively deliver aid (Senlis Council, 2007). The idea here is that if civilian-run agencies in Afghanistan are proving to be ineffective due to the ongoing conflict, then there is a larger role for the military in development and reconstruction efforts and certainly in the promotion of civilian–military integration.

To some extent this is nothing new; the Canadian Forces has never limited its mission to a combat role, but has been increasingly working towards winning 'hearts and minds' among strategically important communities by offering food, tools, and assistance with infrastructural development in exchange for support. To be sure, from the perspective of military strategy, there are a number of political benefits to bringing aid and reconstruction into close quarters with military operations. Rather than contradicting the use of violent intervention, the aid and reconstruction efforts involving NATO members, including Canada, can serve as strategic components of the broader objective of the mission, which is not simply to defeat the Taliban but to transform Afghanistan as a whole. On track with this objective, Canada's whole-of-government approach serves as one expression of how commensurability is fostered between war-making and peace work. Here, humanitarian work does more than offset the use of violence; it is a calculated and at times integral component of the war effort.

For example, while an important goal of the intervention is to identify and eliminate insurgents, the interventionist strategy also entails a 'biopolitical' purpose (Foucault, 2003). Here, strategies of aid control purposefully determine who lives and who dies, not by directly 'killing' but by 'letting' people die. Rather than slay, aid deliverers can simply *deny* aid to unco-operative, suspicious, or even strategically unimportant locals groups, while making it available to co-operative, trustworthy, and strategically important ones. Within this framework, the policies and decisions of local communities and the conduct of particular groups and actors are not simply interpreted as expressions of local politics, but become calculated into the evolving strategy of coalition warfare. To put it in crudely metaphorical terms, this looks like a game of 'good cop/bad cop' in which civilian–military teams become hands that feed, hands that decide not to feed, and hands that strike. Such a strategy of aid control is, to be sure, well within the tactical objectives of the mission to eliminate Taliban supporters and to win strategically relevant public support. Moreover, with calls by some NGOs to have the military play an even larger role in the distribution of aid, this strategy is likely to become used more widely. For Canada, the militarization of aid, to put it in different terms, appears to be the unwavering trend of the future.

While at first glance this shared space of aid and military activity might seem to be inconsistent with humanitarian principles of neutrality, impartiality, and independence, it is consistent with received and widespread opinion among aid donors since at least the end of the Cold War that development ought to be 'a structural form of conflict prevention' (Duffield, 2001: 121). Very recently, this view has been instrumental in the revival of counter-insurgency methods, rarely practised by Western states since the Vietnam War. Preventing and addressing conflict, according to counter-insurgency strategy, require more than responding to outward symptoms, but must intervene upon the internal conditions that purportedly lead to insurgency internally and terrorism externally. Improved governance and the promotion of behavioural change are directly concerned that Afghanistan 'never again serves as a terrorist haven' (Canada, 2006: 1). Historically, security and development have often been envisaged as separate processes, and even as processes at odds with one another, yet Canada's whole-of-government approach conflates them into one goal. In doing so, securing Afghanistan is not simply about limiting the activities of insurgents, but is also concerned with finding ways to promote acceptable forms of behaviour among the population more broadly. Significantly, the mission, in seeking to shape conduct, binds international security to social transformation.

International security, so we now are told, hinges on social transformation in distant lands. Rather than being principally concerned with the more traditional issues of territory and state, or even limited to apprehending 'enemies', securing Afghanistan has become intimately focused on the claim that underlying social problems—systemic forms of violence, poverty, and corruption—in poor and fragile states are a significant source of insecurity to the West. In one respect, the intervention surpasses traditional military operations by focusing on the role of development and social transformation, yet in drawing reconstruction and aid into the terrain of war it also remains intimately tied to traditional state-centric goals. Countering the problem of terrorism now requires a social makeover for Afghanistan, a makeover that is charted by Canada and its NATO partners.

Enlightened Self-Interest and the Image of Danger

The policy framework guiding the intervention in Afghanistan collapses what counts as an international security problem into the professed interests of coalition states. Certainly, Canada's Prime Minister, Stephen Harper (2007), employed the concept of global security to increase the legitimacy of Canada's mission when he announced that '[i]f we fail in Afghanistan, if that country relapses into anarchy and once again becomes a haven for extremists and terrorists, the world will be manifestly more dangerous.' Yet the reverse case is also made by the Canadian government. Here, Canada's national security interests are featured as primary, with global and Afghan interests secondary. As former Minister of National Defence Gordon O'Connor stated, staying the course in Afghanistan is important

'for the future of Afghanistan', for the 'stability of the region', and for 'international security'. But in stating these reasons O'Connor (2006a) noted that they are
actually second to the fundamental reason:

> most of all, our mission in Afghanistan is in our national interests. On
> September 11th 2001, terrorists attacked North America and Canadians were
> killed. Let me be clear: when terrorists attack Canadians, Canada will defend
> itself. That's why we're in Afghanistan . . . it's important to address threats to
> our security before they reach our shores.

What is professed by these varied claims is a collapse in distinction between the
security of Afghanistan and the national security concerns of intervening parties. In
tandem, they are an expression of enlightened self-interest (Duffield, 2007), a logic
claiming that what is good for Canada is also good for Afghanistan. Conversely,
waging war in Afghanistan is not only good for Afghanistan, but is also good for
Canada. Yet, the reality is that what is 'good' for Canada and its coalition partners
takes precedence over what might be good for Afghanistan. Consequently, Afghans
will have their fate decided elsewhere.

This lopsided and troubling logic is further harnessed by the security and
defence intellectuals who play a disproportionate role in defining what constitutes Canada's national interest. The Canadian Forces, for example, has gained
much from dramatic increases in defence spending amounting to over $18 billion
per year in 2006–7, with projections for further increases. Despite protracted and
popular depictions of Canada as a defence 'free-loader' by many in the defence
intelligentsia who have long argued for budgetary increases, Canada has now
moved to the thirteenth highest military spender in the world and the sixth highest
spender in NATO in real dollars (Staples and Robinson, 2007). In adjusted dollars,
today's military spending, in fact, surpasses Canada's peak output during the Cold
War. It is worth noting, too, that these budgetary gains have been directly lucrative for Canadian manufacturers of military equipment. A cursory perusal of the
Department of National Defence press releases shows a ream of new or renewed
multi-million dollar contracts struck with military equipment suppliers such as
Lockheed Martin, Boeing, and the IMP Group International.

This enlightened self-interest, which tells us that intervention is not only good
for Afghanistan but also good for Canada, is further buttressed by a recurrent way
of representing strategically relevant poor, Southern nations such as Afghanistan
(often alongside other nations such as Iraq, Iran, Syria, and North Korea) as zones
of danger. While some may claim that descriptions of danger and disorder are in
fact appropriate, it should not be ignored that the image of danger has long been
a politically valuable tool for legitimating the intervention into and the reorgani-
zation of other societies. Rather than treat these images as simply benign, from
a critical vantage it is important to consider how images of danger are attached
to some states (those that are intervened upon) and not others (those who intervene), and to understand the consequent courses of action that become possible
and legitimated as a result of such labelling.

In the first place, strategically important states such as Afghanistan are constituted as ineffective, wayward spaces plagued by disorder and mismanagement. It is no secret that the Taliban's legacy of rule in Afghanistan was repugnant, as were the Soviet rule that preceded it and the British rule before that. But today's Afghanistan is associated with the image of the terrorist. In particular, it is presented, overwhelmingly, as a 'haven' for terrorism. And as emblematic of terrorism, Afghanistan is positioned in diametrical opposition to images used to represent the West. In contradistinction to the values of 'evil' used to characterize insurgents, for example, Prime Minister Harper (2006a) rallies for the intervention in Afghanistan on the basis of 'freedom' and 'democracy' that Canadians 'cherish' and 'must defend'. While terrorists supposedly wish for the opposite of freedom and 'hate freedom', Canada, by contrast, is presented as wholly committed to freedom. It loves freedom and tries to spread it, and does so through intervention in Afghanistan and support for the US-led War on Terror. As George W. Bush (2005) said, this war confronts 'a global campaign of fear' with a 'global campaign of freedom'.

Representations of Afghanistan as a 'terrorist haven' also effectively mark not simply terrorists, but underdevelopment itself as a source of dangerousness and disorder. We might think about this as a process of securitization in which development and humanitarian efforts are moved increasingly into the realm of risk/threat (Abrahamsen, 2005). The movement is away from the idea of poverty as a problem of political and economic injustice, towards defending the West from dangerous 'others'. This view is consistent with developments in the post Cold-War era that, as Mark Duffield (2002: 1066) notes, have seen a 'transformation of borderlands', those imagined spaces from which 'chaos' supposedly emanates, 'from a series of strategic states into a potential dangerous social body'.

Yet a humanitarian impulse as it is applied to Afghanistan extends further still. It is asserted in claims about the 'burden' of Western intervention. This is a view recently re-popularized by prominent commentators such as Michael Ignatieff (2003). It recalls the 'white man's burden' and is reminiscent of the view that colonial interventions and the desire to 'civilize' Southern peoples was a benevolent duty bestowed upon the white peoples of the European world (Doty, 2006). Without question, it was one of the beliefs that have instrumentally shaped enduring political and economic inequality between Northern/Western regions of the world and Southern/Eastern regions. The so-called burden on the shoulders of the white man was to enlighten and morally improve subject populations, which initially involved authoritarian means and extended to the gradual introduction of self-governance and self-reliance. To see intervention as a burden is to present it as an ethical move to emancipate distant populations from social inadequacy, corruption, and poverty. Today, this idea is deployed as an imperative to address what is taken to be a failure of modernity, which is said to make Southern states 'breeding grounds' for terrorism against the West. As Ignatieff (2003) espouses, the cost of these interventions, while troublesome, may be worthwhile in the effort to secure a broader international good. Thus, the acclaimed moral character of the West's burden today is derived not merely from an imperative to 'improve' the conditions of Southern populations, but derives from Western values themselves, which are taken to offer the requisite capabilities to achieve success. As Gordon O'Connor (2006b) asserts, the Canadian Forces in Afghanistan 'are helping to improve the lives of people struggling to achieve the rights and privileges that many of us Canadians take for granted.' This burden is also 'shared', so that individual members of the international community must 'pull their weight'. As O'Connor (2006a) notes, '[w]e've never been a nation that shies away from its responsibilities. We will shoulder the burden. We will stay the course in Afghanistan.'

These representations can be made sense of as undeniably Orientalist not only because they privilege Western interests, but also because they treat the West as though it is beyond the troubled precincts of global order. In other words, these representations depict the West in ahistorical terms and as morally superior. They subscribe to an economy of representation that posits an identity—geographically, politically, and culturally—of the South in ways that promote a vision of politically intractable difference and inherent inequality between the familiar (Europe, West, 'us') and the strange (the Orient, the East, 'them') (Said, 1979). As Edward Said recounted, the 'Oriental' is regarded as irrational, depraved, conflictual/violent, illiberal, childlike, animal-like, different, while the European is none of these but is rational, virtuous, peaceful, liberal, logical, mature, normal. The West, in this view, is at liberty to wrestle with and give shape and meaning to the 'Orient', and to uncover its 'inner workings'. The latter is merely an object to be disciplined, formed, and moulded, while the former is the agent imagined to have the unique capabilities to drive this process.

Orientalism affirms the enlightened self-interest that informs Canada's role in the War on Terror in general and through its deployment to Afghanistan in particular. It echoes the words of George W. Bush (2004) as he addressed a Canadian audience in December 2004 on the shared values of both Canada and the US that currently guide Western foreign policy objectives. As he proclaimed, '[w]e know there can be no security, no lasting peace in a world where proliferation and terrorism, and genocide, and extreme poverty go unopposed. . . . The United States and Canada face common threats in our world, and we share common goals that can transform our world.' Thus, in subscribing to the War on Terror, Canada's foreign policy approach is designed to contribute to ongoing Western counter-terrorism strategies that flow from a view that the West's role is to shape the world in ways that, while claiming to address the problems of 'others', are poised to guarantee its own security. In more parochial moments no mention is made whatsoever of interests beyond those of NATO members. Offering a variation on the domino theory that guided US interventionist policy during the Cold War, General James L. Jones of the Atlantic Council for the US commented, '[i]f Afghanistan fails, the possible strategic consequences will worsen regional instability, do great harm to the fight against Jihadist and religious extremism, and put in grave jeopardy NATO's future as a credible, cohesive and relevant military alliance' (Escobales, 2008). Driven less by the desire to ameliorate suffering in its own right or to bring about global change that would require redressing structural forms of inequality in which the West is implicated, the intervention simply equates the securitization of Afghanistan with securing the West itself.

The vision of political difference attached to Afghanistan, then, not only compels remedial programs of discipline, but has, multiple times, shored up arguments to extend the length of the mission. Such a vision tells us that the West's pursuit of its own interests is good for Afghanistan, but its actual framework offers more direction on the path towards global containment than global change. What is incontrovertible is that the West's strategy of enlightened self-interest is not the *savoir-faire* remedy to the dismal conditions in Afghanistan. But it might be able to tell us something about the appalling humanitarian situation after eight years of the most recent intervention and about the growth of local resistance to foreign agents.

Canada as Moral Responder

The representation of Afghanistan as a source of danger and disorder casts a particular image of Canada as a 'responder' to the problem of terrorism and poverty, rather than as implicated in the creation of these problems to begin with. What we might see as a 'will to govern' in Afghanistan both veils and separates North–South relations in ways that obscure historical, political, and material relations that produce and sustain global inequality. Rather than drawing attention to these relations, indeed, figuring the role of the West, including Canada, in them as more than simply reactive, the intervention in Afghanistan relies instead on distinguishing the irrationality and excess of 'them' from the civility and reason of 'us'. As Canada and its NATO allies position themselves as knowing what is best for the future of Afghanistan, they assert a claim of moral advantage that affirms current global political and economic relations, while also obscuring how these relations figure in the production of conflict and poverty. Canada, in the popular story of its interventionist role, not only has legitimate security concerns to pursue, but also is an innocent responder to the interplay of terrorism in global politics.

We see this view expressed by Stephen Harper (2006b) when he tells Canadians that terrorists are not people with any real grievances, but people who 'hate open, diverse and democratic societies like ours because they want the exact opposite'. According to George W. Bush, 'terrorists have endless ambitions for imperial domination, and they wish to make everyone powerless except themselves . . . they are people who have built a culture of victimization, in which someone else is always to blame and violence is always the solution.' For years, mainstream media told us that suicide bombers are losers; they are often young, poor, uneducated, hopeless, and full of rage (Atran, 2006). Having nothing to live for, and no morality to speak of, they seek the annihilation of Western civilization. And we can identify the religious commitments of terrorists by any number of names—'evil Islamic radicalism', 'militant jihadism', 'Islamo-facism'. According to these views, the deeds of terrorists can be explained by religious pathology and a hatred of freedom. The West is a target of terrorism that is unrelated to any particular conduct on its part, but, as Harper remarks, because of 'who we are and how we live, our society, our diversity and our values . . . [v]alues such as freedom, democracy and the rule of law'. As Bush puts it, the actions of terrorists are not derived from history or social relations; they simply 'hate our freedom'.

But, of course, the West, including Canada, is not innocent. While the words of political leaders are always worthy of some discursive analysis, even a positivist causal analysis of the politics of terrorism and insurgency is disquieting to popular claims. For instance, Robert Pape (2005) has analyzed every documented case of terrorism from 1980 to 2004. He concludes that common patterns suggest that foreign occupation—not religion—is the core motivating factor behind suicide terrorism. From the actions of Lebanon's Hezbollah and Hamas in Israel/Palestine to the Tamil Tigers in Sri Lanka and the so-called jihadists of 9/11, the motivation was largely nationalist. While it may be true that Al-Qaeda terrorists are twice as likely to come from a country where radical strands (Salafist/Wahhabist) of Islam are practised, they are also, according to Pape, 10 times more likely to come from a country with US troops stationed in it. In addition, countries said to contain some of the most extreme religious groups do not appear to be correlative. For example, no suicide bomber has ever come from Iran, where there are no foreign troops, and Iraq had never seen suicide bombing until US troops arrived in 2003.

Focusing more specifically on terrorism since the attacks on the US in September 2001, Scott Atran (2006) and Jessica Stern (2004) both offer especially nuanced analyses, arguing that terrorism is not just a response to foreign occupation, but is about redressing a 'deep pool of perceived humiliation' that is not limited to military occupation. It can also include Western support for corrupt local regimes, Western cultural imperialism, economic exploitation, and the abuse of civilians and detainees—in other words, a number of actions that the West, including Canada, has been implicated in. The claim that terrorists are acting simply out of religious zeal, are 'evil', or 'hate freedom' is, however, not only less than insightful, it also works well to garner domestic support for the War on Terror by closing down considerations of how the West ought to take stock of its own contributions to fomenting the current interplay of global violence.

There are, moreover, specific ways in which Canada's current foreign aid practices in Afghanistan, as part of its whole of government approach, are working to reinvent the very same relations of inequality and oppression that have helped to produce conflict and violence to begin with. In addition to the problems of civilian–military aid distribution noted earlier, broader aid efforts are contributing to the highly questionable management practices of international financial institutions. The World Bank, for example, currently holds an Afghanistan 'trust fund', which collects and distributes aid dollars from donor governments for development and reconstruction projects. For the fiscal year 2007, reported Alastair McKechnie, the Bank's country director for Afghanistan, 'Canada is the largest contributor to the Afghanistan Reconstruction Trust Fund' (World Bank, 2008). The World Bank, however, attaches its aid provisions to economic policy and maintains a commitment to economic liberalization and the privatization of industries and services with the tacit support of wealthy countries that are seen as 'shareholders'. A 2005 Bank report on Afghanistan's investment climate argued for the liquidation and privatization of state-owned enterprises and for making the public sector more 'commercially oriented'. Where privatization and liquidation will lead to substantial job losses and be controversial, the Bank speaks against 'unduly generous' severance payments that will purportedly set a damaging pattern for future public-sector job losses (World Bank, 2005).

Both the World Bank's and the International Monetary Fund's overt commitments to privatization have been met with criticism in recent years, as in a 2006 Oxfam policy brief. Both of these international institutions, which are disproportionately controlled by Western nations, especially the US, use aid control to force poor nations to adopt policies that often undermine national development policies, result in inexcusable delays in aid provision, and have an especially harmful effect for poor people (Oxfam, 2006). These practices continue with the tacit support of wealthy nations such as Canada, despite an emerging consensus that aid conditionality is not only ineffective, but exacerbates the conditions of poverty that these institutions purport to address. Such capitalism-friendly, market-based practices have contributed enormously to the conclusions reached by a number of critical commentators that aid levels are insufficient and that no tangible evidence indicates that the conditions of life have improved for most Afghans. While there have certainly been changes in Afghanistan, development looks to be largely non-material.

It is also the case that reconstruction has become a markedly lucrative exercise for private contractors. Naomi Klein (2007) reports that a 'democracy-building' reconstruction business has sprouted up around the shattered economies of Iraq and Afghanistan, with contracts of $10 billion to Halliburton and a slew of public-sector consulting firms (who are often subcontracted to run government services and advise governments on selling off public assets) that have seen massive profit margin increases in recent years. According to Oxfam, a significant portion of the overall aid to Afghanistan 'is absorbed by profits of companies and subcontractors, by non-Afghan resources and by high expatriate salaries and living costs'; indeed, '[e]ach full-time expatriate consultant costs up to half a million dollars a year' (Hemming, 2007). A more recent study by Acbar, an alliance of aid agencies working in Afghanistan, reports that while $10 billion of promised aid for Afghanistan has never materialized, 40 per cent of what has appeared has been recycled into the pockets of donor countries via consultancy fees and company profits (Norton-Taylor, 2008). The problem for Afghans is not that they need to become more self-reliant, as the model of privatization suggests, but that, unlike the populations of the West by and large, they already are. The aid industry, it appears, aims to keep it that way.

Few Afghan authorities, let alone local Afghan people, play a decisive role in shaping patterns of aid distribution, as these remain discretionary conduct for donor states or are governed by agreements between donor governments, international financial institutions, and private contractors. To be sure, the desperate need for aid dollars, even those with untenable conditions, makes negotiations and political organizing seem like an exercise in opulence. Much of the population is occupied with the struggle to access basic necessities of life while dodging bombs and gunfire exchanges. Whole communities have been driven from their homes, only to become refugees or internally displaced persons, while coalition forces attempt to 'weed out' insurgents. A number of key decisions about the direction of the economy, it must also be noted, took place years before there was even an elected government. Even now, however, Afghanistan lacks the political autonomy to resist changes sought by the 'international community'. According to international 'agreements' between Afghanistan and the international community, the country is in a state of 'conditional' or 'limited' sovereignty. Afghanistan takes direction much less from its own citizens than from its Western-backed political elites, donor governments, the World Bank, and coalition forces.

Conclusion

The most recent reports on the situation in Afghanistan suggest that the NATO mission has brought neither security nor the alleviation of poverty. After so many years of intervention, Canada's self-image as a force for peace in the world thus requires sustained critical scrutiny. Yet there are a number of ways in which this popular image works as a kind of self-fulfilling prophecy, not because it actually produces change, but because it tells us much about how war and systemic forms of violence can be carried out in the name of peace and human betterment. If we think about how violent practices are configured in the name of peace, it becomes readily apparent that we must move beyond the naive view that aid and reconstruction efforts are simply designed to alleviate human suffering or that development initiatives hold the promise of a better future for those they claim to act on behalf of.

Instead, there are important ways in which developmental and aid efforts are strategically bound to the military mission. This is not simply a process that has been put into motion despite the better judgement of powerful institutional actors in the aid sector, such as the World Bank and the IMF; rather, it has come about at their beckoning. Aid and reconstruction, in other words, must be thought about not simply as undergoing militarization, but as strategies of war against populations in their own right. Canada's whole-of-government approach flows from an under-criticized self-interest that claims that what is good for Canada is also good for Afghanistan. This does not denote a view that Canada and Afghanistan have similar political realities or even aspirations, but is rooted in long-standing views of nations of the global South and their peoples as lacking the values and capabilities that the West claims to uniquely champion. These views are prevalent today in representations of Afghanistan as internally chaotic and, externally, as a source of danger and disorder to the West. This image of Afghanistan also constructs Canada as merely a responder to the problems of terrorism and internal strife in Afghanistan, rather than as a contributor to these problems to begin with.

To be sure, a lack of any tangible evidence of reflection on Canada's role in contributing to relations of global inequality, marked by misery for many and prosperity for few, is clearly evident in its continued foreign policy practices. The shape of aid disbursements, military–civilian operations, and, indeed, the whole-of-government approach in Canada's foreign policy carry political vogue as a comprehensive strategy in the field, but offer little in the way of material improvement and substantive political self-determination for the people who are purported to be the prize of the intervention in Afghanistan. It is not simply the traditional aspects of the military mission that ought to be controversial; equally controversial should be those forms of civilian intervention that too often and too easily gain their rectitude from discursively aligning themselves with the building of 'peace'.

Chapter Six

Canadian Border Policy as Foreign Policy

Security, Policing, Management

Mark B. Salter

A crucial aspect of Canada's recent national security strategy and foreign policy approach has been a fundamental shift towards deeply integrated and intense flows of global trade and international mobility. Border agreements are at the core of a network of trade, migration, policing, and national security policies. With the reinvigoration of national security concerns at the border, or rather a retranslation of security concerns at the border, it becomes important to re-examine how we understand border policy. Border politics are the co-ordination of foreign policy and domestic policy: immigration and entry requirements are framed in terms of economic security; customs regulations protect or integrate our economy; population movement and the larger geopolitical picture of the 'War on Terror' are framed in terms of intelligence and police co-operation; ecological and pandemic concerns are framed in environmental regulations. In short, border policy is a foreign policy with both foreign and domestic audiences. In particular, the mainte-nance of the possibility of a secure border lies at the very heart of the claim by sovereign states to demarcate an anarchical outside, against which they are the sole political agents that can offer protection. Without border security there can be no territorial sovereign state in international relations.

Similarly, without the ability to police the population flows across the border, there can be no strong claim to a national population. The border is the primary frontier where representatives of the sovereign demand obeisance for all citizens and define all foreigners (Salter, 2006). Border politics are the foundation of foreign policy: it is a signal, a claim, and an assertion of security, territory, and population. That signal, claim, or assertion is in continual need of rearticula-tion. The particular modalities of rearticulation illustrate important political aspects of foreign policy, the conceptions of the *state* of the state, and the *real* of international relations. Border policy is foreign policy—it represents the state's ability to define itself and its population, and its ability to interact with and influence its neighbours. This dual audience is described by Reg Whitaker: 'Canada's legitimate antiterrorist tasks are undertaken to assure Americans of the safety of their northern border, and thus to alleviate the threat of economic insecurity arising from intrusive American border security measures. Such obligations are also assumed to assure the Canadian public that its government is protecting it' (Whitaker, 2004–5: 55).

There have been two significant shifts in the past 20 years in the dominant border policy strategy: from a focus on border *security* through border *policing* towards the contemporary emphasis on border *management*. This change is a result of external factors such as the increased flows of goods and people, the impact of the capture of Ahmed Ressam, the Millennium bomber, and the attacks on the United States of 11 September 2001, in addition to internal changes in the way that the Canadian government organizes its border 'services' agency. With the consolidation of a number of agencies and bureaucratic goals, the border itself has become dispersed throughout many spaces within and outside the national frontier, and the border function now requires more surveillance of data, goods, and populations. The risk management approach, even if it is being supplemented by a revanchist militarization of the border, supplements the expansion of global surveillance because it mandates the collection of personal, social, and commercial data that are then examined through a security frame. From the North American Free Trade Agreement to the Smart Border Declaration, the Smart Border Accord, and the Security and Prosperity Partnership, this chapter will examine how Canadian border policy, as a particular variety of foreign policy, through the adoption of a risk management approach has made possible the wider securitization of other sectors and spaces.

Inside/Outside: Defending the Border

Thinkers across the social sciences have written about the impact, persistence, and rearticulation of borders (Amoore, 2006; Andreas, 2003a; Newman, 2003; Walters, 2006). Borders are a unique and contested site of international relations where the inside/outside frontier is determined, policed, and negotiated. Traditional analyses focus on the management of border issues, or the degree of equivalence between sovereignty and territory: these analyses often take for granted the fact of the border, and represent simply one side of the border story. Borders are not simply about the inside protecting itself, but also about the inside and outside mutually constituting each other. Andreas points to this:

> border controls have politically important perceptual and symbolic effects that are too often ignored or taken for granted. To judge border policing strictly in terms of whether or not the instrumental goal of deterrent is attained partly

misses the point . . . it is also about projecting an image of moral resolve and propping up the state's territorial legitimacy. (Andreas, 2003a: 110)

Two scholarly movements with critical approaches to security studies show great potential for the study of borders and foreign policy. The Paris and Copenhagen schools orient our attention to two sets of questions, as framed by the c.a.s.e. (critical approaches to security in Europe) collective (2006). The Paris School of international political sociology, led by scholars such as Didier Bigo, is concerned with the erosion of this inside/outside in terms of border policing (Bigo, 2001). Bigo (1996) demonstrates that the European networks of border agencies, police forces, military organizations, intelligence operatives, and risk specialists have ceased to talk in terms of national/international. The Paris School examines how the key concepts of security, borders, and policing are defined in their daily use by the 'field' of experts, bureaucrats, and other agents. Bigo demonstrates how the particular transnational field of immigration professionals share a similar vocabulary, imagination, and policy tool kit for the management of borders (2002). This approach requires a rethinking of the traditional foreign policy analysis that, even in its bureaucratic politics guise, generally treats national foreign policy communities as distinct actors. These perspectives are useful because, as Drache (2004: 2) puts it: 'Some one hundred and fifty cross-border agreements govern the [Canada–US] border. . . . much of the governance function is also conducted through informal contacts and ad hoc arrangements between US Departments and Canadian ministries.'

The Copenhagen School, on the other hand, argues that through illocutionary or performative speech acts a particular political issue can become a security issue (Wæver, 1995). Over the past 20 years, and with increasing intensity, migration has become securitized within the European scene (Wæver et al., 1993, Huysmans, 2006). State elites are consequently able to expand their executive power and avoid public debate about policies by labelling them existential threats that require emergency actions. In this theory, there is no necessary correlation between describing something as a threat and real danger. As Campbell (1993: 3) explains, 'the boundaries of a state's identity are secured by the representation of danger integral to foreign policy.' By examining the international agreements on border security, the move towards the delocalization of the border away from the physical frontiers of the state, and the discursive shift towards border management, this chapter concludes that the foreign drivers of border policy intrude deeply into arenas of domestic Canadian policy.

Following on the work of Walker and others from the critical tradition, we are already convinced that an essential part of foreign policy is the representations of self/other, in particular, the representation that the boundary between inside/outside is natural, necessary, and manageable. Walker (1993: 62) summarizes: 'spatially, the principle of state sovereignty fixes a clear demarcation between life inside and outside a centred political community. Within states, universalist aspirations to the good, the true and the beautiful may be realizable, but only within a spatially delimited territory.' Consequently, the border is one of the most important sites of the representation of sovereignty—both in terms of independence and also in terms of relations with other states. It is a limit of the possibility of politics and the beginning point of international relations. Representations of the national 'security, territory, population' are each secured to some extent on the representation of the border, precisely because the border is a filter of goods, people, and ideas in circulation within the state (Foucault, 2007). The performance of the national border is fundamental to the appearance of security, the territorial limit of the state, and the integrity of the population. This is true for both domestic and international audiences. The border appeals to the container metaphors so foundational to the discourse of sovereignty, state, and security (Chilton, 1996). Even under the sign of globalization, borders maintain a strong hold over the political imagination, and the integrity of borders is read as the integrity of identity, community, and particularity. In the next three sections, I will look at three dominant modes of border policy: security, policing, and management.

Security as Process

There has been no time when the frontier or the border (especially with the United States) was not important to Canadian foreign policy (Laxer, 2003). While relatively settled in the sense of legal jurisdiction (although some lingering issues persist), the economic and political meaning of border security has indeed changed over recent history. The Copenhagen School has proposed a model of securitization that is constructive: an actor utters a securitizing move, which is constituted by the description of an existential threat that requires extraordinary means, that move is accepted by an audience, and the issue becomes depoliticized, no longer available for public political debate (Buzan et al., 1998: 25). Rather than securitization being a *coup de grâce* that occurs only once, and then an issue is banished to the realm of security forever, securitization, instead, is a continual process of threat construction and justification. Politics itself and political resistance always challenge dominant narratives of securitization. In short, security is a 'thick signifier' and must be unpacked and placed in a particular temporal, spatial, social, and political context (Huysmans, 1998: 228). We accept that borders are a continuing security issue—but the ground on which that securitizing move is accepted has changed over time. Traditional appeals to militaristic, geopolitical security imply the state's exclusive dominance over a particular territory, indicated by the ability to protect a frontier from an invasion by a foreign army or subversion through crime. Economic security is figured in not dissimilar ways through the protection of an economic market against predation by pirates or sabotage through foreign ownership. Population security has been figured chiefly in terms of migration, but always is justified on the grounds of public health, public order, and crime/security.

During the Cold War, the 'longest undefended border in the world' was not a security issue in the military sense, but it was difficult to separate the Canadian military imperative to secure the border and the American imperative to play a wider geopolitical strategy through the Permanent Joint Board on Defence established in the Ogdensburg Agreement (1940), the North American Aerospace Defence Command

(1958), and US Northern Command (2002). One could also make the argument that economic security, in the form of customs, and population security, in terms of immigration, have dominated the post-Cold War era. To focus on military security, the shared Canada–US border was displaced onto the remote Canadian border in the Far North and the potential of a Soviet circumpolar attack (Lackenbauer and Farish, 2007) and onto US–Canada border posts. The Distant Early Warning (DEW) Line was a projection of the American border into the Canadian Arctic: 'It was a physical presence, then, that gave the DEW Line its imaginative significance as a political boundary. A series of scattered construction sites became a technological wall that was also a moral divide, marking the boundaries of security and certainty' (Farish, 2006: 184). Military technology made the physical border a geographical Maginot Line that could be avoided by strategic bombers and ballistic missiles. This historical displacement of the border can also be seen in the US–Canada pre-clearance agreements started in 1952, by which Canadian air passengers bound for US destinations may clear US customs and immigration officials while present on Canadian territory (Salter, 2007a: 56). Within the larger geopolitics of the Cold War, the US–Canada border was figured in terms of population and economic flows, rather than straight military invasion. The construction of the DEW Line in 1957 and the creation of NORAD a year later pushed the US border deep into Canadian space. This is not to say that security is not still the justification for these border projects, but the calculus of the securitization of the Arctic and of civil aviation passengers takes place on different registers. The DEW Line was an electronic tripwire, figured in a traditional military-strategic narrative; consequently, the existential threat of nuclear annihilation is relatively easy to prove, and acceptance by American and Canadian audiences was widespread. Securitization of the Arctic was easy. The placing of US border posts on Canadian soil, however, was a security measure that took place in an entirely different language. There was no existential threat—the pre-clearance of US-bound passengers was seen as entirely technical, and was exemplified by bureaucratic co-ordination rather than formal treaties. In essence, the American securitizing move of Canadian air passengers went unnoticed: there was no crisis, no emergency, and no extraordinary powers required—the border was depoliticized. The changing ground for border security demonstrates that, as with national interest, security is a process of interpellation or recognition and of negotiation.

Policing: NAFTA and Ever After

The passage of the Canada–US Free Trade Agreement (FTA) and the subsequent North American Free Trade Agreement (NAFTA) represents a change in the focus of border policy. This is not to say that in the 1990s there were not some important initiatives between the US and Canada: the Shared Accord on the Border in 1995 focused on the facilitation of trade, the reduction of transaction costs at the border, and policing concerns such as smuggling, narcotics, and illegal movement of people. Here, border security is defined in terms of policing. The 1997 Border Vision Initiative continued this focus on co-ordination, facilitation, and 'low politics'.

A strong argument can be made that the asymmetric nature of Canada–US–Mexico relations made Canada very much the beggar at the continental feast. The FTA framed border security within the context of Canadian economic health; NAFTA represented a different structure. Rather than being an initiator of the widening of the FTA, the United States saw that NAFTA could, in some way, be a long-term solution to its southern border security problems, in addition to serving economic interests. The US–Mexico dilemma is dominated by the 'war on drugs' and the question of illegal migration. Since the 'pull' and 'push' factors for both illegal narcotics and migrants remain strong, there are escalating incentives for individual entrepreneurs to evade any new border security measures. NAFTA is in part an attempt by the United States to guarantee that market imperatives are attuned to national security concerns; in other words, economic security was more important than military security. The treatment of individual illegal migrants was seen as a policing issue rather than a military issue (Andreas, 2000; Walters, 2008), and so American border security was perceived as either an economic foreign policy issue or as an internal domestic policing issue. As Andreas (2003b: 78) argues, 'more intensive border law enforcement is accompanying the demilitarization and economic liberalization of borders.'

The best examples of this policing mentality are the Integrated Border Enforcement Teams (IBETs). They are now present along both sides of the border from coast to coast and are comprised of the RCMP Customs and Excise Section; local, provincial, and federal drug enforcement agents; Immigration and Passport officials; the Canada Customs and Revenue Agency; the US Border Patrol; and the US Customs Service. Though formalized after the 11 September 2001 attacks, IBETs started in 2000 from the actual practices of co-operation of border and policing agencies along the border near Vancouver (Schneider et al., 2000: 88). Originally focused on drug smuggling, IBET teams matched operational co-ordination with technical co-operation. Jurisdictional issues, which had inhibited trust-building, were dealt with on a longer-term horizon by the Cross-Border Crime Forum started in 1997. Also, it was felt by the police on the ground that co-operation would be productive. This ground-level co-ordination, which may have happened informally in the past, could be formalized and made part of practice and of policy precisely because it functioned within the working environment of the security experts at the border. Transnational crime could be dealt with in the international forum, but real operational co-operation was a result of relationships. This directly supports Bigo's notion of policing policy being constructed by actors and agents in the field, enabled precisely because it was not considered 'high' foreign policy.

Risk Management: Facilitation and National Security

The Smart Border Accord was signed on 12 December 2001 and represented a fundamental sea change in how the US–Canada border was framed (Kitchen, 2004).[1] After 9/11, and with elite and public perceptions that the US–Canada border was 'leaky', both governments agreed to a new conception of border security: a border based on risk management. National security becomes plural: the protection of safe flows of goods and people, the continuing co-operation on policing issues, and the protection against national security threats, which figured predominantly in terms of terrorism. Since the breaching of the border by Ahmed Ressam[2] and the scale of the 9/11 attacks, and the multiple interactions between the 9/11 hijackers and US Immigration and Customs officials (US Department of Justice, 2002), it became clear to Canadian and American border security officials that they needed to change their 'policing' models into a co-ordinated 'homeland security' model. Following wide-scale bureaucratic and corporate practice, Canada successfully argued for a risk management approach. Risk management, as a set of knowledge practices, ranks threats to an organization or state according to impact and frequency, and then applies a four-square solution grid: accept, avoid, mitigate, transfer (Salter, 2007a). The Canadian government was successful in pushing for this strategy to border security in the immediate aftermath of 9/11, despite previous, unsuccessful attempts to advocate a risk approach before 9/11. The Smart Border Accord and 30-point Action Plan could be signed so quickly because DFAIT officials had previously been working on the project. A combination of high-level political pressure and regular ministerial meetings (and the personal relationship of Canadian Foreign Minister John Manley and Tom Ridge, the US Secretary for Homeland Security) also led to co-operation between the mid-level foreign policy bureaucracies (Belelieu, 2003: 3). Framing border security in terms of risk management allowed agencies to facilitate the safe passage of goods/people (i.e., high-frequency, low-impact events) while focusing their resources on unknown or risky goods/people (i.e. low-frequency, high-impact events).[3] Low-risk frequent travellers could be accommodated in the updated NEXUS program, which provided expedited examination in return for pre-registration, and the FAST (Free and Secure Trade) regime, which provided a similar facility for freight. Separate from the empirical arguments one could make about the adoption of risk management as a strategy for border policy, at a minimum it represents a widening of the objects, practices, and politics that fall under 'border security'. We can point to three areas of this widening of border security, and its signal securitization: data exchange,[4] refugee protection (see Bell, 2006; Nyers, 2003; Salter, 2007b), and public health. In each of these areas, new techniques of surveillance and control have been implemented by the Canadian government as part of the Smart Border agreements or the National Security Policy. Risk management depends on being able to assess the individual or freight in terms of danger, and thus requires greater domestic and international surveillance. The management approach to border security attempts to rationalize the border: in other words, a depoliticization of the security issue into a statistical, technological question of governance. While this seemed initially appealing to both governments, the emphasis in the United States on security, through the new War on Terror and the creation of the Department of Homeland Security, in fact restricted the success of the Canadian government in desecuritizing border policy through risk management.

Protecting the Canadian border was a central plank of Canada's National Security Policy, as was the creation of a unified Canadian Border Services Agency. These moves were met with great appreciation from the United States, which interpreted these signals as an indication of the gravity with which Canada was taking the 9/11 attacks. But by 2003 Canada was losing the initiative in its border relationship with the United States, in part because of an American perception that 'Canadians think the security and border issues are only US problems' (Meyers, 2003: 15). Whitaker framed the Canadian perception: 'post-9/11 offers the opportunity to negotiate economic security for Canada in exchange for national security for the US' (Whitaker, 2004–5: 54). Two major American programs, neither of which involved serious consultation with the Canadian government, indicate the loss of Canadian leverage: the Western Hemisphere Travel Initiative (2004) and the Secure Border Initiative (2005).[5] The WHTI requires a passport or similar approved secure identity card and proof of citizenship for entry into the United States by air, land, and sea. Currently, the Canadian passport or a NEXUS card, which in itself requires a Canadian passport, is the only document accepted by the Department of Homeland Security. Enormous demand for Canadian passports, because of the dominance of US-bound travel by Canadians, has caused significant delays in passport processing.[6] The SBI is a much wider program, aimed at militarizing the Mexican and Canadian borders. Through the use of unmanned aerial vehicles (UAVs), new fences, remote detection technologies including cameras and sensors, enhanced lighting, and an integrated detection/communication/intelligence network, SBI and SBInet represent a move towards the unilateral hardening of the American border between ports of entry. The Canadian government was not consulted in the planning of the SBI and is not a partner: SBI essentially lies next to other border agreements and is a unilateral attempt to 'secure' borders against illegal migration.

The attacks of 9/11 facilitated the securitization of the border, making social and political capital available for the American and Canadian governments to describe border security as representing an existential threat that required emergency action. However, the sense of urgency in Canadian popular and foreign policy circles has faded. Meyers reports that 'Canadians admittedly focused on their economy and the facilitation of people and goods, [and] question whether the United States isn't overly focused on security to the exclusion of all other items, including economics and common sense' (Meyers, 2003: 16). Other advocates, policy-makers, and scholars support this attempted 'desecuritization', a discursive process by which a security issue is contested as not existential, not an emergency, and not requiring emergency measures. In this case, the desecuritization is partial: the Canadian audience has accepted that the border is not a military or national security emergency, but the American audience has not.

Dispersion: Delocalization of Foreign Policy

The border is being dispersed as a set of conditions—border politics, i.e., the policing and protection of the territory and population of a particular sovereign state, is occurring at multiple sites both inside and outside Canada. As Nyers (2003) argues, for migrants at risk, any meeting point with the agents of the government can become the site of a border decision. However, the border is not everywhere (Balibar, 2002: 80). What makes a *border* decision—regardless of the physical or bureaucratic location—is the exclusion from the protection of the state, the drawing of limits in the population. And these decisions take place at the airport (both in Canada and outside of Canada), in the embassies, in the hospitals, in the manufacturing plants, in the flight reservation call centres. When the airline representative informs a passenger that he or she may not board an airplane because of a 'no-fly' program, here or in America, that is a foreign policy decision about defining borders and their porosity. Too often, the discussion of border policies, passport requirements, and exchange of security intelligence takes place within a discourse of legal sovereignty that misses two crucial points. First, issues considered to involve security operate differently from normal political foreign policies, and more must be done to understand the process of the securitization and desecuritization of border policies. Second, these issues are in constant definition and redefinition by practitioners of foreign policy and also other agents of the state, such as border officials, police, transportation security agencies, privacy advocates, etc., and more must be done to understand the bureaucratic field of play and the friction that may occur between elite and front-line foreign policy actors.

There are a number of pressing avenues for future research on the border as foreign policy. This sketch will indicate the parameters of two of those avenues: the Canadian public imagination of the border and the widening of the object of border policing. In regard to public imagination, how is Canada's identity tied up with the imagination of the border? In this, literary Canadian studies, anthropology, and sociology are further advanced than foreign policy analysis (New, 1998). How does the image of Canada as an international promoter of human rights, human security, and the protection of refugees work within a sovereignist discourse of the arming of border guards, the issuance of security certificates, and the surveillance of refugee claimants and suspect ethnic organizations? A productive avenue for foreign policy research could be the public perception of 'leakiness' of the US–Canada border (in both American and Canadian publics), which can lead to a 'conspicuous consumption' of security measures (Salter, 2007b). For example, politicians playing to domestic audiences can have a dramatic foreign policy impact. The Senate Standing Committee on National Security and Defence issued a report in 2005, *Borderline Insecure*, that advocated the raising of customs exemptions and the arming of border guards. American proposals have included a call to 'prevent students in border communities from attending school part-time in the other country . . . limit the stay of most tourists to 30 days' (Meyers, 2003: 15). One of the key insights of the Copenhagen School, which can be fruitful for critical foreign policy scholars, is that of the delimitation of 'security' in terms of scrutinizing moves and audience acceptance: when and how do Canadian and American foreign policy audiences make and accept the classification of an issue area as a 'security' issue? A second area for creative analysis of the border as foreign policy may be the general widening of what is counted as 'border' policy. Analysts of foreign policy must take note of the advances in surveillance studies and political sociology to understand the impact of transnational data flows that precede, complement, and shadow the actual movement of goods and people. Because of the stress of information and intelligence in the assessment of cases within the risk management paradigm, there is a real pressure to 'share' as much information as allowed by law (and maybe a bit more in cases regarding terror). In this regard, the Paris School approach of fieldwork in the communities of mid-level bureaucrats, experts, and specialists can demonstrate how domestic/foreign policies are broken down by actual international networks of actors.

This chapter has demonstrated a prima facie case for the use of the Paris and Copenhagen schools of critical security studies to examine border policy, which is a foundational foreign policy. The changing nature of border security, even in a relatively settled relationship, illustrates that, as the Paris School analysts have shown, internal/external boundaries are being complicated by actual networks of policy actors who, though nominally employed by a particular state, are involved in the formulation and implementation of policy in consort with officials from other states. Of similar import, the Copenhagen scholars have shown that the changing nature of security involves the 'securitization' (and audience acceptance) of particular classifications, whereby, if a threat to security is asserted and accepted within a public discourse, that threat becomes accepted as real and state actions can follow. The US–Canada border, seen in this light, is understudied as a complex of cultural, political, economic, and foreign policies, and more critical work is needed.

Notes

1. This chapter is less concerned with how 'smart' the smart border is, or if 'smart' co-operation is a possible model for future co-operation, than with how border policy and foreign policy are entangled in processes of securitization (Kitchen, 2004; Meyers, 2003).

2. Ahmed Ressam, the 'Millennium bomber', planned to attack Los Angeles International Airport on New Year's Eve 2000, but was stopped at the Port Angeles post on the American border between British Columbia and the state of Washington. Though unrecognized at the time, this was the first sign that national security threats, and particularly terror attacks, against the United States would need a much more discriminatory tool for analyzing risk and threat of individuals at the border.

3. Kitchen (2004) convincingly argues that part of the success of 'smart' co-operation was not harmonization of rules and regulations, which would be extremely difficult, but rather confidence-building between the two countries' elites and bureaucracies so that trust could be built alongside different policies.

4. See discussions of Maher Arar in Kitchen (2004) and Andreas (2004), but also the British Columbia Civil Liberties Association (2004) and Bennett (2008).

5. Paris (2007) also has made the argument that the 2005 Security and Prosperity Partnership lacks an overall plan. He argues: 'It is little more than a hodgepodge of bilateral and trilateral working groups on issues such as border security, food safety, migratory birds, and so on. Most of these groups existed long before the SPP was announced in 2005. When the SPP was created, the groups were organized into two broad clusters—security and prosperity—and

a new mechanism was created to oversee their activities. The goal was to nudge their work forward by requiring them to deliver semi-annual progress reports to ministers from all three countries.'

6.   It could also be argued that this demand, and the consequent delays, led to changes in the passport application process. After the experience of Ahmed Ressam, who had obtained a false but completely authentic Canadian passport by using a baptismal certificate and a student identity card, Passport Canada tightened its screening process. But, faced with massive delays because of the demands created by the WHTI requirements, security requirements for passport applications have been relaxed.

Part III

Security and Self after 9/11

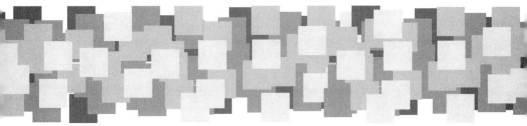

Chapter Seven

Clandestine Convergence
Human Security, Power, and Canadian Foreign Policy

Kyle Grayson

Mapping Terrains of Contestation in Canadian Foreign Policy

It is hardly contentious to propose that the seemingly diverse orientations in Canadian foreign policy in the post-World War II era have generated a considerable amount of debate within the overlapping rings of academic, popular, and policy circles. As analysts of foreign policy we are trained to identify these ruptures and to carefully delineate the areas of disagreement. The point is to determine the practical implications of these contending orientations and what kinds of policies they make possible, and to offer a judgement as to whether we think that a particular way of viewing foreign policy meets our own criteria for an effective policy posture.[1]

Mainstream analysts tend to give too little attention to identifying the similarities between contending positions, whatever the subject area. Within the field of foreign policy analysis, very rarely is the question asked: what is being held in common between seemingly diverse orientations in Canadian foreign policy? The oversight is extremely important in terms of the political element that defines foreign policy as a set of practices in the popular imagination and the tangible political outlook of the Canadian foreign policy community.

However, this oversight becomes understandable when one turns to the results of analyses that have asked this probing question. For example, Mark Neufeld's (1995) examination of the middle-power debate revealed how commonly held definitions by all parties helped to discipline the actions of the Canadian state in international politics by stunting what was considered to be politically possible. Similarly, J. Marshall Beier and Ann Denholm Crosby (1998), in their examination of the grounds open for contention during the Ottawa Process that led to the Convention to ban landmines, were able to clearly demonstrate that a shared notion of bounded accountability pervaded among key actors. This view tacitly excused those states who had previously been involved in the production and distribution of these weapons from any formal sanction.

Gender analyses have been at the forefront of questioning the 'common sense' of Canadian foreign policy and, by extension, the hegemonic structures that shape Canadian society, including neo-liberalism, militarism, and the idea of the national interest. A rigorous research agenda has investigated a range of issue areas, from the concepts of human security and humanitarian intervention to the (re)production of the military family, gender mainstreaming, immigration policy, migrant workers, Canadian development policy, the projection of Canadian values, and trade—all integral aspects of foreign policy. Feminist scholars and activists, using a variety of approaches,[2] have revealed the structural asymmetries that contribute to the marginalization of dissent and to the proactive and passive silencing of alternative perspectives on Canadian 'statecraft'. These analyses have all raised uncomfortable questions about the roles of gender and race in the processes and practices of Canadian foreign policy. They also present a series of challenges to the supposed moral fortitude of 'Canadian values', the constitutive identification of Canada as being beyond ethical reproach, and the (violent) practices of Canadian pluralism that are not recognized within the 'values' discourse.

Thus, the question posed above is not merely an intellectual exercise; it is a form of inquiry that gets to the very heart of politics: what ideas, principles, understandings, and beliefs are held in common by a set of actors? In other words, what is taken to be common-sense in a given context and therefore not worthy of critical investigation (Weber, 2005)? Common sense is an important site for political analysis because it reveals the ways in which power relations within a given society can create hegemonic foundations for the practices of politics, which, despite different branding, ultimately reproduce very similar results (Edkins, 1999: 2–6). As Steve Smith (1996: 13) has remarked, common sense sets the limits of a community's 'practical and ethical horizons'. Moreover, the maintenance of hegemony perpetuates all of the structural imperfections of the status quo, a cost most heavily borne by those who are positioned on the margins (Cox, 1994). Therefore, common sense is very often beneficial to the interests of the powerful and serves as a means of reproducing current states of affairs through different forms of political packaging (Murphy and Tooze, 1991; Edkins, 1999; Smith, 1997).

But common sense need not be accepted as commonsensical. The rest of this chapter will attempt to add to the growing body of critical literature that seeks to rupture the common sense of Canadian foreign policy. It will do so by examining a specific debate that raged for nearly a decade beginning in the mid-1990s over the concept of human security. For this purpose, I have adapted three questions posed by Michel Foucault (1990: 10, 18, 30) in his groundbreaking study of sexuality:

1. Did concepts of human security as put forth in Canadian foreign policy debates during the 1990s and 2000s act in opposition to power mechanisms

that had operated unimpeded until that point in time, or were they a part of the same historical-political network as those things they denounced?

2. How did the 'institutional incitement to speak' of human security, 'the determination on the part of agencies of power to hear it spoken about, and to cause it to speak through explicit articulation and endless accumulation [of] detail' shape debates? In other words, how did the multiplication of discourses concerning the appropriateness of human security as a foreign policy issue constitute an exercise infused with the promotion of a particular set of power relations?

3. In what ways did silences (i.e., those things not articulated in the debates over human security) function alongside those things that were said to further particular relations of power in Canadian society?

In providing preliminary answers to these questions, another issue of significance comes to the forefront: who or what is responsible for this management of the parameters open for debate and who or what should be held to account? This chapter will conclude with a brief discussion of how answers to this final question can be conceptualized.

The Historical-Political Network of Human Security

The Golden Age?

As Barry Buzan (1991) has famously noted, security is an essentially contested concept with multiple definitions that compete for political saliency. As a comprehensive set of shared principles, it is usually argued that human security first gained prominence in the mid-1990s, reflecting both deep structural changes in geopolitics brought about by the end of the Cold War and associated intellectual moves to reconceptualize security in response (Paris, 2001).[3] Human security was said to encapsulate all these developments: it widened the definition of security beyond concerns with the threat of external military attack to potentially include issues like intra-state conflict, environmental degradation, human rights violations, poverty, crime, and communal violence. Human security also contested the long-standing claim that the state should be the primary referent object (i.e., the focus) of security policy. Instead, it was argued that security policy should endeavour to widen the choices and opportunities available to individuals and communities by tackling those issues that constrained the ability of people to live their lives to the fullest capacity (UNDP, 1995). Thus, in the absence of the 'clear and present threats' of the Cold War era and with the inertia of a polarized international system, human security proponents argued that new opportunities were available to ensure that people all over the world would be free from fear and free from want.

The Department of Foreign Affairs and International Trade (DFAIT) officially records the year 1996 as the starting point for human security as a formal policy posture, coinciding with Lloyd Axworthy's appointment as the Minister of Foreign

Affairs and the creation of the Canadian Peacebuilding Program. It would be under Axworthy's leadership that human security would reach its zenith in rhetoric as an organizing concept for Canadian foreign policy. The idea of a people-centred approach to security was claimed to be a major catalyst for Canada's efforts to orchestrate—with the help of the International Campaign to Ban Landmines—the Ottawa Convention banning landmines, as well as Canada's position of leadership among like-minded states for the creation of the International Criminal Court (Axworthy, 1997; Axworthy and Taylor, 1998). The human security agenda under Axworthy was always presented as a development that had considerably *transformed* both the practices of Canadian foreign policy and key forms of governance in the international system (Axworthy, 2001). 'Soft power' through moral suasion, it was believed, would allow a middle-power nation such as Canada to have a significant and beneficial impact on international relations and on state–civil society behaviour. Not only were issues previously ignored by state actors and institutions in the international community—such as child soldiers, conflict diamonds, and gender violence—gaining attention as areas for concern and policy formulation, but Canada was garnering global recognition by playing a leading role in the championing of human security on the international stage (McRae and Hubert, 2001).

Despite the apparent successes, these claims did not go unchallenged (see, e.g., Hampson and Oliver, 1998; Nossal, 1998; Stairs, 1999). It was at these early stages in which the grounds for debating the meaning of human security, its efficacy, and legitimacy would be established. Primarily, contention focused on how human security should be defined for the purposes of Canadian foreign policy and on the wisdom of actively pursing a human security agenda. What becomes clear through deconstructing the positions put forward in the literature is that, rather than operating in opposition to the power mechanisms of the time, the human security debate was a central circuit for their operation. Specifically, the common-sense constraints fostered by the acceptance of neo-liberalism and militarism, and the ontological saliency of the Canadian national interest, were reproduced and perpetuated, despite the claims that human security represented a transformation in security thinking.[4]

During the mid- to late 1990s, how human security should be defined for the purposes of Canadian foreign policy formulation was an area of significant disagreement. Initially, Lloyd Axworthy (1997) had put forward a wide definition of the concept, mirroring the definition initially advocated by the United Nations Development Program. This understanding included 'freedom from fear' issues such as civil rights violations, small arms, landmines, and intra-state warfare, as well as 'freedom from want' issues such as underdevelopment, poverty, and environmental degradation. The placement of these phenomena onto the human security threat matrix did not represent a shift to an overtly moralist Canadian foreign policy, as some critics contended (Hampson and Oliver, 1998). Rather, as first stated in the UNDP report and later implicitly echoed in Axworthy's (1997) *International Journal* article on the subject, the point was that if left uncontained, things like intra-state warfare, societal dissolution, and poverty could spread and undermine global stability. Furthermore, the probability of proliferation of these problems to new sites became far more likely in an international system that was becoming increasingly shaped by the forces of globalization. The message was clear: while the problems may seem at a distance from the territorial borders of Canada, left unchecked, these problems sooner or later would lead to detrimental outcomes for the Canadian people and their allies.

Axworthy (1997: 193) argued that Canada was well positioned to offer credible leadership for human security issues because of its existing international reputation and the absence of a domineering colonial past. In practice, this reputation would translate into a heightened ability to secure multilateral co-operation with like-minded actors. Using its significant soft-power capabilities, particularly the use of moral suasion, it was thought that Canada would be a prime architect in the creation of new institutional structures and forms of governance. Canada would also be in a position to manage key issue areas like humanitarian intervention that had thus far escaped formal incorporation into the global system. As such, the human security agenda was presented as the evolution of Canada's previous internationalism and commitment to functionalist principles.

In sharp contrast, critics alleged that such a broad agenda could never be adequately operationalized (Nossal, 1998; Khoong, 2001).[5] Given the competing priorities, diverse interest areas, and potential ambiguities of such an agenda, it was argued that, at best, human security would contribute to an incoherent foreign policy where Canada attempted to be a jack-of-all-trades while being a master of none. At worst, having an agenda that attempted to address issues as diverse as child soldiers and micro-credit finance without the ability to determine specific priorities would lead to policy paralysis (Paris, 2001). Moreover, some argued that to underemphasize the traditional concerns of military security, particularly defence commitments to European allies and the United States, was short-sighted (international conditions could change) and would irreparably damage Canada's international standing (Stairs, 1999).

If traditionalists conceded ground, it was to argue, if a human security agenda could not be wrestled away, that Canada should prioritize the 'freedom from fear' aspect as this would best ensure that Canada's hard-power capabilities, i.e., military capabilities, were not neglected. A 'freedom from fear' orientation would still necessitate a standing army capable of being rapidly deployed to engage in conflict intervention, peacekeeping, and peace support operations (Hampson et al., 2002: 125–49). The flip side was that, unlike a strong development program, traditional hard-power capabilities could be used both for human security missions and for those that might arise from more traditional state security concerns, thereby helping to maintain some credibility in key forums (Hampson and Oliver, 1998). As such, by focusing on 'freedom from fear' issues, Canada would continue to maintain its tradition of (military) internationalism through security contributions to NATO and to North American territorial security while upholding its image as a pre-eminent peacekeeper (Maclean, 2002).

So, was this time a period of great debate? At first glance, the human security adherents and the traditionalists (or narrowers) appear to have been at complete loggerheads with very different conceptions of the purposes, priorities, and goals of Canadian foreign policy. However, they shared common ground on at least three interrelated principles: the invocation of a shared understanding of Canada's tradition in international affairs, the acceptance of the continuing relevance of state security concerns, and a geopolitical logic focused on containment.

All sides of the debate made use of the same representations of Canadian identity, including such traditional tropes as internationalism, functionalism, and peace-keeping, as well as specific actor types such as 'middle power', 'international citizen', and 'helpful fixer', to make their case for a particular foreign policy orientation. The political effect was that there was no sustained scrutiny of the accuracy of these depictions or critical investigation of Canadian foreign policy actions that would not neatly fall within their confines. For example, the lack of an imperial and colonial legacy in Canadian foreign policy was taken at face value, a contentious claim given the historical and present-day policies with respect to Indigenous peoples (Beier, 2007). The terrible atrocities committed by Canadian peacekeepers in Somalia and the decades-long toxic combination of a poorly funded foreign development assistance program primarily based on tied aid[6] were also not interrogated within these discussions as there was no discursive space to do so (Busumtwi-Sam, 2002). Thus, whatever one felt about the appropriateness of human security as a foreign policy agenda, the discursive and institutional structures of Canadian foreign policy and those who held positions of authority within them went unchallenged. The central question for debate was how to best steer the ship rather than whether it needed to be completely rebuilt from the ground up.

Despite the desire to look back upon this period nostalgically as a golden age for human security within which national security held no sway over the Canadian foreign policy community, it is important to note that at no time was there any official talk of abandoning the concept of national security or of fully demobi-lizing national security structures. Even Axworthy's passionate appeals only went as far as to say that, given the geopolitical environment at the time, human security promotion should be a priority; this is not the same as arguing that national security was totally irrelevant (Axworthy, 1997; Axworthy and Taylor, 1998). Thus, human security was a reform engineered to work in tandem with traditional security thinking, not its complete replacement. Moreover, the ways in which organizations like the UNDP and conceptual entrepreneurs like Axworthy justified human security implicitly appealed to the belief that addressing these issues would actually protect the security and interests of states, particularly wealthy industrial-ized Western states.

In protecting the security and interests of Western states, the geopolitical logic focused on containment: keeping the sources, carriers, and consequences of human insecurity locked within specific geographic locales so they would not be able to spread their damaging effects. The connection to a prime element of traditional national security discourses, that is, to the West's attempts to contain communism during the Cold War, is obvious. But what might not be so obvious is how this geopolitical logic concurrently defined those areas that were safe and free of human insecurity by mapping out areas of danger that must be kept sealed. The shared agreement that human insecurity was something 'out there' in the global South, therefore, meant that it became a logical impossibility within the debate to locate its presence within the territorial confines of the Canadian state (Smith, 2003).

Heather Smith (2003) has illustrated that the consequences were very powerful as the political, economic, and social status quo within Canada became de facto legitimated in one sweep. This was during a time of significant social dislocation in Canada brought about by the austere neo-liberal economic reforms engineered by Finance Minister Paul Martin to balance the budget, reduce the national debt, and promote economic growth (Grayson, forthcoming). Numerous studies have shown that while considerable gains were made in these areas, they came at the expense of social protections funded by the state (see, e.g., Jackson, 2000, 2004; UNCESR, 2006). Neo-liberal reforms had a disproportionately negative impact on those who were already marginalized in Canadian society, including children, Aboriginal peoples, the poor, women, and visible minorities. Yet, the idea that there might be *human insecurity* at home was not expressed in discussions of Canadian foreign policy, nor did the recognized problems get framed as human security issues within broader public policy discourses (Smith, 2003).

Maturity?

By 1999, it can be reasonably argued that the explicit promotion of a human security agenda had reached maturity for the purposes of Canadian foreign policy. Debates between wide and narrow proponents were made moot by the Lysøen Declaration (see DFAIT, 1998a, 1999b) signed by Canada and Norway, the purpose of which was to establish a framework for consultation and action on important human security issues, and by the publication of the policy brief, *Human Security: Safety for People in a Changing World*, drafted by Paul Heinbecker, a long-serving and distinguished member of the Canadian foreign policy community (DFAIT, 1999a). The report argued that human security was a complement to national security, not a replacement. Moreover, the report asserted that although human security and development concerns were related, for the sake of policy coherence and direction they must be kept apart in Canada's human security agenda.

While the narrowing of human security was ostensibly undertaken for the sake of producing a manageable foreign policy outlook, the decision to focus primarily on forms of violence against people and the communities to which they belong worked in tandem with budgetary moves already well underway (Busumtwi-Sam, 2002; Pratt, 2000–1). Specifically, the 'freedom from fear' emphasis made it possible for the ongoing dismemberment of the Canadian foreign aid program to avoid being represented within official policy discourses as at cross-purposes to the aims and objectives of Canadian foreign policy.

Although defence spending was not being prioritized to the extent that it was during the Cold War and the idea of soft power was greatly disliked by the Canadian military establishment, the revamped human security agenda maintained the perception of a need for well-equipped and well-trained armed forces at a time when a strong case could have been made for a significant downsizing (if not complete dismantling) of Canada's military (Sokolsky and Jockel, 2000–1).

Thus, by preserving the idea of the Canadian military as a provider of security against myriad threats and by allocating the requisite levels of funding to make this claim appear at least partially credible, 'the Canadian human security agenda gave Canada the means by which to claim membership with authority and voice within evolving international and regional security architectures by functionalist criteria. Far from breaking with the militarism of the Cold War, human security helped to maintain it in Canada during the pre-9/11 stages of the post-Cold War era' (Grayson, 2004: 58).

With the participation of 18 CF-18 fighter planes alongside NATO allies in the bombing of Serbia as a response to the Kosovo crisis, Lloyd Axworthy (1999) and other Western leaders, most notably British Prime Minister Tony Blair, argued that a chord had been struck for the promotion of human security, democracy, and human rights around the world (Chandler, 2003). In the humanitarian hubris that surrounded the events of the war, there was little official discussion of how targeting critical civilian infrastructure and the citizens of Serbia in order to protect the human rights of Kosovars directly led to human security promotion. Nor was much concern publicly voiced from inside DFAIT about what the failure of NATO to receive UN Security Council recognition for the action might mean for human security on a global scale.

In contrast to the public front put forward by DFAIT, the Canadian foreign policy community was less than unified on the legitimacy of the action. Debates centred on whether it was morally just for Canada to be 'exporting' its values abroad. Interventionists felt that Canada and other like-minded actors had a duty to promote democracy, human rights, and free markets around the world; moreover, this duty translated into meeting key national interests, including improving the economic prosperity of Canadians. Others argued that values promotion, through force or otherwise, was, at best, a misuse of time and energy or, at worst, a dangerous form of cultural imperialism (Bain, 1999: 93; Owens and Arneil, 1999: 4). Yet, a shared deference to a notion of 'Canadian values' became the common ground for agreement. In other words, the idea that as a political unit Canada embodied values that were wholly appropriate—good for good governance and good for the well-being of its citizens—was not challenged, though the exact values in operation and their effects remained largely undefined (Howell, 2005).

But in other regions of the world, the 'Canadian values' being promoted were profit and human rights violations as Canadian corporations engaged in a host of activities abroad that generated human insecurity even under the terms of the narrow operating definition of the government (UN, 2002). The most public incident was the discovery that Talisman Energy, a Calgary-based oil firm, was in partnership with the Sudanese government in the Upper Western Nile region of the country to exploit hydrocarbon resources. Compelling evidence arose of Talisman's complicity in gross violations of human rights, and the conclusion reached by a special governmental commission was that its presence was exacerbating the ongoing civil war (Harker, 2000; Gagnon et al, 2003). Yet, Axworthy and the Canadian government never took substantive action against Talisman, nor did the government introduce measures to regulate the actions of Canadian corporations abroad to ensure that they would not contribute to human insecurity (Grayson, 2006). It was argued that voluntary self-regulation through the establishment of industry codes of conduct was the most effective means of governance, demonstrating that neo-liberalism and the human security agenda could operate hand in hand (Grayson, forthcoming).[7]

Thus, even at maturity, the human security agenda was neither willing nor able to effectively confront the structures of the status quo, let alone its beneficiaries who made human insecurity possible. The argument is not that if the human security agenda had had the requisite level of political power it would have confronted the status quo; rather, the point is that given the essential assumptions the human security agenda shared with other power structures (such as neo-liberalism and militarism), it would never feel compelled to address certain issues surrounding how foreign policy might or should be pursued. Human security in Canada, then, did not seek to challenge the status quo—it was firmly ensconced within it.

Decline?

With the stunning attacks on the World Trade Center and Pentagon of 9/11, a growing consensus emerged within the Canadian foreign policy community that global politics had changed and hard power would once again regain currency, particularly as the preferred method to deal with terrorism. Canada's human security agenda embraced the robust counter-terrorism agenda of its American ally, elevating the issue to the top of its list of human security threats to which the Canadian government was extending priority.[8] However, rather than argue for a measured response to ensure that the physical safety and human rights of innocent people were protected in the invasion that looked to be inevitably imminent, the government of Canada stood silent. Along with its NATO allies, Canada participated in a military operation whose initial goals were to remove the Taliban from power in Afghanistan and capture those responsible for the 9/11 attacks. Domestically, the Canadian state adopted a range of controversial counter-terrorism strategies, banking on the legitimacy of the argument that normally guaranteed constitutional rights and freedoms did not necessarily apply in the exceptional circumstances of a global 'War on Terror'.[9]

Exceptions were also continually made in Canadian foreign and defence policy. Canadian officials highlighted the legitimating rationales in the 2001 report of the Canadian-led International Commission on Intervention and State Sovereignty, *Responsibility to Protect*, to justify its involvement in Afghanistan. Values such as democracy promotion, human rights, economic development, and the emancipation of women were presented as positive by-products of the Afghan mission. Yet the speed with which the government was willing to resort to the use of organized violence while ostensibly promoting human security for the peoples of Afghanistan was never formally flagged as a potential contradiction.[10] In 2003, reflecting the explicit acknowledgement of the merging of human security and geopolitics, Foreign Minister Bill Graham stated that 'Canada's commitment to a person-centred, as well as state-centred, approach to security policy has only become stronger with time' (DFAIT, 2003a). As such, rather than representing a marked difference with the logic of traditional national security outlooks, the Canadian concept of human security was being shaped as much by realpolitik as by any commitment to humanitarian principles.

By 2003, with the War on Terror in full swing and growing concerns over what directions Canadian foreign policy should take in response, the need for a new foreign policy review grew increasingly clear. Prior to the formal process, a series of questions were published for public input as part of the *Dialogue on Foreign Policy* (DFAIT, 2003b). These questions provided an institutional incitement to speak about human security and were ostensibly drafted to generate debate and diverse responses. Yet, key questions, if answered directly, necessarily funnelled debates down particular tributaries and not others.

Key Questions within the Dialogue on Foreign Policy

An important assumption was that the three pillars identified ('the protection of our security within a stable global framework; the promotion of prosperity and employment; and the promotion of the values and culture that Canadians cherish') were in fact the three pillars underpinning Canadian foreign policy since the release of *Canada in the World*, the foreign policy white paper issued in 1995. Moreover, it also assumed that the three pillars had been in balance, an assumption that incidents like the Talisman affair might call into question.

In its framing of security promotion as only concerned with Canadians, the *Dialogue* questions reverted to a traditional understanding of foreign policy as a set of practices that must serve to protect national interests. Thus, even with the term 'Canadians' as opposed to the state, and the listing of 'broader security measures', questions did not directly elicit answers that would focus on policies that might augment global human security, regardless of the direct benefits to be experienced by Canadians. Moreover, the explicit use of the word 'combatting' as the verb of choice in managing global public goods issues revealed a predisposition towards retaining a traditional understanding of security where, by definition, there must be a role for the military in any response.[11]

The *Dialogue* questionnaire also took for granted that the military serves Canadian foreign policy objectives in some capacity and that it is the primary provider of security for Canadians, an assumption that really deserved critical scrutiny in light of other kinds of security and other means of security provision (e.g., a strong social safety net). The tendency detailed above to locate the places and sources of (human) insecurity beyond the confines of the Canadian state, conferring a degree of legitimacy on the social, political, and economic status quo in Canada, can also be found in the questions opened for public response. Therefore, the Canadian government's right (through the possession of the requisite expertise) to assume a responsibility to protect and intervene elsewhere was upheld.

With regard to questions about the future of values promotion, coherence could only be obtained if the reader shared the assumption that Canada had been advocating values like human rights, democracy, respect for diversity, and gender equality in all parts of the world. With the interventions in Kosovo and Afghanistan and their ambiguous results, Canadian security practices, including indefinite detention for terror suspects based on classified information, the Maher Arar affair, the turning over of insurgents in Afghanistan to US and Afghan forces for torture, the refusal to regulate Canadian corporate conduct abroad, and continuing class, gender, and racial inequalities at home with the embedding of neo-liberalism, this question again served to dissuade the respondent from critically interrogating the contingent claim that certain values were avidly pursued abroad or at home.[12]

With the routes of critical interrogation cut off within the *Dialogue on Foreign Policy* and the long list of (questionable) foreign policy practices able to be operationalized under a human security agenda, the ground shared with traditional matrices of security and foreign policy continued to expand. Human security was now being deployed to aid and abet practices to which one could reasonably assume that it might have been opposed at first principles. Moreover, a stunning silence existed in terms of an assumption that was unexamined by all sides: that being identified as an individual or group or population experiencing human insecurity would necessarily lead to improvements in one's quality of life through the practices of Canadian foreign policy. While people were arguing over what policies would best lead to a greater range of 'life choices' in places like Afghanistan, questions about the consequences for the exercise of political agency and voice for those classified as insecure were not included within the normal parameters of debate.

Demise?

It would be easy to mark the end of the human security agenda with the Conservative government's abandonment of ear-marked funding for the Human Security Program, the subsequent downsizing of significant academic–policy interfaces such as the Canadian Consortium on Human Security, and informal directives that funding would not be forthcoming for projects that made explicit reference to the concept.[13] This absence is particularly conspicuous given the high profile of the human security agenda in the *International Policy Statement* (DFAIT, 2005). Within this document, the first major government statement on foreign policy in nearly a decade, human security was recognized as a policy priority with many of its practical tenets featuring prominently, including the promotion of democracy, the responsibility to protect, and the augmentation of international law to deal with issues of human rights. What, then, might account for the overt abandonment of a rhetorically powerful concept that had been thought to have brought considerable status and prestige to Canada?

My tentative proposal would be that although the label of human security has, for the most part, been dropped in the official discourses of Canadian foreign policy, the concept remains a nodal point through which specific policy postures have continued to be promoted. In other words, the human security agenda has not been demolished; it has remained intact.[14] The perception of a reticence on the part of policy-makers to articulate the concept of human security misses a crucial development: there is no need to do so. The supposed aims, objectives, focal points, and rationales of the human security agenda have been subsumed within neo-conservative visions of foreign policy that have gained considerable currency within Ottawa since the 2006 federal election. Issues once considered to be the proprietary domain of the human security agenda now feature as a central part of dominant national security narratives, particularly those of key allies like the United States on such issues as democracy promotion, human rights, and (humanitarian) intervention. To be sure, human security principles are not central to every aspect of recent high-profile policy postures, and human security is no longer evoked by Canadian policy-makers. However, this is not because human security is necessarily at odds with the neo-conservative foreign policy outlook of the Harper government; rather, a shift stems from the (piecemeal) incorporation of this outlook within the concept of human security. There is no reason to articulate a concept when it has already been assumed as 'what goes without saying' in key areas of policy formulation (Barthes, 1972: 11, quoted in Weber, 2005: 4).

Conclusion

Returning to the three questions posed at the outset, the answers are now clearer. Despite claims to the contrary, which have been made by both opponents and proponents, human security has never been in critical opposition to the status quo at the national and global levels. Nor did human security ever seek to seriously challenge those structures that comprise the status quo.[15] Canada's human security agenda was always content to work within them and now has blended into their confines. Thus, the answers given above are both counterintuitive and perplexing. The counter-intuition comes from breaking free of mainstream perceptions of difference that tend to accentuate surface-level variation at the expense of underlying similitude. The perplexity derives from leaving the critical foreign policy analyst in a rather difficult position in terms of questions of accountability.

Traditionally, when outcomes fail to meet the intended aims and objectives, the role of the analyst is to pinpoint why suboptimal results were obtained. In the study of foreign policy, this generally takes the form of holding particular actors accountable—whether they are specific individuals, committees, political parties—for poor implementation (e.g., the Prime Minister interfered). Another common tactic is to directly criticize the policy itself (e.g., policy x was so ill-conceived, it could never have achieved outcome y). Less often, analysts concede that circumstances arose beyond anyone's imagination and control to derail a particular policy outcome despite the best of intentions.

But given the form of critical analysis undertaken here, which has primarily focused on human security as a discursive formation, these traditional ways of assessing accountability seem ill-equipped to get at those things that made hollow policies possible. This suggests that the driving force behind the story of human security in Canadian foreign policy cannot simply be reduced to bad behaviour or elite manipulation. Rather, as is suggested through the deployment of a Foucauldian analytic, the problem is two-pronged but interrelated. The first prong is cultural and is deeply embedded within the understandings and practices of the Canadian foreign policy community and general public. It is important to remember that culture (as a set of understandings and practices) helps to shape structures. The second prong is structural, that is, it is embedded within forms of governance that guide practice and inform our understandings of the possible. These two prongs feed back onto one another, perpetuating particular ways of thinking about things (i.e., common sense) and of acting, given perceived opportunities and constraints.

To be clear, my argument is not that we should abandon more traditional forms of accountability, as there are moments when individuals and groups are very self-aware of how they are deploying language and using discursive frameworks. Rather, what the case of the human security agenda in Canadian foreign policy points to is that if we (as citizens) are serious about transforming Canadian foreign policy—and, by extension, the global political environment—we face a more expansive, more diffuse, and more difficult task than simply voting for a new governing party, demanding different spending allocations, or changing policy priorities. The task requires a complete rethinking of what we mean by 'foreign policy', 'security', and even 'Canada', as well as the energy, willingness, and awareness to expose, challenge, and reconfigure the relations of power that will inevitably shape our answers.

Notes

1. These criteria can be anything from the cost-effective achievement of predetermined aims to normative considerations of what it means to be a good global citizen.

2. See, for example, Smith (2003, 2005), Turenne Sjolander (2005), Howell (2005), Whitworth (1998, 2004), Jeffrey (2005), McDonald (2003), and Tiessen (2003). This list is far from exhaustive as there is a diverse range of research from perspectives sensitive to gender and the constitution of the political in Canada.

3. At the danger of being pedantic, while this may have been true in policy circles, particularly with the publishing of the 1994 *United Nations Development Report*, which formally articulated a conception of human security that captured the attention of the international community, it is important to remember that the idea of placing individuals and/or the communities they belong to as the referent object of security policy was forwarded well before this time by peace activists, dissidents, civil rights movements, Indigenous rights movements, trade unions, and other actors who opposed the (in)security logics of the Cold War. For a broad overview, see Booth (1991). For an analysis of the Canadian context, see Ross (2001).

4. Ontological saliency simply refers to a political situation in which all participants believe that something exists. In other words, the debate was being framed in part by a shared understanding that there was a single, coherent, and undeniable Canadian national interest.

5. For a more contemporary presentation of this argument, see Hataley and Nossal (2004).

6. Tied aid is development aid given under the condition that the recipient will purchase products and/or services from the donor, often, though not necessarily, at inflated prices.

7. For a broader discussion of the connections between neo-liberalism and human security, see Neufeld (1999).

8. For evidence, compare the differences between *Freedom From Fear: Canada's Foreign Policy for Human Security* (2000) and the second edition published in 2003.

9. For a detailed discussion of states of exception, see Agamben (1998). For critical commentaries on counter-terrorism in Canada, see Bell (2006a, 2006b), Côté-Boucher (2008), Daniels et al. (2001), and Human Rights Watch (2003).

10. For an archive of the official understanding of the Afghanistan mission, see <geo. international.gc.ca/cip-pic/afghanistan/menu-en.aspx>.

11. Hugh Gusterson notes that members of a community 'are bound together both by shared allegiance to explicitly formulated propositions about the world . . . and by common consumption of aspects of discourse that exist on the edge of awareness' (Gusterson, 1999: 326). The use of the word 'combatting' would be an example of the latter as opposed to the former.

12. It also bears noting that these practices of response management were also taking place in some of the public forums organized by DFAIT. For example, I personally noticed a significant deterioration in the critical content of questions being posed to policy-makers during the Canadian Peacebuilding Committee's annual symposium in 2003 as compared to the previous year. I would later find out from a confidential informant that DFAIT had in fact planted operatives in the meetings and arranged for them to have first opportunities at microphones during the very limited time period open for questions. With question periods from the previous year proving quite pointed, the hope was to keep discussions within comfortable parameters.

13. The program has been rebranded as the Glyn Berry Program For Peace and Security in memory of Glyn R. Berry, an esteemed Canadian diplomat who was killed in Afghanistan in 2006.

14. It is not the case that the Canadian state has manipulated an otherwise unproblematic human security agenda that arose from within the United Nations; rather, it bears noting that human security has always been a status quo-oriented policy framework (see Grayson, 2008; Shani et al., 2007; Wibben, 2008).

15. Challenging and transforming underlying structures—as opposed to making changes to particular policies that these structures make possible—is the very essence of critical approaches, as discussed in the Introduction to this volume.

Chapter Eight

No CANDU
The Multiply-Nuclear Canadian Self

David Mutimer

What is Canada's policy on nuclear weapons? This is a seemingly simple question, and one to which there is even a clear answer: Canada is a leading proponent of international arms control, non-proliferation, and even disarmament. Yet when we turn a critical gaze onto that question, neither the answer nor the question itself is all that simple after all.

One of the earliest and most extensively explored insights of critical International Relations has been the conditional nature of identity. From the early forays into constructivism through the more recent turn to performativity and hybridity, critical approaches to international politics have rendered the assumed, singular identity of international actors problematic. Performativity in particular draws our attention to the multiple ways in which the self can be constituted. The sites of performance will alter the selves that are thereby produced: I can produce myself as scholar, teacher, colleague, friend, and singer all on the same day, depending on the place and the performance.

This chapter is animated by the complexity introduced to the question of Canadian policy on nuclear weapons when Canada is considered to be constituted performatively. It considers the production of the Canadian self in relation to nuclear weapons within three discursive locations. The first is the set of global non-proliferation, arms control, and disarmament practices, in which Canada performs its international arms-controlling self. However, Canada performs its nuclear weapons policies in places other than this arena, and so the chapter then considers an additional two. The first is Canada as a member of NATO and the second is as the developer and salesman for the Canadian Deuterium-Uranium nuclear reactor: the CANDU.

Following a short discussion of the performative constitution of identity and its relation to the production of a 'Canada' that can have nuclear weapons policy and other foreign policy, the chapter considers the Canada produced at each of these three sites. The three Canadas that emerge pursue policies in relation to nuclear weapons that are not necessarily in concert, and so the chapter concludes with a consideration of a site in which Canada's nuclear-Eve[1] came together: the indefinite extension of the Nuclear Non-Proliferation Treaty (NPT) in 1995.

Performing Canada

In order to ask the question about Canada's policy on nuclear weapons, it is necessary to make a number of important, and generally unacknowledged, assumptions. The one of most concern to this chapter is the assumption that there is something known as 'Canada' that can have a policy of any kind. We assume, in other words, a particular identity for 'Canada': generally, that identity is of a coherent 'international actor', which adopts and executes 'policy' in international relations. This assumption of an international identity that is simply taken as given and about which questions of policy can be asked has been systematically challenged by the critical perspectives that animate this volume. Before continuing to explore Canada's relation to nuclear weapons, I will consider briefly the performative constitution of international identity, beginning with the work of David Campbell.

In *Writing Security*, Campbell took dead aim at the unquestioned assumption of an identity for the state acting internationally. He argues for:

> the performative constitution of the state. Specifically, I want to suggest that we can understand the state as having 'no ontological status apart from the various acts which constitute its reality'; that its status as the sovereign presence in world politics is produced by 'a discourse of primary and stable identity'; and that the identity of any particular state should be understood as 'tenuously constituted in time . . . through a *stylized repetition of acts*,' and achieved, '*not* (through) *a founding act, but rather a regulated process of repetition*.' (Campbell, 1998: 10)

The state performs itself, not through the enactment of some pre-given script, but rather as an ongoing improvisation, built on the repetitions of previous acts. Identity is therefore performed, and the performance is guided (regulated), not by any external authority, but rather by the memory and interpretation of what has gone before. That is to say, identity is both reproduced and produced at the same time and in the same way. It is reproduced inasmuch as it is a 'stylized repetition of acts', but it is simultaneously produced as the present act is constitutive of the state's identity every bit as much as those acts which have preceded it. This duality of the productivity of performance is often then indicated by saying that identity is (re)produced, with the parentheses indicating that there is both production and reproduction, while at the same time refusing to divide the one from the other by using separate words.

In making his argument, Campbell is building on the work of Judith Butler, who in turn has drawn from that of Michel Foucault to explore how natural persons are performatively constituted. Specifically, Butler shows how our genders—a central element to most of our identities, and often considered to be natural, as we seem to be born either 'a boy' or 'a girl'—are actually constituted performatively.

> In this sense, *gender* is not a noun, but neither is it a set of free-floating attributes, for we have seen that the substantive effect of gender is performatively produced and compelled by the regulatory practices of gender coherence. Hence, within the inherited discourse of the metaphysics of substance, gender proves to be performative—that is, constituting the identity it is purported to be. In this sense, gender is always a doing, though not a doing by a subject who might be said to preexist the deed. (Butler, 1990: 24–5, see also Butler, 1993)

In *Writing Security*, Campbell makes the case that, similarly, the state is always 'a doing', and also a doing by a subject that does not pre-exist the deed.[2] He shows how the United States, seemingly the most sovereign, most powerful, most secure state in the international system, is (re)produced in contingent fashion in and through its foreign policy.

In an elaboration on Campbell's central claims, Cynthia Weber has explored the (re)production of the United States in its ongoing relations with its Caribbean neighbours, and shows a United States that is somewhat at odds with Campbell's, at least visually. Weber's text begins with the following startling image:

> This is the United States as I see it today—a white headless body of indecipherable sex and gender cloaked in the flag and daggered with a queer dildo harnessed to its midsection. This figure finds its global footing on Caribbean islands and its hegemonic identity reflected in the Caribbean Sea. ... It is America's caped crusader. It is an American body politic. Cartoonlike in its heroic pose, it stands ready for action of whatever sort in whatever locale. (Weber, 1999: 1)

The rest of Weber's *Faking It* builds up this image through a series of readings of the history of American performances in the Caribbean: the Cuban revolution, the attempted assassinations of Castro, the invasions of Grenada and Panama, among others. While perhaps not everyone would find there a United States that (re)produced itself as a flag-draped, dildo-sporting hermaphrodite, what most would find is a United States that seems somewhat different from that (re)produced in acts of the Cold War contest with the Soviet Union that animate Campbell's text.

Such multiplicity and variability in state identity should not, however, be surprising if we stop to think about it for a moment. Butler's point was that we are constituted as 'a gender' through our performances of gender. Yet, we are all more than just 'woman' or 'man'. These other identities—mother, professor, friend, woman of colour, Englishman, North American, golfer—are similarly (re)produced performatively. We often perform our various selves in different places and at different times. Indeed, in foreign policy analysis, this aspect of our lives has been elevated to an analytic insight: where we stand depends on where we sit.[3] We also, however, face situations in which we are hailed to perform different selves at the same place and time, and this can cause us considerable anxiety—parent/professional and lover/worker being among the most noted examples, but by no means the only ones. If this multiplicity of selves is true of natural persons who are, by and large, physically coherent, how much more likely is it to be true of states, which are performed by a range of individuals and institutions in a stunning array of settings? Performative identity is, therefore, not just tenuous and stylized, but also multiple and contextually contingent.

For the purposes of considering Canada and its relation to nuclear weapons, there are two important implications to the performative constitution of the foreign policy state:

1.   We can look at multiple sites for the performative constitution of Canada in relation to nuclear weapons. This I will do at the sites I have mentioned above: the global NACD (non-proliferation, arms control, and disarmament) discourse, the NATO alliance, and the global marketplace for nuclear reactors.
2.   The Canadas that emerge from these three performative sites will not necessarily be compatible. Thus, when I consider the indefinite extension of the NPT, there is the possibility for the multiply-nuclear Canada to come into some conflict with itself.

Canada and NACD

On the official website of the Canadian Department of Foreign Affairs is a simple statement of Canada's policy on nuclear weapons:

> Canada has long held a policy objective of non-proliferation, reduction and elimination of nuclear weapons and other weapons of mass destruction. (DFAIT, 2007)

Indeed, that long-held objective stems from one of Canada's core claims: that we are the first country to have voluntarily renounced nuclear weapons. As a member of the Manhattan Project, Canada was one of only three countries in 1945 to possess nuclear weapons technology. In the autumn of 1945, following the first use of nuclear weapons by the United States over Hiroshima and Nagasaki, Canada announced that it would not build its own weapons. There is no doubt that this was a notable decision. On 15 November 1945 Canada had joined with the other two states capable of producing nuclear weapons, the US and UK, to issue a joint declaration, which began by noting the significance of the new technology:

The President of the United States, the Prime Minister of the United Kingdom, and the Prime Minister of Canada, have issued the following statement: (1) We recognize that the application of recent scientific discoveries to the methods and practice of war has placed at the disposal of mankind means of destruction hitherto unknown, against which there can be no adequate military defense, and in the employment of which no single nation can in fact have a monopoly. (Truman et al., 1945)

Canada, therefore, was renouncing a weapon of unparalleled destructive potential, one that would likely vault the country into the top tier of post-World War II military powers (Canada ended World War II with one of the largest militaries in the world, including the third largest navy and fourth largest air force). The renunciation of nuclear weapons was a virtually unprecedented act, and it forms an important element in the narrative we tell to ourselves and to the world about who we are as Canada. We produce ourselves, in other words, as champion of nuclear disarmament through telling a story about our willingness to disarm.

Canada has performed this first nuclear self in a range of locations, though particularly through the multilateral NACD practices:

Canada has worked strenuously to promote and reinforce multilateral efforts that, directly or indirectly, contribute to constraining the proliferation of nuclear weapons and work to reduce existing arsenals. (DFAIT, 2007; for a detailed, conventional history of Canada's involvement in these practices, see Legault and Fortman, 1992)

Canada has been a member of the various UN and UN-related efforts at multilateral disarmament since the founding of the United Nations. Canada was a member of the original Disarmament Commission, and from 1960 onward it has been a member of the series of Geneva-based multilateral arms control and disarmament negotiating fora: the Ten Nation Committee on Disarmament (1960), the Eighteen Nation Committee on Disarmament (1962–8), the Conference of the Committee on Disarmament (1969–78), and finally the Conference on Disarmament (1979–present). Through these memberships, Canada has played a leading role in the negotiation of all the major multilateral arms control agreements, including the Nuclear Non-Proliferation Treaty, and is party to all such agreements to which it can belong.[4] Canada also took a lead in the first UN Special Session on Disarmament, held in 1978, and not long afterwards, then Prime Minister Pierre Trudeau launched a peace initiative that, among other things, included a call for 'suffocating' nuclear development. The suffocation proposal was to ban the further production of fissile material for use in atomic weapons, an idea now known as 'the Fissile Materials Cutoff'. A Cutoff Treaty continues to be discussed at the Conference on Disarmament, and remains a priority of Canadian arms control policy to this day (DFAIT, 2007).

The present Canadian government, headed by Prime Minister Stephen Harper, despite seeking to strike a different tone in foreign affairs from its Liberal predecessors, still maintains a broad commitment to disarmament through multilateral means. Peter MacKay, then Foreign Minister and currently the Defence Minister, addressed the Fiftieth Anniversary Pugwash Conference in 2007:

> This Canadian government continues to advance the nuclear disarmament agenda.... Canada strongly supports the multilateral nuclear non-proliferation, arms control and disarmament regime, especially efforts to strengthen and universalize the Nuclear Non-Proliferation Treaty. (MacKay, 2007)

Canada, therefore, has consistently performed its identity as a committed arms controller for more than 60 years, despite changes in government and changes in policy in a myriad of other areas. Yet, as Gordon Edwards has suggested, to a degree this vision of Canada as a promoter of the peaceful atom is a myth (Edwards, 1983). Edwards's point is that despite what we say, Canada is hardly disconnected from the violent use of the atom: 'Canadian nuclear research, it was said, would be dedicated exclusively to bringing the peaceful applications of nuclear energy to commercial fruition. Nevertheless, for twenty years after World War II, Canada sold plutonium (from Chalk River) and uranium (from Ontario, Manitoba, Saskatchewan and the Mackenzie District) for use in the American and British nuclear weapons programs.' Nonetheless, to call the arms-controlling Canada a myth is not to say it is untrue, but rather that it is a story we tell ourselves precisely to enable the performance of a particular form of nuclear self. There are, however, other stories and other selves that Canada performs.

Canada and NATO

If we return to the Foreign Affairs website and its initial statement of the core Canadian policy on nuclear disarmament, we find that the text quoted earlier continues as follows:

> We pursue this aim [of non-proliferation and disarmament] steadily, persistently and energetically, consistent with our membership in NATO and NORAD and in a manner sensitive to the broader international security context. (DFAIT, 2007)

What does membership in NATO have to do with Canada's policy on nuclear weapons? Put another way, which nuclear Canada is performed in the context of the Alliance? The first place to look for an answer is the strategy that guides NATO and its relationship to nuclear weapons.

Soon after the events in Eastern Europe that marked the end of the Cold War, the Alliance produced a new Strategic Concept that, for the first time publicly, set out the strategic principles of NATO. In the section entitled 'Guidelines for Defence—Principles of Alliance Strategy', NATO made the following commitment:

To protect peace and to prevent war or any kind of coercion, the Alliance will maintain for the foreseeable future an appropriate mix of nuclear and conventional forces based in Europe and kept up to date where necessary, although at a significantly reduced level. Both elements are essential to Alliance security and cannot substitute one for the other. (NATO, 1991: para. 38)

These principles were articulated in 1991, a time of tremendous promise but even more uncertainty. The end of the Cold War had been entirely unexpected, and it was by no means clear what would follow. NATO security had been founded on the deterrent mix of nuclear and conventional arms, and so it is not surprising that this mix would be retained in a document issued a month *before* the formal end of the USSR.

However, with the end of the Soviet Union in December 1991 and the rapid transformation in Europe that followed, the Alliance was forced to rethink its role—a good number of commentators, in fact, argued that NATO was no longer necessary.[5] Part of that rethinking involved a reconsideration of the role of nuclear weapons in Alliance strategy. The re-evaluation culminated in 1999 when NATO adopted an updated Strategic Concept. In 1991 the shape of the new Europe was rapidly changing, but by 1999, a decade after the fall of the Berlin Wall, members of the former Warsaw Pact were joining NATO—Poland, Hungary, and the Czech Republic already had, and in only a few years former constituent republics of the Soviet Union would also join—and Russia was linked formally to NATO in a 'Euro-Atlantic Partnership Council'. It might well be expected that NATO's strategy would take a rather more pacific, and certainly less nuclear, direction. Yet, remarkably, in the comparable section of the new document, 'Principles of Alliance Strategy', NATO makes an astonishingly similar claim:

But the Alliance's conventional forces alone cannot ensure credible deterrence. Nuclear weapons make a unique contribution in rendering the risks of aggression against the Alliance incalculable and unacceptable. Thus, they remain essential to preserve peace. (NATO, 1999: para. 49)

The Strategic Concept is a fundamental document of the Alliance, setting out the military strategy of the organization, and thereby it also is a statement of the strategic policy of each of the members of the Alliance. The Strategic Concept, therefore, is a statement of Canada's strategic policy. In a recent statement of Canada's defence policy, the 2005 *Defence Policy Statement*, the section on NATO begins by recalling the centrality of the Alliance to Canada's security: 'NATO is an essential collective defence structure and embodies the transatlantic link that continues to be critical to the security of our country' (Canada, 2005a). Membership in that 'essential' structure, which is 'critical' for Canada's security, demands that we profess the unique contribution nuclear weapons make to providing for our security.

Canada performs at least two identities internationally in relation to nuclear weapons. On the one hand, Canada performs a nuclear self that is at the forefront of global disarmament efforts, in part because it is the first and one of the very few states to have 'renounced' nuclear weapons, having in some sense possessed them. On the other hand, however, Canada is part of an alliance that not only has nuclear-armed states as members, but as part of that collective, Canada performs itself as nuclear-armed.[6] Nuclear weapons make a 'unique contribution' to Alliance (Canadian) security and 'remain essential to preserve peace.' The Canada that performs itself within the Alliance, therefore, is a nuclear-armed self rather than a nuclear disarmer. It would seem that the question of Canada's policy on nuclear weapons is not as simple as it first appeared. Indeed, there is a third performance of Canada that complicates the question still further: Canada the nuclear salesman.

Canada CANDU

Canada performs two selves in relation to nuclear weapons in two potentially contradictory places: as an advocate for nuclear disarmament claiming legitimacy from its having relinquished nuclear weapons in the 1940s, and as a member of a nuclear-armed alliance in which nuclear weapons are 'essential'. There is, however, a third performance of a nuclear Canada that warrants examination. Atomic Energy Canada Limited (AECL) is a Crown corporation, which, in its own words:

> is one of the world's leading nuclear technology companies, providing services to nuclear utilities on four continents. Established in 1952, AECL is the designer and builder of CANDU® technology, including the CANDU 6, one of the world's top-performing reactors. (AECL, 2008a)

In other words, Canada is a nuclear salesman, hawking its wares globally. Indeed, AECL brags about being perhaps the best nuclear salesman in the world:

> AECL has been building reactors almost continuously for the past 30 years and has the strongest project management delivery capability of any nuclear vendor in the world. A leader among nuclear vendors, AECL has designed, built and delivered six CANDU 6 reactors to international customers in the last decade. All of these projects have been delivered on or ahead of schedule, and on budget. (AECL, 2008b)

The CANDU, of course, is an energy generator, designed to provide (relatively) cheap and (relatively) efficient power to its customers. Consider, in trying to sell new CANDUs to Ontario, AECL claims the following, on a page with a lovely maple leaf symbol proclaiming 'Canada is a CANDU country':

> Ontario's electricity sector is facing one of the most challenging periods in its history. Our electricity system has less capacity today than it did 12 years ago, while demand has continued to increase. This could create a gap of up

to 24,000 megawatts (MW) by 2025—about 80 per cent of Ontario's current capacity.

The solution: CANDU nuclear technology—a proven, world-class performer, operating in Canada and around the world with an unmatched safety, reliability and power production track record. (AECL, 2008c)

Canada thus performs itself as a salesman of nuclear technology, but is very clear to say that this is peaceful technology: the CANDU provides energy, and AECL also provides isotopes for medical uses.[7]

How does the sale of nuclear power reactors relate to nuclear weapons policy? Well, the problem is that there is no break between the technology and material for nuclear power and that for nuclear weaponry. Once you have the ability to generate power, and a full fuel cycle to support that ability, you have the capacity to launch a nuclear weapons program. As Frank Barnaby has written: 'A country with a nuclear-power programme will inevitably acquire the technical knowledge and expertise, and will accumulate the fissile material necessary to produce nuclear weapons' (Barnaby, 1994: 1). By exporting the technology to provide for a nuclear power programs through the CANDU reactors, Canada is, therefore, providing the foundations for potential nuclear weapons programs in those countries that purchase the technology. Indeed, Canada discovered this to its chagrin in the 1970s, when Canadian nuclear technology contributed to the development of the nuclear 'explosive' that India tested in 1974. Despite that explosive test, and the general recognition that both India and Pakistan were pursuing nuclear weapons programs, Canada continued civilian nuclear co-operation with both countries.[8]

When other countries export the capacity to manufacture nuclear weapons they are called 'proliferators' and are primary targets of Canada's nuclear disarmament policies. As a result of the experience Canada had in relation to the Indian test, we joined with other suppliers of nuclear technology to form two supplier cartels that set rules about who can have nuclear technology and under what conditions, so that the line between civilian and military uses can be policed by the suppliers themselves (see Mutimer, 2000). More recently, Canada has joined the 'Proliferation Security Initiative', which describes itself as follows: 'In essence, the PSI aims to help prevent the proliferation of WMD, their delivery systems, and related materials, *through enhanced interdiction efforts*' (PSI, 2008; emphasis added). 'Enhanced interdiction efforts' refers to the use of member states' militaries to intercept ships on the high seas and planes in the air, forcibly stopping and searching these vessels to prevent the spread of 'WMD . . . and related materials'. In the case of nuclear weapons, there is little that is more 'related' than a robust nuclear-generating capacity and the skills and technologies that go along with it.

Canada and NPT-95

Canada performs its nuclear selves in at least three relatively distinct contexts, (re)producing at least three Canadas in relation to nuclear weapons. We perform ourselves as a committed arms controller, the first to renounce possession of nuclear weapons, in the context of global, multilateral arms control. We rather paradoxically perform as a nuclear-armed ally in NATO and again in NORAD. Finally, we perform as the global nuclear huckster through AECL and the CANDU. Just as natural persons can generally keep their contradictory selves from bumping into one another by performing their parts at their proper times and in their proper places, so, too, can states like Canada. But similarly, just as we are occasionally forced to face our contradictory performances, there are times when the multiple state cannot ignore that multiplicity. For Canada such a moment came in 1995.

In 1995, the nuclear-Eve that is Canada set about working with partners to secure the indefinite extension of the Nuclear Non-Proliferation Treaty (NPT-95). The policy of the Canadian government going into these negotiations was that the indefinite extension of the NPT was a necessity for the continued success of the nuclear non-proliferation regime. Indefinite extension was, indeed, the outcome that was achieved, but in the process the contradictions of the triply-nuclear Canadian self were brutally exposed.

The central deal of the NPT is fascinating:

- Those states that had tested nuclear weapons by 1967 are recognized as nuclear weapons states and allowed to keep their weapons (Article IX.3) *but* they commit to the negotiation in good faith to the eventual elimination of nuclear weapons (Article VI).
- Those states that had not tested nuclear weapons by 1967 agree never to acquire them (Article II) *but* in exchange they are to be provided access to peaceful nuclear technology (Article IV) (NPT, 1970).

The review and extension conference of the NPT convened in New York in May 1995. At the time of the conference there were more than 170 states party to the treaty, including the five nuclear weapon states, and most of the other states in the world. The exceptions were significant, however: Israel, India, and Pakistan had all refused to join the NPT. Israel is widely assumed to have a small nuclear arsenal, and both India and Pakistan would test nuclear weapons in 1998. Virtually all of the rest of the world, however, had formally accepted the NPT's bargain, and gathered in New York for a most unusual conference. Most treaties are open-ended, and so those that include review conference provisions use the conferences to assess the progress of the treaty's objectives. The NPT, by contrast, was set to expire after 25 years, unless the 1995 conference made an explicit decision to extend it. Article X.2 of the treaty reads: 'Twenty-five years after the entry into force of the Treaty, a conference shall be convened to decide whether the Treaty shall continue in force indefinitely, or shall be extended for an additional fixed period or periods. This decision shall be taken by a majority of the Parties to the Treaty.'

The unusual nature of Article X made the 1995 conference rather more significant than any other review conference of the NPT or other multilateral agreement. The very future of the NPT was at stake, as was the nature of the nuclear non-proliferation regime that would emerge from the conference. As the conference neared, three broad options emerged in the preparatory discussions. The first was that the majority of the states party would not vote to extend the treaty, and so it would expire. For the Western states in particular, including Canada, this was seen as a disastrous outcome, to be avoided at almost any cost. These states supported the second option, the indefinite extension of the NPT. A third position, however, was garnering significant support as the conference approached. This position grew from the language of 'additional fixed period or periods' in Article X, and came to be known as the 'rolling extension'. There were a number of variations on the theme, but essentially they all involved extending the NPT conditionally, with the parties meeting at fixed intervals to approve its further extension.

The rolling extension appealed to a number of non-nuclear weapon states that were not, as Canada is, protected by a nuclear alliance with the United States. The threat of the NPT not being extended in 1995 had contributed, in the early 1990s, to some of the most significant advances in the history of nuclear disarmament. The proponents of the rolling extension saw it as a means to maintain the pressure on the nuclear weapon states to continue disarming by retaining the threat that the next conference might not vote to extend the NPT. These states argued that a world without the NPT was more appealing to them than a world in which the nuclear-armed states continued to hold their weapons indefinitely, without fulfilling their commitment to disarm.

Despite our commitment to nuclear disarmament, Canada opted to join the push for indefinite extension, which removed the pressure from the nuclear weapon states to disarm (a position, incidentally, that some officials in Canada now recognize as a mistake). However, of particular interest in the present discussion is the way that the different Canadas were brought into conflict externally by the pursuit of this goal. Officials from DFAIT, in general, and from the the the Non-Proliferation, Arms Control and Disarmament division, in particular, performed Canada in the processes surrounding the review and extension conference. As such, they were performing the Canada that has long held 'a policy objective of non-proliferation, reduction and elimination of nuclear weapons', and developed a policy to pursue non-proliferation through indefinite extension even at the cost of pressure for reduction and elimination.

However, the interlocutors on the extension debate included a large group of countries seeking a rolling extension to maintain the pressure for fulfilling the disarmament commitments of the NPT. These were all non-nuclear weapon states, which had willingly forsaken nuclear weapons as a means to guarantee their own security in exchange both for the commitment by the nuclear weapon states to disarm and for guaranteed access to the peaceful fruits of nuclear technology. These were also, by and large, Canada's allies in the global arms control arena. The other Canadian performances in relation to nuclear technology significantly undermined the position Canada was adopting in calling for an indefinite extension of the NPT:

- Most notably, the NATO alliance had begun to rethink its strategy and recently had released the 1991 Strategic Concept asserting that nu-clear weapons remained essential for Alliance security. NATO is the singly strongest military organization on the planet, anchored by the only remaining military superpower, and collectively accounts for roughly 60 per cent of the world's total military expenditures (SIPRI, 2007). For Canada to claim that other countries could safely renounce their potential right to acquire nuclear weapons while, from perhaps the safest place on earth, claiming that we needed nuclear weapons for our own security was a stunning hypocrisy. This hypocrisy was noted, and served to undermine Canada's capacity in the lead-up to the conference (Mutimer, 2003).

- Second, the NPT that Canada was seeking to enshrine indefinitely and without amendment guaranteed the non-nuclear weapon states access to nuclear technology for peaceful purposes. The International Atomic Energy Agency through its Safeguards program was tasked with monitoring the use of that technology to ensure it was not used for prohibited purposes (NPT, Article III). However, as noted above, following the Indian test of a nuclear explosive in 1974, Canada joined with other suppliers of nuclear technology to form what would ultimately become two nuclear technology cartels with considerable overlap in membership: the Zangger Committee and the somewhat larger Nuclear Suppliers Group.[9] Both of these groups, and particularly the Nuclear Suppliers Group, serve to restrict access to nuclear technology on the basis of their judgements about the potential recipients—regardless of the commitments of the NPT and practices of the IAEA.

Conclusion

I began this chapter by asking: What is Canada's policy on nuclear weapons? This seemingly simple question proved to be far from simple, however, when it was examined in a critical perspective. The question assumed that there is a singular 'Canada' that can and does have 'a policy' on nuclear weapons. Social critique teaches us to question those assumptions and to ask, among other things, how they came to be. This chapter has examined Canada's relationship with nuclear weapons through the lens provided by the performative constitution of identity. Performativity reveals identities that are (re)produced in performance and constituted iteratively, which are both contingent and contextual.

Seen in this perspective, Canada becomes multiple, produced in at least three generally distinct realms of practice in relation to nuclear weapons. In the global non-proliferation, arms control, and disarmament arena, Canada performs the identity we generally expect: a Canada committed to multilateral arms control, with authority derived in part from having renounced nuclear weapons before any other country. Different Canadas emerge in the two other spheres in which Canada performs its nuclear weapons policy. Among its NATO allies, Canada performs as a military power for which nuclear weapons are essential to its security, a Canada, in other words, that is all but nuclear-armed. Canada's multiply-nuclear self is even more complex than its NACD and NATO selves suggest, however. Through its civilian nuclear energy program, Canada performs a nuclear-salesman identity, working hard to spread civilian technology globally, the same technology that is at the heart of a nuclear weapons program, as the Indian experience amply demonstrates.

The three realms in which these three Canadas are performed are generally distinct. The NPT in general, and the 1995 Review and Extension Conference in particular, however, brought the three together in ways that those performing Canada found profoundly uncomfortable. Canada was performed by one of its 'selves' in the NPT process, and so was performed as the champion of non-proliferation, arms control, and disarmament. The position was consistent with one vision of that 'long-held objective', that is, the centrality of non-proliferation, in general, and of the NPT, in particular, to the larger NACD agenda. Any policy this Canadian self adopted at the review conference would conflict with the other two Canadas that were performed elsewhere and by others. A rolling extension of the NPT would still have conflicted with the NATO-Canada and the AECL-Canada as member of the suppliers' groups. The NPT Review Conference was enlightening precisely because the multiple performances of Canada's nuclear self were *irreconcilable* within its practices: staunchly defending the commitment to disarmament under the NPT would necessarily bring Canada into conflict with itself within NATO; full commitment to the principle of access to nuclear technology would violate the commitments to the Nuclear Suppliers Group.

What, then, is Canada's policy on nuclear weapons? This chapter provides no answer to that question. Instead, it demonstrates that there are profound limits to the question itself, and counsels asking other, prior questions about the conditions under which it is possible to ask the question at all.

Notes

1. As in the 1957 film starring Joanne Woodward, *The Three Faces of Eve*, about a woman with multiple personalities.

2. Campbell and those who follow him are not arguing that individuals are constituted performatively and then come together collectively as settled individual identities to forge a collective identity such as Canada, but rather that the state forms *its* identity in a way analogous to the performative constitution of gender. Campbell is explicit on this point (Campbell, 1998: 10).

3. The phrase is shorthand for an approach to foreign policy analysis developed by Graham Allison and Morton Halperin, and usually is referred to as 'bureaucratic politics' (see Allison, 1971; Halperin, 1974). The suggestion is that people's positions on foreign policy issues within a complex bureaucratic structure such as the Canadian government are in large part determined by the jobs they hold. Today's Minister of Foreign Affairs may take a completely different position than she did yesterday when she was the Minister of Employment.

4. There are a number of arms control agreements to which Canada could not be party: the bilateral agreements between the US and USSR, for example (SALT, START, and the ABM), as well as those establishing regional nuclear weapons-free zones: for example, the Treaty of

Tlatelolco, which covers all of Latin America and the Caribbean (1967; in force since 1969), and the Treaty of Pelindaba, which covers Africa (1996; not yet in force).

5.   The continued relevance of NATO was largely secured by the inability of the European Union to respond adequately to the wars that erupted around the breakup of the former Yugoslavia. The Belgian Foreign Minister, as President of the EU, fatefully announced that 'this is the hour of Europe' in 1992 when the violence was beginning. 'Europe', outside NATO, lacked institutional capacity to respond to the crises. NATO is seen as having 'saved' the European mission, and thereby proved its post-Cold War relevance.

6.   The NATO Strategic Concept is the most recent instance of the contradiction between 'renunciation' and 'possession', and the most important in the context of NPT-95, but it is by no means the only one. Canada co-operated with the United States throughout the Cold War in ways that undermined its non-nuclear status. The following are the best known, but not the only examples: in 1957 Canada agreed to allow the United States to fly air defence missions over Canada using planes equipped with the nuclear-armed 'Genie' interceptors; two years later Canada agreed to build two bases for Bomarc missiles, which could carry nuclear weapons; and in the 1980s, Canada agreed to allow the United States to test its newly developed cruise missiles over Canada's Siberia-like landscape. For an account of Canada's involvements with US nuclear weapons, see the trilogy by John Clearwater (1998, 1999, 2007).

7.   The production of isotopes became news in Canada towards the end of 2007 when problems at the Chalk River facility caused production to cease. The government fired the head of the regulatory body that oversees safety at Canada's nuclear facilities as a response, which led to a political scandal. More interesting for our purposes is that Chalk River was part of Canada's contribution to the Manhattan Project and what followed thereafter, providing nuclear material to the US and UK weapons programs.

8.   For example, both India and Pakistan joined the CANDU Operators Group in 1989, which provides 'programs for co-operation, mutual assistance and exchange of information for the successful support, development, operation, maintenance and economics of CANDU Technology' (COG, 2008). The CANDU Operators Group was formed by AECL and the Canadian utilities using CANDU reactors, with foreign owners of the technology, including India and Pakistan, joining later.

9.   The Nuclear Suppliers Group consists of: Argentina, Australia, Austria, Belarus, Belgium, Brazil, Bulgaria, Canada, China, Croatia, Cyprus, Czech Republic, Denmark, Estonia, Finland, France, Germany, Greece, Hungary, Ireland, Italy, Japan, Kazakhstan, Republic of Korea, Latvia, Lithuania, Luxembourg, Malta, Netherlands, New Zealand, Norway, Poland, Portugal, Romania, Russian Federation, Slovakia, Slovenia, South Africa, Spain, Sweden, Switzerland, Turkey, Ukraine, United Kingdom, and United States. The Zangger Committee is comprised of: Argentina, Australia, Austria, Belgium, Bulgaria, Canada, China, Croatia, Czech Republic, Denmark, Finland, France, Germany, Greece, Hungary, Ireland, Italy, Japan, Kazakhstan, Republic of Korea, Luxembourg, The Netherlands, Norway, Poland, Portugal, Romania, Russian Federation, Slovakia, Slovenia, South Africa, Spain, Sweden, Switzerland, Turkey, Ukraine, United Kingdom, and United States of America.

Chapter Nine

The Art of Governing Trauma

Treating PTSD in the Canadian Military as a Foreign Policy Practice

Alison Howell

In recent years significant attention has been focused on the prevalence of post-traumatic stress disorder among members of the Canadian Forces.[1] The military's former Ombudsman, in particular, became active in raising concern about the mental health of Canadian soldiers, as well as their treatment (both social and medical). In this context, one piece of art has become particularly prominent. Colin Gill's 1919 painting, *Canadian Observation Post*, which depicts a soldier suffering from 'shell shock' in World War I, is featured in various special reports, opinions pieces, and other publications that were produced by or about the Ombudsman. The painting is also prominently displayed in the recently reconstructed Canadian War Museum. After being relegated to storage for 80 nearly uninterrupted years, why has this painting been the subject of renewed interest? What can this painting, and moreover, its current *uses*, tell us about Canadian foreign policy?

This chapter questions why this painting from World War I has been featured so regularly in recent years, how it has become useful, and how it functions within emergent governmental rationalities (Foucault, 1991) surrounding post-traumatic stress disorder (PTSD) in the Canadian Forces. It is argued that the painting has been called upon to visually constitute PTSD as an illness that soldiers have always experienced. The recent 'discovery' of PTSD and the medicalization of trauma are then positioned as evidence of progress (in the military and in medicine) and improved care. This chapter disrupts such narratives by questioning the political effects of treating trauma as an illness (Young, 1997; Edkins, 2003). Such an approach does not deny that soldiers may experience trauma, but questions the politics of treating such trauma as a medical problem. It is argued that the diagnosis of PTSD functions to render trauma a medical problem, thus focusing our attention on the psyches of individual soldiers. What is lost in treating war trauma as a medical problem or by medicalizing trauma? I argue that we lose the ability to sufficiently politicize sources of trauma: that is, decisions by Canadian foreign policy-makers to use military force in both 'peace' and combat missions, such as the recent deployment of Canadian troops in Afghanistan. In this sense, PTSD is used to medicalize trauma rather than politicize it. Our responses to trauma are then individualized—we treat traumatized soldiers as individuals in need of medical care, rather than questioning the political sources of their trauma: war and the use of force. This marginalizes important political questions about war and militarism in Canadian foreign policy.

The approach taken in this chapter stems from the view that we should investigate the politics of the uses of psychiatry. As such, this chapter is grounded in the belief that we can and should investigate the power of authoritative knowledge, or what Foucault called regimes of truth, especially in the case of the psy disciplines[2]—psychology, psychiatry, and their sub-disciplines. Following from this, it is important to understand that post-traumatic stress disorder, as with other diagnostic categories, is an invention, not a discovery. The American Psychiatric Association's *Diagnostic and Statistical Manual of Mental Disorders* (*DSM*) includes and excludes different disorders in successive editions:

> With each new edition some disorders are classified for the first time (where were they before?) and others disappear (where did they go?). This is a reminder that a psychiatric diagnosis is primarily a way of seeing, a style of reasoning, and (in compensation suits or other claims) a means of persuasion. (Summerfield, 2001: 97)

Many diagnoses—such as the fugue or multiple personality disorder—have either disappeared or fallen into disuse (Hacking, 1995). This signals to us that diagnoses are inventions: they constitute the very objects that they claim to identify. By the same token, psychiatry also invents new diagnoses. The *DSM* includes new diagnoses in each edition: PTSD was not included until 1980, in the wake of the Vietnam War. Thus, the disorder is not a discovery but an invention: it is 'an *achievement*, a product of psychiatric culture and technology' (Young, 1997: 116). In the psy disciplines this is represented as a series of progressive discoveries. Treating trauma as a medical problem is considered evidence of progress.

Authorities in the Canadian military share this belief as well. There is a widespread conviction in the Canadian Forces (CF) that the 'condition' or 'problem' has always existed, but that the diagnostic category of PTSD has allowed for progress in the treatment of soldiers. Colin Gill's World War I painting is used to prop up such faulty claims. The purpose of this chapter is to scrutinize the treatment of trauma as a medical problem. I argue that war trauma is fundamentally a political issue, because it is produced by foreign policy decisions to make war, and even purportedly 'peace' through military deployments. War trauma is the result of the militarization of Canadian foreign policy. As such, trauma is fundamentally a political problem rather than a medical one. Viewing trauma as a political problem, instead of a medical one, can guide us in forming a critical approach to Canadian foreign policy, and especially the use of force in foreign policy. The aim of this chapter is not to deny that trauma exists, but to challenge its medicalization in order to better understand the political contexts through which trauma is produced in the first place.

To make these arguments, the chapter proceeds in three sections. The first describes how Gill's painting came to be displayed and exhibited much more frequently after 2000. The second section places the sudden prominence of the painting in the context of increased calls for improvements in the medical and social treatment of soldiers diagnosed with PTSD, as well as resistance to such calls in the military. The final section then draws out the importance of these observations for the study of Canadian foreign policy by asking the question: what is at stake in our approach to war trauma?

Canadian Observation Post

Colin Gill, *Canadian Observation Post* (1919). CWM 19880266-003. Beaverbrook Collection of War Aart. © Canadian War Museum.

Gill's *Canadian Observation Post* (1919) made a sudden and marked re-emergence in the context of increased concern for the mental health of Canadian soldiers, though it had existed in relative obscurity for 80 years after it had been painted. The artist, Colin Gill, joined the British Army at the outbreak of World War I, and in 1915 was sent to France as a member of the Royal Artillery. The following year he was seconded as a camouflage officer in the Royal Engineers. Gill was recruited as an official war artist in 1918 and all his paintings on the war were completed after the Armistice (Keegan, 1999). *Canadian Observation Post* remained in storage for many years, only to come to prominence in 2000. Indeed, early records show a marked disinterest in the painting. It was placed in storage in the Public Archives, was exhibited once, at the Canadian National Exhibition (CNE) in Toronto from 9 August to 11 September 1941, then was returned to storage again. It remained in storage until 2000, when it suddenly came to garner significant interest. It was put on display in the Canadian Museum of Civilization in 2000, and later became part of the 'Canvas of War' travelling exhibit, making its way across the country between 2001 and 2005. It then landed in its current place of display, just inside the main entrance of the Military History Research Centre at the newly rebuilt Canadian War Museum in Ottawa. After being displayed only once in the 80 years between 1920 and 2000, it was exhibited in no less than 10 museums across Canada in the five years between 2000 and 2005, ending up on permanent display in a place of prominence.

Yet of even greater importance than the painting's recent history of frequent display is its rapid rise in being *reproduced* in a wide variety of publications and policy documents. For instance, it appears as the cover art for Canadian novelist Alan Cumyn's 2003 work of fiction, *The Sojourn*. It also appears on the cover of the Canadian Museum of Civilization's Corporate Report for 1999. More notably, though, it has appeared in several documents produced by or about the Canadian military's former Ombudsman, André Marin, who was central to instituting the military's new policies and programs for the treatment of the mental health of Canadian soldiers. The painting has appeared in newspaper and other media reports about Marin. For instance, in the winter of 2005 it appeared in Carleton University's alumni magazine, accompanying an article titled 'Trauma on the Front Line' that featured an account of the efforts by Marin (a Carleton alumnus) to bring PTSD to the forefront in the Canadian military. Yet probably the most prominent positioning of Gill's painting is as the cover art for the Ombudsman's *Special Report on the Systemic Treatment of CF Members with PTSD* (2002a). Of significance in these positionings of the painting is the attention paid to its lower right-hand corner, where a soldier is depicted hunched over, sitting, and covering his ears with his head in his hands, in what has come to be considered a representation of 'shell shock' or PTSD.

This chapter questions why this painting from World War I has suddenly been featured so regularly, how it has become useful, and how it functions within emergent narratives concerning PTSD in the Canadian Forces. In order to question the role of this work of art in such narratives, it is important to place the painting in context. The following section thus traces an assemblage of programs, technologies, and strategies that have increasingly problematized the psyches of Canadian soldiers, as well as resistance to such programs.

PTSD in the Canadian Military

Beginning in the mid- to late 1990s the mental health of members of the Canadian Forces came to be an issue subject to increased attention. There has been a rise in the number of programs, statistical surveys, special reports, and public discourse on the topic of PTSD in the Canadian military. In conceptualizing this shift, Gilles Deleuze's concept of assemblage is useful. Deleuze identified in Foucault's work the idea of assemblages, that is, sets of concrete practices or material 'technologies' that are a result of abstract ideas while also productive of them (Deleuze, 1986: 37). Assemblages are cobbled together through various strategies, and are both the result of and reproductive of particular ideas or forms of knowledge. The increase in programs for the treatment of soldiers with PTSD can be thought of in this way: it has simultaneously relied on and reproduced the notion that the psyches of Canadian soldiers are particularly in need of medical care and treatment. The purpose of studying problematizations is to emphasize their contingency and thus changeability. In this sense, this chapter traces how soldiers' psyches came to be a 'problem' for the military and for Canadian foreign policy, and seeks to expose the contingency of this problematization and to question its effects.

In part, the very public narrative of Roméo Dallaire's experiences with PTSD served to bring the issue to the forefront. Dallaire had been the commander of the failed military portion of the UN operation in Rwanda, leading up to the 1994 genocide. Dallaire's account of his experiences has come to prominence through the publication of his book, *Shake Hands with the Devil* (Dallaire, 2003), which was awarded the Governor General's Award for non-fiction in 2004, along with a documentary and a dramatic film by the same title, in addition to his numerous speaking engagements and his current position in the Canadian Senate. In this narrative, he recounts how a lack of support from the UN Security Council contributed to the failure of his mission to prevent the genocide, leading to Dallaire's own struggles with post-traumatic stress disorder and several suicide attempts. This account by a senior Canadian Forces member was one factor in bringing PTSD to the forefront.

Beyond this, concern with the state of the psyches of soldiers was also highlighted by the Department of National Defence's Board of Inquiry on Croatia, which was originally tasked with assessing the health consequences for soldiers of exposure to environmental contaminants during a tour of duty in Croatia from 1993 to 1995. The Board of Inquiry concluded that veterans of this mission were experiencing difficulties not as a result of identifiable environmental contaminants, as had originally been thought, but due to 'a complex web of physical and psychological stressors' (DND, 1999: 1). It was concluded that a large number of the veterans of this mission were suffering from PTSD, but that they were reluctant to come forward due to fear of stigmatization. This review, then, constituted another way in which the mental health of soldiers came to be problematized.

Yet, the attention directed at the state of the mental health of Canadian soldiers reached a crescendo with the release of three successive 'Special Reports' on PTSD in the Canadian Forces by the military's former Ombudsman, the first of which featured Gill's painting on the cover (Ombudsman, 2002a, 2002b, 2003). These reports were originally undertaken in response to a complaint arising out of one particular incident: in the early morning hours of 15 March 2001, Corporal Christian McEachern smashed his Nissan Exterra SUV into the headquarters of the Edmonton Garrison, then proceeded to slowly drive around inside the building, knocking over desks and computers (he did not cause injury to anyone) (CTV, 2002). After calmly surrendering to military police, he asked to be 'put out of his misery', and later attempted to grab another soldier's service revolver, presumably in an attempt to commit suicide (ibid.). McEachern had served as a peacekeeper in Croatia and Uganda, and had previously been diagnosed with PTSD. He later stated that this incident was a 'cry for help': that he had been treated poorly by his commanders, abandoned and stigmatized by his unit, and generally ostracized. Following from this event, McEachern filed a complaint with the then-Ombudsman for the Canadian Forces, André Marin, who conducted an exhaustive study resulting in the publication of a 217-page Special Report (Ombudsman, 2002a) on the treatment of military personnel with PTSD.

The report did not look into the specific circumstances surrounding McEachern's case (since this was a matter before the courts), but instead investigated the systemic ill-treatment of Canadian Forces members diagnosed with PTSD. The report focused on the need to address the stigmatization of soldiers who seek psychological help and the need for education and training in order to effect this change. In addition, the Ombudsman called for improved services, not only through the Operational Trauma and Stress Support Centres, where soldiers could receive the care of psychologists and psychiatrists, but also through peer-to-peer support programs and the creation of the position of 'PTSD co-ordinator' to oversee such activities. It was argued that this would be beneficial both to soldiers who suffer from PTSD and to the efficiency of the military in general.

Further, the report identified a lack of sufficient data on the prevalence of PTSD in the Canadian Forces, and called for a database, statistical reports, and other calculative technologies to be instituted. In September 2003, a survey was conducted by Statistics Canada, resulting in a 259-page document enumerating the purported prevalence of PTSD through survey data (Statistics Canada, 2003). Attempts to enumerate—to create data—are intrinsic to problematizations: in this case, the problematization of soldiers' psyches (Rose, 1999: ch. 6). Such efforts to enumerate the 'problem' of PTSD in the military thus constitute one more aspect in the assemblage targeting soldiers' psyches.

The Ombudsman's Special Report was followed up with another one nine months later, which assessed the extent to which the recommendations laid out in the original report had been implemented (Ombudsman, 2002b). It praised the changes that had occurred, but highlighted the continued prevalence of a military culture in which negative attitudes about soldiers with PTSD prevailed. The Canadian military continues to develop programming to prevent and treat PTSD, including: screening programs for soldiers returning from deployments for possible PTSD; a 24-hour hotline staffed with counsellors; and programs (such as stress and anger management or healthy lifestyle courses) specifically aimed at enhancing the 'psychological self-help skills' of soldiers (Jaeger, 2006: 31). These efforts, taken together, form an assemblage that relies on and reproduces the problematization of the psyches of soldiers. It is within this assemblage that Gill's painting has come to such prominence in recent times, after spending most of 80 years in storage. Such programs, however, and the more general call for a shift in military culture have been met with significant resistance, and have been critiqued by many within the Canadian military community.

At the unit level, resistance to the call for new attitudes towards soldiers with PTSD was nowhere more apparent than in what came to be called the 'Crazy Train' incident, which occurred during an annual event called the 'French Grey Cup' celebrated by the Princess Patricia's Canadian Light Infantry (PPCLI) at CFB Winnipeg. This event includes a parade featuring floats made by each battalion in the PPCLI. The annual event became the object of much scandal in 2002. During that year's celebration, one of the floats portrayed a mythical 'crazy train', which was a well-known and widely used derogatory term to describe soldiers suffering from PTSD (it originates from an Ozzy Osbourne song of the same name) (Ombudsman, 2003). The float featured a black locomotive pulling a pink jail cell. The battalion's male contestant for 'Miss' Grey Cup rode inside the cage, dressed in women's lingerie, and reportedly acted 'crazy'. In addition, the float featured signs that read 'Next Stop: North Side'. The term 'North Side' is commonly used in reference to the north area of CFB Winnipeg, where psychiatric services are located, and where soldiers diagnosed with PTSD are often sent. The float not only belittled soldiers diagnosed with PTSD, but did so through the homophobic act of putting the 'crazy' soldier in drag. The entire scenario was clearly an act of opposition to changes taking place in the military concerning the treatment of soldiers diagnosed with PTSD.

Resistance to calls for better treatment of soldiers diagnosed with PTSD has occurred not only at the unit level, but also more broadly in the military community. Several critiques of the Ombudsman's recommendations came to prominence through a series of newspaper 'opinion' features. The most prominent of these were pieces in the *National Post* written by retired Major-General Lewis MacKenzie, who commanded troops during the Bosnian civil war in 1992. MacKenzie argued that the stigma attached to soldiers with PTSD is 'understandable' because 'there is no capacity to indefinitely keep handicapped soldiers in uniform who are suffering from PTSD' (MacKenzie, 2002: A14). He cast suspicion on the validity of such diagnoses by asserting that only a minority of soldiers 'genuinely have problems' while the rest 'soldier on and do the dirty work for the rest of us' (ibid; see also MacKenzie, 2003). Such sentiments reflect the broader view within the military that soldiers claiming to be suffering with PTSD are most often 'fakers' and 'malingerers'.

At first, this may appear to be a debate between two opposing sides. Yet both proponents and resisters to PTSD diagnoses in the military share a number of commonalities. Both, for example, advocate for increased military spending and for making the military more efficient. So, although these two sides appear to oppose one another, upon closer inspection they are both deeply invested in militarism. As Enloe (2000) has noted, there is a need to focus less on changes within militaries and more on challenging militarism itself. This is just as true of the Canadian military as of any other country's military. While the Canadian military is often represented as an altruistic and 'kinder, gentler' force involved in peacekeeping instead of war-making, this has been disputed by Marxist, feminist, and anti-racist scholars (Whitworth, 2004; Razack, 2004).

Beyond the shared belief in militarism, the debate operates by focusing attention on individual soldiers and the state of their psyches. The debate centres on the question of whether PTSD is 'real', with one side asserting that it is, and the other asserting that it (usually) is not. Those espousing the view that PTSD claimants are malingerers or fakers express an anxiety over PTSD claims as a means to escape military service. In a sense, it can be helpful to take this anxiety seriously. By considering the possibility that claims to be suffering from PTSD could indeed be acts of resistance, or a 'way out' of military service, we can shift attention to the sources of such acts. In other words, we need to shift the debate from one focused on individual soldiers (and the 'realness' of their mental states) towards a focus on the political effects and context of PTSD claims in the Canadian military. This contestation over the medical and social treatment of soldiers diagnosed with PTSD forms the context in which Gill's *Canadian Observation Post* came to such prominence in the years following 2000. A closer examination of the place of Gill's painting can help to move beyond this limited debate on PTSD in the Canadian Forces.

Gill's World War I painting is used in two central ways. First, it is used to support the medicalization of trauma, and second, it is used in broader governing strategies aimed at rendering soldiers fit for redeployment in the service of an increasingly militarized Canadian foreign policy agenda. These two related claims are developed in the following section.

War, Trauma, and Canadian Foreign Policy

Debates in the military have centred on whether or not PTSD is 'real', and Gill's painting has been positioned as evidence of its 'realness' despite the fact that PTSD had not yet been invented—it did not exist—when the painting was completed. As suggested above, however, we need to move beyond debating whether PTSD is 'real', because such debates have failed to question militarism. So, it is important to shift the debate away from assessing the validity of PTSD and the legitimacy of PTSD claimants. Instead, the balance of this chapter directs scrutiny at the political effects of the problematization of soldiers' psyches in order to make two related claims. The first is that the medicalization of soldiers' experiences is an individualizing process that marginalizes broader political questions about the Canadian military and its deployments, and about Canadian foreign policy in general. The second is that psychology and psychiatry are used to manage war trauma through this medicalization in order to govern soldiers and thus render them fit for redeployment in the service of an increasingly militarized Canadian foreign policy agenda.

In this context, the reproduction of Gill's painting on the cover of the Ombudsman's initial Special Report is especially noteworthy. Here, the painting is captioned with this statement:

With his head buried in his hands, the man in the lower right corner of Colin Gill's 1919 painting, *Canadian Observation Post*, appears to be suffering from 'shell-shock'. Today, this condition is called post-traumatic stress disorder (PTSD). (Ombudsman, 2002a: i)

This caption positions the painting within narratives concerning soldiers' psyches in some very specific ways. The painting, though predating the invention of PTSD, is used to frame the 'condition' as singular and unchanged—only what it has been 'called' has changed (i.e., from 'shell shock' to 'PTSD'). As discussed in the first section of the chapter, the psy sciences position PTSD as a discovery and as evidence of progress in terms of diagnosis and treatment, and authorities in the Canadian military share this view. Major Stephane Grenier, a soldier diagnosed with PTSD who then created a peer-support program, makes an argument common in the military's approach to the issue. In an article titled 'OSIS: A New Way to Look at an Old Problem', he asserts that even though PTSD was 'discovered' only relatively recently, 'military organizations have had to deal with the realities of stress induced injuries since the beginning of time' (Grenier, 2005: 1). The painting is important also in that it depicts World War I soldiers, who have an aura of toughness. If these soldiers could suffer from 'what we now call' PTSD, then the illness must be valid, real, and enduring. Gill's painting, then, is used to 'prove' that PTSD has always existed (though under different names). It is also used to propel the notion that the diagnostic category of PTSD has allowed for progress in the treatment of soldiers.

The trend towards increased diagnoses of PTSD and the more generalized focus on soldiers' psyches in the Canadian military problematizes individual soldiers at the expense of politicizing the deployment of Canadian troops. Yet PTSD is not inherently depoliticizing: its invention was actually achieved, in part, through political struggle. Summerfield (2001) explores how the invention of PTSD is a legacy of the US war in Vietnam and the chilly reception that veterans received upon returning to America. Veterans who saw psychologists were originally diagnosed with having an anxious state, depression, substance abuse, personality disorder, schizophrenia, battle fatigue, or war neurosis—diagnoses that were later supplanted by PTSD (ibid). Proponents of PTSD were often anti-war activists who were resisting the ways in which military psychiatry served the interests of the military. The new diagnosis 'was meant to shift the focus of attention from the details of a soldier's background and psyche to the fundamentally traumatogenic nature of war' (ibid., 95). This shift also positioned veterans as victims of war, rather than as perpetrators or offenders, and also guaranteed them disability pensions (ibid.).

However, with the entrenchment of PTSD into the psy disciplines and into militaries, the original intent of shifting attention away from soldiers' psyches to the nature of war has not borne out. So, rather than solely examining the history of the invention of PTSD, it is important to study how the category *'came into being as a category that could be used'* (Edkins, 2003: 45). Indeed, this is particularly important because PTSD is not a static category: its uses have varied over time. It is an ever-expanding diagnosis, one that continues to swallow up a wider variety of experiences. Several theorists of the psy disciplines have pointed out that anything from involvement in road traffic accidents to witnessing a fire or a riot are now considered sufficient to cause post-traumatic stress disorder (Rose, n.d.: 6). The most recent version of the *DSM* states that PTSD has lifetime prevalence rates of up to 58 per cent among combat veterans and others at risk. Paying attention to the expanding nature of the diagnosis does not suggest that it is less authoritative (or that traumatic experience is unreal), but that PTSD is actually becoming a more authoritative diagnosis. Thus, the expansion of what is included in the category of PTSD is 'not so much a debasement of the terminology as *an extension of the methods of discipline and control* that were forged in the context of post-Vietnam combat trauma, to, on the one hand, the victims of reality TV, and, on the other, the survivors of Nazi camps' (Edkins, 2003: 51).

While the original purpose of lobbying for the recognition of PTSD may have been to focus attention on the traumatogenic nature of war, instead we have seen the emergence of the problematization of soldiers' psyches through PTSD diagnoses: it is used in ways that individualize the experience of combat, as well as 'peace' operations. In the Canadian military it is acknowledged that PTSD is the result of deployments:

> PTSD is an operational hazard. . . . [it] is not a new problem, nor is it one that can be avoided. It is the cost of Canada's continued involvement on the world stage as a nation committed to preserving peace. (Ombudsman, 2002a: ix)

At first blush it might seem that PTSD thus focuses attention on soldiers' trauma, on war, and in particular on recent Canadian Forces deployments. But ultimately, the expectation is that soldiers are supposed to reconcile these experiences through psychological help instead of politicizing traumatic events. Consider, for instance, the following statement of one military official concerning soldiers diagnosed with PTSD: '[they] have had their image of fairness or stability of the world so disrupted that they are forced to devote much time and energy adjusting to the emotional disturbance this has caused' (Grenier, 2005: 2). What if soldiers were called upon not only to adjust to their emotional disturbance, but to explore the politics of the lack of 'fairness or stability' that they have witnessed? Moreover, this raises the question of whether trauma should be treated as a medical problem, or whether it points to political 'problems', namely, Canada's military deployments and its war-waging actions. The point is not to deny such trauma, but to place it within a political rather than a medical context.

Yet, as Edkins argues, PTSD often acts to depoliticize trauma in that those diagnosed 'are to accept the route to cure suggested by therapy. Political action is ruled out. Any attempt at such action . . . is interpreted as an expression of their disease. It is an "acting out" of their symptoms, nothing more' (Edkins, 2003: 50). Consider, for example, the incident that sparked all of the interest on the part of the Canadian Forces Ombudsman—a corporal driving his SUV into the Edmonton Garrison and causing property damage. This incident came to be understood as the soldier 'acting out' his disease. His diagnosis with PTSD rendered this action symptomatic of the disorder: pathological rather than political. Through the diagnosis of PTSD, attention is focused on the individual, for example, on the soldier's psyche, rather than on the conditions of his deployment, the role of the Canadian military, or the conduct of Canadian foreign policy. At best, this has resulted in a call for destigmatizing those diagnosed with PTSD. But questions about peace operations and about Canada's place in the 'war on terror' or in producing liberal world order are left unexamined because ultimately the focus is on curing the disordered (and disorderly) individual.

What is lost through the medicalization of soldiers' experiences is that survivors of events 'have something to tell us about . . . power and political community in the contemporary western world' (ibid., 51). The medicalization of Canadian soldiers' trauma, which is achieved in part through the use of Gill's painting, removes their memories from the realm of the political—wherein the decision of the state to deploy soldiers could be examined—and is instead supplanted through a focus on the disorder of individuals (ibid., 42). Distress is relocated from the political and social arena to the clinical arena, allowing for sources of distress to escape scrutiny (Summerfield, 2001: 98).

The medicalization of trauma thus individualizes war trauma and marginalizes political debate over the uses of the Canadian military, Canada's actions abroad, and about Canadian foreign policy in general. This is the first of two claims about the medicalization of trauma. The second claim I make is that there is a need to examine how psychology and psychiatry are used to manage war trauma and govern soldiers in order to render soldiers fit for redeployment. Programs of governance draw on a variety of sources of authority, and sometimes these sources of authority are disparate and unexpected. In the case of governing the psyches of Canadian soldiers, it is not only the psy disciplines that are called upon, but also Gill's painting.

Bennett has argued that art is involved in 'a variety of governmental programs aimed at bringing about changes in ways of life' (Bennett, 2000: 1425). He traces this to the second half of the nineteenth century, and to the position that art museums played in attempts to curb drunkenness among working-class men. Rather than adopting coercive measures (such as prohibition), liberal reformers saw museums as capable not only of getting such men out of the public houses, but also of elevating them to a 'higher plane of existence' such that they would no longer desire drinking and would govern themselves accordingly (ibid.,1414). Bennett argues that such nineteenth-century programs of liberal governance have a legacy in the present context. He traces the way in which art is now harnessed in programs of governance aimed at various communities, for instance, the provision of arts training skills for disaffected youth (ibid., 1421). Bennett's work is instructive in showing how art can be enlisted in programs of governance. Gill's *Canadian Observation Post* can be understood in just this way. Its rediscovery in 2000, after spending 80 mostly uninterrupted years in storage, coincides with the emergence of governmental rationalities aimed at managing the psyches and conduct of soldiers in the Canadian military. Gill's painting, captioned with the claim that it represents PTSD and positioned on the cover of the central report driving military changes, serves as an authoritative visual text in the problematization and thus governance of Canadian soldiers.

Psychology and psychiatry are primarily called upon in the governance of the psyches of soldiers. As Rose (1998: 115) asserts, the psy disciplines are individualizing technologies that render subjects 'amenable to being calculated about, having things done to them, and doing things to themselves'. Thus, the medicalization of trauma is a disciplinary technology. As Edkins (2003: 51) writes, 'It is the intersection of trauma and political power that makes it necessary for survivors to be disciplined.' The medicalization of trauma, then, not only focuses our attention on the psyches of individual soldiers, rather than on the political context of the production of such trauma. It also serves to discipline and govern soldiers in order to render them fit for redeployment in the service of an increasingly militarized Canadian foreign policy. According to the former Ombudsman:

> Canadians are living in increasingly troubled times. Canadians wish to have a military that they can depend on to contribute to the defence of freedom and security in the world. . . . [Psychological] resources must be there to care for CF soldiers when they return from battle, so they will be healthy and ready to respond in the future. (Ombudsman, 2002a: 207)

The treatment of PTSD in the Canadian Forces is meant to produce a population of orderly soldiers, fit for redeployment in the name of securing an orderly and free world. This has become especially pressing in the context of Canada's war-waging actions in Afghanistan. As such, practices aimed at rendering the psyches of Canadian soldiers orderly are deeply implicated with the militarization of Canadian foreign policy. And yet, these very missions go unquestioned when the focus is shifted to the psyches of individual soldiers. Put simply: when the problem is located in the psyches of soldiers, instead of in the act of making war, then the 'solution' to this problem is deemed to be medical rather than political. The answer is always more medical treatment, not the cessation of the use of force. PTSD has thus come to be used in ways that individualize the experience of military missions, while marginalizing questions about military deployments abroad, and thus about Canadian foreign policy in general.

PTSD, understood in this manner, should be viewed as a military technology of governance—but one that calls on some disparate sources of authority. This governance of soldiers' psyches certainly relies on and reproduces the authority of the psy disciplines. Gill's *Canadian Observation Post*, a forgotten painting from World War I, has also been employed in the creation of a narrative concerning the medicalization of trauma. The painting has been positioned in such a way that it supports the faulty idea that the condition has always existed, when PTSD was only invented in 1980. Further, the painting is used to promote the idea that PTSD is a marked improvement over the diagnosis of shell shock in the care for Canadian soldiers. I argue otherwise: the PTSD diagnosis is not a sign of progress but a technology of governance that seeks to make soldiers fit for redeployment in the service of the use of force in Canadian foreign policy. In this sense, the painting is implicated in the medicalization of trauma in the Canadian Forces. Medicalization has two central effects: first, it individualizes the experience of war and focuses our attention away from the politics of militarization; and second, it governs soldiers' psyches and behaviours such that they can be returned to duty in the service of an increasingly militarized Canadian foreign policy agenda. By paying heed to the multiple sources of authority that produce the medicalization of war trauma, such as the use of Gill's painting, we may view these developments as political, contingent, and therefore changeable.

Notes

1. This chapter was first presented as a paper on a series of panels on critical Canadian foreign policy analysis organized by Professor Rob Aitken and myself for the annual meetings of the Canadian Political Science Association in 2006 and the International Studies Association in 2007. I am grateful to the participants of these panels for their engagement with this work. David Mutimer, Sandra Whitworth, Elizabeth Dauphinee, and John Grundy have also provided exceptionally useful feedback, as have the editors of this book.

2. The term 'psy' refers to all those disciplines that take the psyche as their object: psychology, psychiatry, and all of their sub-disciplines and cognates. This is not to say that such disciplines should be treated as monolithic, coherent, or undifferentiated (see Rose, 1998: 2). Despite the difference between these sub-disciplines, however, what they all share in common is their problematization and medicalization of psyches.

Chapter 10

'Happy Is the Land That Needs No Hero'

The Pearsonian Tradition and the Canadian Intervention in Afghanistan

Mark Neufeld

Introduction: 'Unglücklich das Land, daß keine Helden hat'

['**Unhappy is the land that has no heroes**'] –Bertolt Brecht, *Leben des Galilei*, Scene XII

I can recall clearly a class discussion in my Grade 13 Canadian history course on the question of Canadian heroes.[1] Our teacher, Mr Pollard, was adept at getting these discussions going with leading questions. The United States is very good at celebrating its heroes—what about Canada? Do we have heroes? Why not? Should we? Who from our past is a candidate?[2]

I didn't realize it at the time, but what we were really discussing was whether any Canadian personalities were central to what Gramsci, borrowing from Sorel, called an animating 'Myth' (see Augelli and Murphy, 1996). Such myths, because of their power, are vital to the efforts of mainstream intellectuals to motivate publics to active support for elite projects. Oppositional intellectuals, too, may be tempted to appeal to those same myths in an effort to reorient public support away from such agendas. Such is certainly the case in terms of the ongoing debate about Canada's involvement in the military campaign in Afghanistan. And what is particularly noteworthy in terms of this chapter is that as both proponents and opponents have worked to stake out their positions, a leading figure in a central Canadian animating myth has figured in the arguments of both sides: Lester B. (Mike) Pearson.

Hey Mike, Which Side Are You On?

There is no question that Mike Pearson—the only Canadian to have won the Nobel Peace Prize—has attained the status of Canadian hero. While not the overall winner, he polled well in the CBC's 'Greatest Canadian' contest in 2004, where his case was championed by actor Paul Gross.[3] It is also perhaps noteworthy that books have been designed to instill a sense of admiration for Pearson among Canadian children (Hughes, 2004; Gibb, 2006).[4] Finally, Canada's largest airport, just outside Toronto, is named for the former Prime Minister.

Given the broad public respect for Pearson, it is hardly surprising that he has become a touchstone for opposing positions on the Afghanistan conflict. To begin, proponents of Canada's continued involvement have been anything but shy in invoking Pearson to support their position. Jack Granatstein, for example, has argued that peacekeeping, while an innovation not completely without merit, was not the sum total of Pearson's security repertoire. Peacekeeping is possible only under specific conditions, including an invitation from the parties on both sides of a conflict to foreign troops. However, as such conditions have not existed in Afghanistan,[5] peacekeeping is not an option. In the same vein, development and diplomacy are not real possibilities until security has been enhanced and the situation stabilized.

Fortunately, argues Granatstein, Pearson provides us with a model of how to behave when peacekeeping is not possible. Noting, among other things, Pearson's support for military intervention in the Korean War—an intervention that was not peacekeeping—Granatstein stresses that 'hard-edged values', 'strength and alliances', and a willingness to fight are also part of the essence of the Pearsonian tradition (Granatstein, 2008). For this reason, he concludes, Prime Minister Stephen Harper deserves support, since it is his 'resolve and strength' on the Afghanistan question that makes him 'Mike Pearson's true heir'.

It is true that Stephen Harper has evidenced a new-found—and, arguably, somewhat surprising[6]—appreciation for the core tenets of Pearsonian internationalism such as multilateralism[7] and 'middle powermanship'. In a 2007 address to the Council on Foreign Relations in New York, Harper stressed that success in the current global context requires not unilateralism, but multilateral co-operation 'among capable, committed, like-minded nations', as well as 'middle powers who can step up to the plate to do their part'. Indeed, Harper concluded that with the positive changes made by his government (for example, rebuilding the fighting capability of the Canadian Forces), Canada is now in a position, in co-operation 'with other middle powers', to make 'a real contribution to protecting and projecting our collective interests, while serving as a model of a prosperous, democratic and compassionate society—independent yet open to the world'.

Logically speaking, opponents of Canada's current involvement in Afghanistan have at least two possible strategies for contesting the efforts to link that involvement to Pearsonian internationalism. The first is to reaffirm Pearson's legacy as being an inherently progressive one, marked by his innovations in peacekeeping, his independent voice, and his support for Third World development, and, as such, one that is inherently at odds with the military intervention in which Canada is participating. A good example of this approach can be found in the writing of journalist Linda McQuaig. In a piece published in the *Toronto Star*, 'Canadian "Peacekeeping" Troops in Afghanistan: Keep Pearson Out of It', McQuaig (2008) expressed outrage at the efforts of former Liberal Foreign Minister John Manley, in a report commissioned by the Harper Conservative government, to invoke the name of Lester Pearson in support of the Afghan mission. In defence of her position, she quoted Francis Boyle, a professor of international law, who noted that the 'offensive use of military force (in Afghanistan) bears no similarity at all to Pearson's peacekeeping force in the Sinai, which was genuine and legitimate peacekeeping', and concluded, therefore, that linking Pearson and the Afghan mission amounts to a 'real desecration of [Pearson's] memory and his monumental achievement for world peace'.

The problem with this response, of course, is that it can be countered by simply reiterating (1) that no one is saying (or should be) that what Canadian troops are doing is peacekeeping (because the conditions for peacekeeping do not exist) and (2) that Pearson was about more than peacekeeping, so to be involved in this kind of security-building exercise is not a betrayal of the Pearsonian internationalist tradition, but very much consistent with it.

Before we concede, however, that the proponents of intervention have won the argument, it is worth considering a second strategy—the critical re-examination of the Pearsonian internationalist tradition.

The second strategy—in essence, a delegitimization strategy involving a critique of ideology—starts from the following understanding of what has been outlined above. To recap, those advocating a continued war-fighting presence in Afghanistan argue that the Pearsonian internationalist tradition is in keeping with the kind of mission Canada is pursuing, and that, therefore, the Afghan mission is worthy of support. The counter, outlined above, argues that the Pearsonian internationalist tradition is not in keeping with the mission in Afghanistan, and that, therefore, the Afghan mission is illegitimate. What is noteworthy is what these two positions have in common: the unspoken—and arguably unexamined assumption—that the Pearsonian internationalist tradition is itself worthy and legitimate, and provides a politico-normative standard against which Canada's foreign policy initiatives can and should be judged. This assumption is long overdue for critical interrogation.

It should be noted at this point that a detailed historical review of the entire record of Pearson's career—from External Affairs apparatchik, to Minister of External Affairs, to Prime Minister and after—is beyond the scope of this chapter.[8] I will simply choose some examples from that record, corresponding to the following three themes that are central to the animating myth of Pearsonian internationalism: security, independent voice, and development.

Security

The story of Pearson's achievements in helping to create the first United Nations peacekeeping force in response to the Suez crisis of 1956 is well known and need not be repeated (see Keating, 2002). Even here, however, one can begin to rethink the 'mythical' casting of this event. The first thing to keep in mind is that Pearson was a product of and active participant in the Cold War. As such, he accepted the basic tenets of what has been termed 'Cold War liberalism': (1) the Cold War was started by an expansionist Communist bloc bent on world domination; (2) the Western response was the response of free people in defence of freedom everywhere; and (3) the West had made no significant errors[9]—no significant errors, that is, until Suez, where the Western alliance allowed its unity to be fractured, with France and Britain on one side and the US and Canada on the other. For Pearson, one of the most serious aspects of the crisis was that the West no longer presented a united front to the real enemy (global communism). Thus, the motivation for the peacekeeping innovation had much to do with restoring unity to NATO—an institution Pearson had been instrumental in creating—so that the 'real' war could be continued in an efficacious manner.[10]

The fact that Pearson shared the hard line anti-Communist views of his counterparts in Washington clarifies other parts of the record. It explains, for example, his willingness to accept US nuclear weapons into Canada, notwithstanding the fact that his decision violated Liberal Party policy. His decision earned a strong public rebuke in the pages of *Cité libre* from Pierre Trudeau, who in a short time would enter federal politics, join Pearson's cabinet, and soon enough succeed Pearson as Liberal Party leader and Prime Minister. Trudeau found absurd the idea that Canada, an independent country, was 'obliged' to accept these weapons because of alliance obligations:

> No importance was attached to the fact that such a policy had been repudiated by the party congress and banished from its program; nor to the fact that the chief had acted without consulting the national council of the Liberal Federation or its executive committee; nor to the fact that the leader had forgotten to discuss it with the parliamentary caucus or even with his principal advisers. The 'Pope' had spoken. It was up to the faithful to believe.
>
> Fate had it that the final thrust came from the Pentagon and obliged Mr. Pearson to betray his party's platform as well as the ideal with which he had always identified himself. Power presented itself to Mr. Pearson; he had nothing to lose except honour. He lost it. And his whole party lost it with him.[11] (Trudeau, 1963: 7)

Finally, and perhaps most importantly, there is the (in)famous hotel-room meeting of Pearson with President Lyndon Johnson on 28 May 1964. Pearson claimed it had been nothing more than a social talk. His account was, regrettably, not entirely accurate. Fortunately, there was an American aide—most probably, McGeorge Bundy—in the room who took notes. These notes were later leaked by Daniel Ellsberg in *The Pentagon Papers*, and indicate the following: (1) the meeting was not social but about Vietnam; (2) Johnson informed Pearson he was planning to escalate the bombing of North Vietnam; (3) Pearson indicated his support for the US intervention (as part of the wider global struggle against communism),[12] with the proviso, as befits a Nobel Prize winner, that he hoped the Americans would make every effort to limit themselves to non-nuclear 'iron' bombs. Nuclear strikes, argued Pearson, would be difficult to sell to an increasingly skeptical public. One can almost hear Mackenzie King intoning in the background: 'Nuclear bombing of North Vietnam if necessary, but not necessarily *nuclear* bombing'.[13]

Independent Voice

Two short vignettes should suffice to make the point here.

In 1954 Canada, having been nominated by the US, joined Poland (nominated by the USSR) and India on the International Control Commission (ICC), established by the Geneva Conference on Vietnam. Poland's job was, of course, to defend Hanoi and its Soviet masters. Canada was there to defend Saigon and the US. Canadian delegation members did this by lying and spying. With regard to the first, members confirmed that though they knew it to be untrue, they reported regularly that all problems were the result of intransigence on the part of the North. With regard to the second, Canadian officers passed on first-hand observations on North Vietnam to the Americans. Once again, Pearson and Paul Martin Sr denied this. However, retired Brigadier Donald Ketcheson confirmed that during his service on the ICC (1958–9) he regularly furnished the CIA with information about Communist troop movements, and that External Affairs knew but 'looked the other way' (Taylor, 1974: 18).

The second vignette relates to Pearson's speech at Temple University on 2 April 1965. For proponents of the Pearsonian legacy as a progressive tradition standing in opposition to business as usual, this speech, second only to peacekeeping, is key. It stands, it is argued, as a clear and unambiguous example of the independent voice Canada has been and could yet be again on the world stage. There is, however, a problem. Despite its reputation, the speech is nowhere near the kind of critical, independent intervention that is so often claimed.

Pearson gave the speech at Temple University on the occasion of accepting a peace award. What is significant—yet regularly overlooked—is that 95 per cent of the speech is a reiteration and reaffirmation of the Cold War tenets and precepts that underlay US intervention in Vietnam. Indeed, given Canada's indirect yet substantial participation in the war (by means of selling war materiel to the Pentagon), and given the fact that Pearson shared the Cold War *Weltanschauung* held by Washington, it would have been curious had he provided any kind of principled critique. He did not. The speech is, first and foremost, a ringing endorsement of the goals and general strategy of *pax Americana*: the 'motives' of the United States 'were honourable', Pearson stressed, 'neither mean nor imperialistic. Its sacrifices have been great and they were not made to advance any selfish American interest.' He continues: 'No nation—and particularly no newly-independent nation—could ever feel secure if capitulation in Vietnam led to the sanctification of aggression through subversion and spurious "wars of national liberation". . . . Aggressive action by North Vietnam to bring about a Communist "liberation" (which means Communist rule) of the South must end. Only then can there be negotiation.' His conclusion is very much in the same vein: 'I know that the policy and the effort of the Government of the USA is directed to this end [of peace, hope, and progress]. Such an effort deserves and should receive the support of all peace-loving people' (Pearson, 1975: 108, 1).

This is not to say, however, that Pearson provided no critique of any kind—just that the 5 per cent of the speech dedicated to critiquing it was 'pragmatic', not 'principled'.[14] What distinguishes the latter is that it is rooted in some kind of fundamental principle of right and wrong. A speech that had detailed how the US intervention violated basic principles of human rights, equality, and sovereignty would have been such a critique. And though such speeches have been given, Pearson's was not one of them.

A pragmatic critique, on the other hand, limits itself to questions of efficacy and cost-benefit analysis.[15] By definition, having accepted the essence of the anti-Communist world view behind the US intervention, all that was left to Pearson was a pragmatic critique. Accordingly, his deviation from the Johnson administration's position was at the level of tactics only. Specifically, Pearson suggested that the US stop bombing the North for two weeks to give the Vietnamese leadership a chance to rethink their position and their options. In short, Pearson was suggesting that a stick supplemented occasionally by a carrot is more efficacious than a stick alone.[16]

That Lyndon Johnson, who had his own reasons for overreacting, did in fact overreact—the President summoned Pearson to Camp David the following day, where he reportedly lifted the much smaller Canadian by his lapels and shouted, 'You pissed on my rug!'—in no way constitutes proof of the supposedly 'radical' nature of Pearson's critique. Pearson's speech has come to be seen as an example of independence of mind and spirit, yet this says much more about the power of myth than it does about an essentially conventional and *pax Americana*-derived reaffirmation of reigning orthodoxy.

Development

Along with peacekeeping and the image of an independent voice, a concern for development is the third aspect of the Pearsonian internationalist tradition. It can be argued that Pearson was involved in development issues throughout most of his career, from the Colombo Plan of 1950, which brought together donor nations such as the United States, Great Britain, and Canada and nations of Southeast and South Asia for the purpose of economic and social development. Here, however, I wish to look briefly at his engagement with these issues at the end of his political career.

In 1968, Robert McNamara, who as president of the Ford Motor Company had overseen the production of countless automobiles and then as US Secretary of Defense had overseen the killing of countless Southeast Asians, decided, in his current capacity as president of the World Bank, to push the development debate forward. Specifically, McNamara formed a seven-person commission to study and make recommendations about international development. Significantly, only two of the seven commission members were from the global South. Even more significantly, when it came to appointing an eighth member who would serve as chair, McNamara chose someone whose Cold War credentials and public support for even the most maligned dimensions of US foreign policy (e.g., US intervention in Southeast Asia) beyond question: the recently retired Lester B. Pearson.

In 1969 the eight commissioners produced a report—*Partners in Development*—authored largely by Pearson (1969). In it, Pearson made his well-known recommendation that developed nations should aim to direct 1 per cent of GDP into development assistance.[17] This target—a target met by some Scandinavian countries though never by Canada (despite years of Liberal governments paying lip service to it)—stands as the most widely cited evidence for the third prong of the progressive interpretation of the Pearson legacy.[18]

Once again, however, a close reading of the report provides a useful corrective to the Pearsonian myth. To begin, in the same way as Pearson viewed security issues through a Cold War liberal framework, he viewed economic issues through a capitalist, market-oriented lens (Cox, 1972). As he made clear in his report, the goal of development policy should be to promote a 'global free-market economy'—the necessary precondition for development in the South. Furthermore, for Pearson it was clear that the main agents for positive change were multinational corporations (MNCs). Accordingly, the surest path to development was for MNCs in the global North to enjoy the maximum freedom possible to exert their influence.

This made the problem of development clear. Largely through barriers and efforts at regulation by states in the global South, northern MNCs found themselves hamstrung. Development aid provided by the North, then, should come with conditions, the most important of which would be to require southern states to liberalize their economies, and to use northern aid to build infrastructure (training, roads, electric power) upon which northern MNCs depend.

This raised a second issue, that of compliance. Pearson argued that northern states dealing one-on-one with southern states created a recipe for a loss of potential influence. Rather, he argued, northern states should deal collectively with their southern 'partners'. To that end, he proposed that a northern-controlled international organization should be mandated to speak to the South on behalf of the North as a whole; to oversee the transfer of any capital from North to South; to enumerate conditions attached to those transfers; and to monitor compliance on behalf of southern states.

As it was, Pearson's vision was ahead of its time. However, 13 years later, when Mexico threatened to default on its debt held by northern banks, Pearson's vision was finally realized. The International Monetary Fund (IMF) was no longer needed to regulate currency fluctuations, as it had been during the time of the gold standard—it was now free to assume the new role Pearson had envisaged. Thus, from 1982 on, the IMF oversaw the restructuring of Third World debt, providing new loans with attendant conditions reflecting the Washington Consensus.[19]

☺ Austerity programs?
☺ They're a Canadian idea!

(And an insufficiently celebrated part of the Pearsonian internationalist tradition as well.)[20]

Conclusion: 'Unglücklich das Land, daß Helden nötig hat'

['**Unhappy is the land that needs heroes**'] –Bertolt Brecht, *Leben des Galilei*, Scene XII

By way of conclusion, let me return to the question of peacekeeping and its relevance for the Canadian mission in Afghanistan. Even if one accepts that peacekeeping is not an option there—that, in the words of John Manley, 'there is no peace to keep'—the Pearsonian tradition on peacekeeping still has something to teach us. On 6 November 1956, as peacekeeping was being devised and tried for the first time, UN Secretary-General Dag Hammarskjöld presented a report that laid down the general principles for successful peacekeeping (Reford, 1992: 69). These principles included:

1. A peacekeeping force would not be a fighting force and would not seek to impose its will.
2. A peacekeeping force would be neutral.
3. The sovereign rights of the nation on whose soil it was stationed would be respected.
4. A nation providing troops would be responsible for paying them and for providing their equipment. Other costs would be borne by the UN.

Finally, and perhaps most importantly, great powers would not be included in the force. The reason for this prohibition—a prohibition that had the effect of making peacekeeping a mission for middle powers (i.e., the only non-great powers with enough resources to undertake such a mission)—was that great powers had colonial legacies that would accompany them into any peacekeeping mission and quite probably undermine it.

Canada is no great power. However, the general principle applies. It is vital for there to be clear recognition that in Afghanistan, Canadian troops have functioned as an invading and occupying force. As this is a fact that has generally been obscured, it is worth addressing the issue in some detail. I shall do so first by reviewing three justifications for the presence of Canadian troops in Afghanistan.

The first way in which the presence of Canadian troops in Afghanistan has been justified has been with reference to UN resolutions. In terms of hegemony construction, this is a particularly potent form of justification as the United Nations—the dominant sponsor of the peacekeeping operations in which Canada has participated—is well regarded by many Canadians. There is a problem, however. It is true that the Security Council passed several resolutions in regard to global terrorism after the 9/11 attacks: Resolutions 1368 and 1373 are most notable. As law professor Marjorie Cohn has observed, these resolutions 'ordered the freezing of assets, the criminalizing of terrorist activity, the prevention of the commission of and support for terrorist attacks, and the taking of necessary steps to prevent the commission of terrorist activist, including the sharing of information.' However, none called or offered justification for an armed intervention (Cohn,

2008). Francis Boyle, professor of international law at the University of Illinois College of Law, agrees, noting that the Security Council resolutions regularly cited by people such as John Manley in no way authorized military action. Rather, they called for the perpetrators of 9/11 to be brought to justice. In other words, the UN resolutions direct us not to military intervention, but to extradition and trial of those responsible for criminal activities within the evolving architecture of international criminal law and its institutions, such as the International Criminal Court (see McQuaig, 2008).[21]

The second way the Canadian presence is rationalized is by arguing that Canada is there as the invited 'guest' of the Afghan government. There is a kernel of truth to this claim: Canada has, in fact, been invited by the current Afghan government to help bring stability and order to the country, by means of troops if necessary. The problem with this argument is that the government that has invited us to stay was put into power as part of the original military intervention that toppled the Taliban government.[22] By this argument, the Soviet invasion of Afghanistan in 1979—also at the invitation of a puppet regime the USSR had earlier put into power—would have to be seen as legitimate.[23]

A third line of argument justifies the intervention in terms of the fact that very few states—by some counts, only three—recognized the Taliban government at the time NATO troops toppled it. The problem here is that international law, in particular, the Montevideo Convention on Rights and Duties of States (1933), states that 'The political existence of a state'—and by extension, rights attached to statehood such as equality, sovereignty, and non-interference—'is independent of recognition by the other states' (see, e.g., Levi, 1991: ch. 6). Put simply, a low quotient of recognition by other states cannot stand as justification for military intervention.[24]

All of this, arguably, is secondary: the real issue is how Canadian troops are regarded by ordinary Afghans. Opinion data are notoriously hard to obtain in the case of a society like that of Afghanistan. There is growing evidence, however, that Canadian soldiers are not regarded as an unqualified force for good. Understandably, much is made of the number of Canadian casualties suffered in Afghanistan; by mid-April 2009, 117 Canadian soldiers had died on the Afghanistan mission. At the same time, it is important to consider the number of Afghans—civilians as well as combatants—that Canadians have killed. As the *Los Angeles Times* reported in July 2007, 'after more than five years of increasingly intense warfare, the conflict in Afghanistan reached a grim milestone in the first half of this year: US troops and their NATO allies killed more civilians than insurgents did, according to several independent tallies' (cited in Fowler, 2008). Canadian troops have been as implicated in 'collateral damage' as any NATO participant. And the perceptions of Canadian troops by ordinary Afghans have not been unaffected.

To repeat, then, Canadian troops have functioned as and are increasingly perceived as an invading and occupying force. And that legacy will have important implications for what Canada can do in the future. Assuming some kind of politico-social stability is achieved—and this remains a big assumption—it will be necessary to think about reconstruction and economic development. And here it is noteworthy that since the release of the Manley Report there has been a growing emphasis on the need for Canada to remain in Afghanistan for the long term, quite apart from the Prime Minister's assurances of a troop pullout in 2011, to contribute to the rebuilding of the country. However, just as great powers with a colonial legacy can have no part in peacekeeping, so middle powers with a legacy of intervention and occupation can have no part in development. Notwithstanding elite desires to generate public support for a continuation of the mission by stressing the popular theme of development, the reality is this: whatever part Canada might have played in rebuilding Afghanistan in the post-conflict setting was almost certainly sacrificed when the decision was made to be an active player in the conflict itself.

Finally, we return to the broader issue with which we began: the role of animating myths in eliciting popular consent for elite foreign policy agendas. *Pace* left-of-centre admirers of Pearson, it seems clear, in light of the historical record, that if the political right has the easier task when it comes to harnessing the Pearsonian legacy to its agenda, this is the case for a very simple reason: Pearson was, quite simply, one of their own.

This is not the end of the story, however. Opinion surveys (Gee, 2008) indicate that the Canadian public continues to identify strongly with the ideals of progressive internationalism—ideals such as peacekeeping, independent voice, and development. Accordingly, we should consider the following: does progressive internationalism enjoy public support because it is seen to be Pearsonian? Or, what seems much more likely, is Pearson held in as high regard as he is because he is (mistakenly) thought to have been a progressive internationalist? If the second is true, the implication is clear. Though we need progressive internationalism, we may well not need the Pearson myth to sustain it. In short, we might be capable of living quite happily—and progressively—'as a land without a hero'. And as such, demystifying and rejecting the Pearsonian legacy may be a more productive use of energies than attempts to harness to progressive causes what is, in reality, a highly contradictory tradition at best.

Notes

1. This chapter was originally prepared for the Canadian Political Science Association annual meeting, Vancouver, June 2008. I acknowledge the support of the SSHRC. In terms of personal links to the Pearson family, I should disclose that while I never met the former Prime Minister, I did come to know his grandson, Michael, when we were studying together at the Norman Paterson School of International Affairs. I also worked for his son, Geoffrey, for about eight months in the 1980s when Geoffrey was appointed head of the Canadian Institute for International Peace and Security. As far as I am aware, I had good relations with both—indeed, despite our differences in political orientation, Geoffrey Pearson (who died in March 2008) proved to be one of the more stimulating bosses I ever had. As such, my critique is not motivated by any personal animosity towards the Pearson family.

2. As I recall, my suggestion that J.S. Woodsworth should stand as a hero for his leading role in the Winnipeg General Strike met with a less than enthusiastic response. Canada's

hegemonic discourse (propagated through civil society institutions such as schools) can tolerate moderately left social democratic figures—witness the fact that Tommy Douglas won the CBC's 'Greatest Canadian' contest—but only if they have made a 'positive' contribution, like universal health care. Participation in excessively 'negative' activities—civil disobedience, extra-parliamentary agitation—is sufficient grounds for disqualification. We can rest easier knowing the latter have all but disappeared from the twenty-first-century social democratic repertoire!

3. Pearson placed sixth within the top 10, out-polled by Tommy Douglas, Terry Fox, Pierre Trudeau, Frederick Banting, and David Suzuki. It is true, of course, that the 'Greatest Canadian' contest is a less than scientific measure of popularity. I would argue, however, that it does give a good sense of where certain public personalities stand in the imagination of Canadians and, more importantly, serves as an example of the very kind of myth-making by a government-elite institution upon which elite manipulation of the public depends.

4. I don't mean to leave the impression that this kind of myth perpetuation is particular to Canada alone. A parallel book series for children entitled 'Uncle Lenin' was a standard feature of Soviet society and those of its satellites as well.

5. John Manley has made this point as well. See the Manley Report (2008), as well as his comments at the press conference at the release of the report. For the latter, see Ivison (2008).

6. It is somewhat surprising since the Harper government has made extraordinary efforts to demarcate itself from previous Liberal governments, going so far as to adopt the phrase 'Canada's New Government' as its moniker. This is clearly at odds with a stance that openly embraces core values—specifically, the internationalism—of a former Liberal Prime Minister.

7. For a historical overview of the Canadian foreign policy record and the place of multilateralism, see Keating (2002).

8. There are an increasing number of relevant histories in the scholarly literature, especially as documents are declassified. On Pearson and the Vietnam period, for example, see the comprehensive piece by Preston (2003).

9. I am indebted to my then graduate supervisor, Professor John Sigler, for pushing me to recognize something my then liberal-internationalist ideological commitments had not allowed me to see. In fact, this recognition is to be found in the work of careful mainstream commentators. See, for example, Preston (2003: 110): 'The anti-communist lenses through which policy-makers in Ottawa and Washington viewed the conflict in Vietnam were very similar.'

10. In the interest of fairness, it should be noted that some mainstream/conservative commentators have viewed peacekeeping in less altruistic and more self-interested terms as well. Granatstein, for example, has accounted for peacekeeping's popularity among policy-makers in terms of its relatively low cost, its contribution to Western solidarity, and its 'fit' with our widespread anti-Americanism. See, for example, Granatstein (1992, 1993, 2007). Notwithstanding some superficial similarities between the arguments of those on the right and those on the left (and foreign policy is not the only domain of apparent convergence—one can think back to the critiques of the left and right directed to the welfare state), the overall frameworks that give the individual arguments their meaning are fundamentally opposed. A left position, which argues that the altruistic foreign policy discourse of Canada's elites is a central element in the construction of a hegemony that preserves the positions of power

and influence of the members of Canada's dominant class, is one not likely to be endorsed by a conservative like Granatstein, for example. For an argument from the left that advocates just this kind of position, see Neufeld (2004).

11. Ironically, Trudeau would later use the same specious alliance obligation argument to defend his agreement to allow the US to test its air-launched cruise missile in Alberta. On Pearson and the Bomarc missiles, and on Trudeau and the cruise, see Keating (2002).

12. And Canada certainly did support the effort by providing billions of dollars, over the course of the war, in military goods and services. This was facilitated by the original free trade agreement—in this case relating to military materiel—the Defence Production Sharing Agreement (DPSA), signed in 1959. In the 1980s, well-known Canadian firms would again make significant profits selling goods to Indonesia, then engaged in a genocide against the Timorese. Arguably, making money off the killing of Southeast Asians is also part of our noble internationalist tradition.

13. On this, see Taylor (1974), as well as excerpts from Daniel Ellsberg, *The Pentagon Papers*, in Granatstein (1993: 255). I wait with bated breath for HISTORICA to produce a 'Canada Heritage Minute' on this meeting.

14. The distinction is Chomsky's (1975). See note 16.

15. To hold that 'torture is wrong because it is wrong to intentionally cause pain to another human' is a principled critique. To say that 'torture is wrong because if we get caught we could go to jail' or, better yet, that 'that kind of torture is wrong because you're not doing it right; here, let me show you a better way that produces greater pain with less effort' is a pragmatic critique.

16. This is the dominant form of public critique of Canada's involvement in Afghanistan. Indeed, Michael Byers, a leading liberal foreign policy critic and professor of international law at the University of British Columbia, in an interview with Michael Valpy, argued that 'you don't need to have any particular ideological or moral perspective to realize that any kind of decision like this [Afghanistan] should be analyzed in cost-benefit terms' (Valpy, 2007). What such a position does, of course, is exclude principled critique and limit discourse to pragmatic assessments alone. Pragmatic critiques, by definition, shy away from questions like 'is it morally justifiable to invade another country?' and limit themselves to arguing that 'if the costs outweigh the benefits, we shouldn't proceed.' As Chomsky notes, what is distinctive about that kind of reasoning is that it is the kind that could have been used—and apparently was—by the leaders of the *Wehrmacht* when their *Führer* ordered them to invade Eastern Europe. 'Of course, we stay away from value judgements—where does it get us to ask, "Do we have the right to invade Russia and kill 20 million people"—rather, we should focus on questions like "Is it doable? And will the benefits justify the expenditure?", and above all, "Can we get away with it?"' Despite Byers's assertions, given what it excludes from discussion, pragmatic critique is highly ideological and morally dubious.

Of course, it can be countered that as unsatisfactory as pragmatic critique might be, it is still preferable to a view that refuses to allow for the possibility that Canada is doing anything wrong. As an example of the latter, see Preston (2003). Though Preston's review of the historical record and documents is excellent, his analysis and conclusions are puzzling, to say the least. A good example is Preston's response to the 'complicity thesis' on Vietnam, advanced by writers such as Taylor, that Canada bears some responsibility for the suffering of the people of Indochina because it was complicitous in the US war effort. The *Oxford*

English Dictionary defines 'complicity' as 'Involved knowingly or with passive compliance'. Certainly Pearson's statements in support of US policy and the freedom given to Canadian business to supply the American war machine would seem to qualify as complicitous, and this notwithstanding Preston's arguments that Pearson tried to 'moderate' US behaviour. Preston (2003: 110) rejects the notion of complicity, however. Still, one hopes that 'pragmatic critique' and 'non-critique' are not our only choices.

17. Seventy per cent of the 1 per cent, or 0.7 per cent of GDP, overall was to come from government sources, with the remainder coming from private donors. On this and the significance of the report overall, see Cox (1972).

18. In this sense, it is rather unfair of Rick Salutin (2006) to single out Paul Martin Jr for promising Bono, the rock musician and social activist, publicly and privately, to boost foreign aid, and then failing to come through on his commitment. Arguably, Martin was just acting in conformity with a long-standing Liberal tradition of failing to come through on progressive promises. Salutin at least softens his critique by noting that while Martin didn't do what he promised, Martin insists he did and—crucially—'seems to believe it'. In other words, notes Salutin, Martin 'can apparently lie and not know he's lying.' Concludes Salutin: 'It's a kind of honesty.' As in the case of critique, however, one hopes we are not limited in political life to only this kind of 'honesty'.

19. The policies reflecting the Washington Consensus are varied, but the general working principle is that the problems in economies result from the fact that the poor have too much money and the rich don't have enough! Policies are thus designed to work to transfer wealth/income from the have-nots to the haves. Enhancing the freedom and influence of MNCs is, of course, central.

20. Again, a Heritage Minute is clearly warranted—where are the HISTORICA people when you need them?

21. There is also evidence that the Taliban government was open to moving down this road after 9/11. Curiously, however, all efforts soon became focused on a military intervention and diplomatic solutions were abandoned.

22. And it was only after Afghanistan was invaded and the Taliban government toppled that UN authorization for the current government and the NATO intervention was achieved.

23. Presumably, this line of thinking would also take us to a positive judgement about the legitimacy of Nazi Germany's 'humanitarian intervention', at the behest of the Vichy government, into France.

24. Any more than a professor's unpopularity in his or her department can stand as a justification for a violation of that individual's human rights.

Part IV
Other Diplomacies

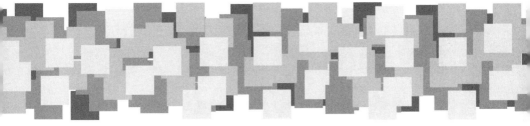

Chapter Eleven

Youth Ambassadors Abroad?
Canadian Foreign Policy and Public Diplomacy in the Developing World

Rebecca Tiessen

Introduction

Young Canadians are going abroad in growing numbers each year[1] and many of Canada's youth[2] are travelling to less developed countries to gain exposure to global issues. The opportunity to travel to another country and to learn about another culture is considered extremely valuable by the youth participants; but how might it also benefit Canada? This is an increasingly important question as Canadians witness low international development assistance spending, declining international activities, and threats of funding cuts to the youth abroad programs of the Canadian International Development Agency (CIDA).[3] In this chapter I examine how youth abroad programs contribute to Canada's public diplomacy and shape a particular image of Canada abroad. The organizations that administer government-funded volunteer or internship abroad programs, and the youth who participate in these programs, play a key role in the projection of Canadian values overseas. References to the significance of sending youth abroad as part of Canada's public diplomacy and global citizenship mandate can be found in Canada's international policy statements, speeches, and volunteer/intern program descriptions. I examine these documents, as well as information gained during interviews with young Canadians, to uncover the perceived impact of youth abroad programs. I begin this chapter by defining and broadening our understanding of public diplomacy in the context of Canadian foreign policy. I conclude by highlighting some concerns for the future of youth abroad and public diplomacy in a time of minimal international development assistance activities on the part of the Canadian government.

Canadian Foreign Policy and Public Diplomacy

The contributions of Canadian youth to public diplomacy, and to the projection of Canadian values abroad, are important to the study of Canadian foreign policy. Research on Canadian foreign policy often focuses on the official business of Canadian government diplomats. However, the state is not always the necessary, or only, starting point of foreign policy analysis (Steinstra et al., 2003). Canadian citizens have the potential to shape foreign policy and international perceptions of Canada because everything Canada and Canadians do abroad (and at home) will reflect on the country and shape perceptions of it. The concept of public diplomacy—the activities and actions of a large number of people working on international issues at home and abroad—expands our understanding of Canadian foreign policy beyond the official business of the state carried out by foreign service personnel.

Canadian foreign policy is well known for its focus on three pillars: the promotion of prosperity, the protection of security within a stable global framework, and the projection of Canadian values and culture. This emphasis on values emerged in the 1995 White Paper, *Canada in the World*. However, Michaud (2007) provides examples of the centrality of Canadian values in Canadian foreign policy dating back to 1947 in the Gray Lecture delivered by Louis St Laurent, the first Canadian Secretary of State for External Affairs. More recent references to Canadian values can be found in the efforts of Foreign Affairs Minister Lloyd Axworthy to end the use of child soldiers and the promotion of human security in the 1990s. These examples reflect Canada's values-oriented foreign policies through diplomacy.

Canada's public diplomacy mandate involves a specific discourse, a range of activities and a broad set of actors. It has been characterized as the 'soft power' (Bátora, 2005; Nye, 2004) or the 'creative statecraft' (Cooper, 1998: 36) Canada demonstrates through diplomatic missions, the liaison work of ambassadors, and in partnership with civil society actors and non-governmental organizations (NGOs) (ibid.). Bátora (2005) defines public diplomacy as that which 'comprises all activities by state and non-state actors that contribute to the maintenance and promotion of a country's soft power'. Thus, public diplomacy and soft power are central to Canada's international negotiation strategies and play a central role in trade relations and domestic security. According to Canada's 2005 *International Policy Statement*, public diplomacy:

> is about projecting a coherent and influential voice to all those who have influence within a society—not just within its government. Canada's credibility and influence abroad will be built not only on Government action but by Canadians themselves—artists, teachers, students, travelers, researchers, experts and young people—interacting with people abroad. Public diplomacy includes . . . youth travel, foreign students in Canada, Canadian studies abroad and visits of opinion leaders. All this cultivates long-term relationships, dialogue and understanding abroad, underpins our advocacy and increases

our influence. (DFAIT, 2005: Diplomacy chapter, 'Strengthening Canada's Overseas Networks', para. 21)

For small and medium-sized states, public diplomacy represents an opportunity to gain influence and to shape the international agenda in ways that go beyond their limited hard power or resources (Bátora, 2005). Public diplomacy is now widely understood as that which a nation does to explain itself to the world (ibid.; Schneider, 2004) and to make it look attractive to other nations. 'Attractive causes', Nye (2004) argues, can include a country's culture, political ideals, and policies, and can be more effective than coercion. The discourse central to public diplomacy reinforces nation's soft power and focuses on key concepts such as good governance, global citizenship, and human security (ibid.). Countries lacking hard power turn to the image or brand they project abroad as a way to identify themselves and to manoeuvre internationally (Potter, 2002).

The image of Canada created for foreign policy purposes is, therefore, a partially fabricated one. Bátora (2005) makes this case when he provides the example of the branding of Canada through a Communications Bureau of the Department of Foreign Affairs and International Trade. The branding involved the creation of a slogan for Canada abroad—'Canada-Cool-Connected'—focusing on themes of captivating, civil, competitive, creative, caring, and competitive. The image generation ran into some challenges abroad, however, and had to be abandoned, as Bátora notes, when China associated the term 'cool' with cold and icy rather than trendy and easy-going. Nonetheless, branding remains an important exercise for Canada and serves many purposes, including the reinforcement of Canadian perceptions of ourselves. Canadians continue to see themselves as worldly and generous while retaining nostalgic notions of international development assistance and peacekeeping (Copeland, 2003, cited in Bátora, 2005).

Diplomats play an important role in the generation of a particular image of Canada. For example, Canadian diplomats have, for years, tried to change widespread international perceptions of Canada as a resource economy. Robert Wolfe describes the tasks of ambassadors as 'representing, protecting, reporting, negotiating, and promoting friendly relations'. Canadian ambassadors 'also engage in public diplomacy, whether promoting Canada (culture or trade) or attempting to influence local opinion, for example, on human rights' (Wolfe, 1998: 1). The exercise of asking what diplomats and ambassadors abroad do is central to examining the image of Canada abroad and 'how the Canadian government pursues the interest of its citizens abroad' (ibid., 4). Nonetheless, diplomacy takes place on many levels through numerous channels. Beyond the work of official diplomats, Canada engages in public diplomacy, which requires the participation of a broader constituency consisting of civil society, NGOs, media, academics, cultural groups, religious leaders, etc. The work of civil society organizations (CSOs) and NGOs to expand Canada's public diplomacy is especially relevant to this analysis since the proliferation of NGOs has played a critical role in shaping Canadian foreign policy since the mid-1990s. Van Rooy (1998: 151) highlights the instrumentalist character of government working with civil society organizations in 'helping Canada undertake the broadening range of tasks now considered part of the diplomatic workload'. The shift in attention to new policy issues (from the hard-power ones like security and territorial sovereignty to soft-power issues such as development and governance) means that more actors now possess and/or have access to information pertinent to official diplomats. Civil society organizations and NGOs therefore provide essential diplomatic services and clout for Canada, especially in a time of 'Canada's shrinking aid budget' (ibid., 152). Nossal (2007: 167) refers to this phenomenon as the 'domestication' of Canadian foreign policy characterized, in part, by 'the practice of wider consultation, and of giving functional groups representation on Canadian delegations to international conferences or negotiations'. Several organizations, such as Project Ploughshares, the Canadian Council for International Co-operation, and Oxfam, offer public education campaigns to Canadians about how poverty around the world is connected to an international economic system that benefits the rich at the expense of the poor. These organizations also reinforce the idea that Canadians have ethical obligations to assist those beyond Canada's borders (Pratt, 2007), thereby promoting Canada's global citizenship mandate.

Public Diplomacy and Youth Abroad Programs

A key mandate for many NGOs interested in human rights and international equity is to offer programs for youth to volunteer abroad in developing countries where development assistance is being delivered. CIDA plays a central role in the administration of these programs and co-ordinates with NGOs in the delivery of youth abroad initiatives. As such, youth abroad programs become a salient feature of Canada's public diplomacy. However, these programs, as a form of public diplomacy strategy, have not been well articulated. Americans have been more overt, and perhaps optimistic, in their understanding of the potential impact of youth abroad, noting that: '[American] [v]olunteers have done tremendous things for our image abroad. The greatest thing the Peace Corps could do for this country is to fight totalitarian and authoritarian governments and work for democracy and grass-roots change in the countries it serves' (Helliger, as quoted in Smith, 1986).

Youth, and civil society more broadly, have the potential to play an important role in image creation among Canadians and abroad. The good deeds (or perception of) carried out by young Canadian volunteers abroad are valued in Canada, and government officials have specifically encouraged youth to join overseas programs. Examples of youth becoming an explicit target group of the DFAIT-initiated public diplomacy program for Canada include foreign service officers giving lectures to young Canadians (Bátora, 2005: 15), the promotion of youth programs such as model United Nations, and a series of websites directed at young Canadians to engage them in image generation and the branding process. In addition, volunteer abroad programs play an important part in the promotion of Canadian values abroad. However small this part of Canadian foreign policy is in funding, the potential impacts for public diplomacy are great. David Kilgour, at that time the

Secretary of State for Latin America and Africa, in a 1999 speech to participants in the Canada World Youth[4] program, highlighted how youth are the future of leadership, and added that the youth participants in this program will play an important role in representing Canada abroad (Kilgour, 1999).

Canada has embarked on several different youth-oriented public diplomacy programs, including the Youth International Internship Program (YIIP) offered by the Department of Foreign Affairs starting in 1997. This program offered youth a first international work experience to further the objectives of Canadian foreign policy. The objectives of the YIIP were to provide underemployed or unemployed youth of Canada with career-related international work experience to prepare and position them for future employment and to enhance partnerships between the Department of Foreign Affairs and Canadian-based organizations active internationally and overseas institutions. The youth internships were expected to further the three main objectives of Canada's foreign policy: the promotion of prosperity and employment, the promotion of peace and global security, and the projection of Canadian values and culture abroad (UNEVOC-Canada, 2002). This example demonstrates how youth are directly involved in public diplomacy and therefore linked to specific Canadian foreign policy objectives. Potter (2002: 4) sees the role of cultural and international education programs as more loosely linked to Canadian foreign policy goals whereby cultural and international educational programs 'help develop a three-dimensional image of a country, leading to a more complete and balanced perception of the country's economic, political and social development.'

CIDA also offers a youth abroad program called the International Youth Internship Program (IYIP). The IYIP is a co-operative venture between CIDA and Canadian organizations. Participants assist with the delivery of international development assistance and contribute to Canada's development projects abroad. According to CIDA (2008), one of the core goals of IYIP is to contribute to objectives of poverty reduction and building a more secure, equitable, and prosperous world. International development assistance is an important Canadian value and an 'integral part of Canadian foreign policy that gives Canadians this warm fuzzy feeling that Canada is a caring country' (Michaud, 2007: 347). The role of aid, in combination with volunteers and youth interns working in less developed countries, helps foster a positive image of Canada abroad and at home.

Past Commitments to the Promotion of Youth Abroad and Global Citizenship

In previous years and under different governments, the importance of promoting global citizenship and youth abroad as part of Canada's foreign policy mandate was spelled out in documents such as *Canada in the World* (1995) under the Liberal Party leadership of Jean Chrétien and the *International Policy Statement* (2005) under the leadership of Paul Martin. The section in *Canada in the World* dealing with youth highlights youth as one of the partners (along with the private sector, universities and colleges, professional organizations, and federal, provincial, and municipal governments) in promoting Canada's development program abroad. The document stresses the importance of partnerships with developing countries and the role Canadian youth can play in building these partnerships, 'especially at the grassroots level' (DFAIT, 1995: Section VI). Specifically, the government sought to encourage youth participation in the developing world 'both to enable them to gain rich experience through international cooperation, and to assist those countries where the talent and energy of Canadian youth can make a difference' (ibid.).

The *International Policy Statement* of 2005 also articulated a role for youth. According to this statement, the Canadian government sends young Canadians abroad as part of its 'global citizenship' mandate. The notion of obligation to help is reinforced with the following statement: 'our responsibility to protect and preserve the values and interests of our own citizens requires us to be a responsible global citizen' (DFAIT, 2005). The document further says that 'The Government is committed to protecting and advancing the global citizenship of all Canadians, but it cannot be done without their strong involvement' (ibid.).

The 2005 *Policy Statement* notes that achieving global citizenship will happen, in part, as a result of the Canada Corps program. Canada Corps was introduced in February 2004 as an opportunity for Canadians of all ages to participate in global citizenship and institution-building around the world. One of the key features of Canada Corps is a focus on young people. According to the Minister for International Co-operation (then Aileen Carroll), this program will allow youth to 'gain valuable international experience' and 'become more engaged globally'. According to CIDA, Canada Corps was established 'as a new vehicle to strengthen Canada's contribution to human rights, democracy and good governance internationally. Canada Corps was designed to develop collaborative partnerships across government, NGOs, the private sector, and with Canadian citizens to bring greater engagement, expertise, coherence and recognition to Canadian governance interventions abroad' (CIDA, 2004a). The overall goal of the Canada Corps initiative is to develop a strategy to engage the Canadian public in the fight against poverty (DFAIT, 2005).

Canada Corps is seen as a vehicle whereby Canadians can also promote global citizenship in Canada. Upon their return from international placements, Canada Corps participants are encouraged to act as domestic ambassadors and use their experiences to stimulate interest in Canada's global citizenship (ibid.). Furthermore, the development co-operation program is promoted as an instrument for making 'this vision a living reality for Canadians as global citizens' as well as for harnessing 'our capacities and advancing Canadian values of global citizenship' (ibid.).

Under the Conservative government, in 2006 the Canada Corps University Partnership Program became the Students for Development, administered by the Association for Universities and Colleges of Canada (AUCC). The Students for Development program allows senior-level undergraduate students and graduate students and faculty members from Canadian universities to work with partners in the developing world to promote good governance. Students participate in three-month internships in a partner country and carry out a work plan designed to support their partner organization's efforts in improving governance. Through these internships, students deepen their own understanding of governance as an essential foundation for development and take part in the search for solutions. A total of 138 students are selected every year to participate in these internships (AUCC, 2008).

The Students for Development program is similar, in many respects, to other government-funded internships for young Canadians such as the DFAIT YIIP and the CIDA IYIP. Since 1997, about 4,500 young professionals have taken part in internship placements with more than 190 organizations and overseas partners (CIDA, 2007). The Netcorps program is another example of Canada's commitment to youth internships abroad. Netcorps began offering internships in 1997 for young Canadians aged 19–30 to provide technical or computer assistance to developing countries. To date, Netcorps has placed more than 2,000 young Canadians abroad, with funding from the Youth Employment Strategy through Human Resources and Skills Development Canada (Netcorps, 2007).

The Canadian government, especially through the Canadian International Development Agency, provides funding to numerous non-governmental organizations and volunteer sending agencies for a variety of internship or volunteering opportunities. Organizations include Canada World Youth (CWY), World University Service of Canada (WUSC), CUSO (formerly Canadian University Services Overseas), Canadian Crossroads International (CCI), and Voluntary Services Overseas (VSO), among other youth-sending volunteer organizations. Non-governmental and governmental agencies sending youth abroad on volunteer or internship programs see these programs as important channels for the promotion of global citizenship. Canadian NGOs such as Canada World Youth and WUSC have also adopted the discourse of 'global citizenship' in publications and reports. Examples include Canada World Youth's *Your Passport to Global Citizenship, Annual Report 2002–2003*, WUSC's report on its student refugee program, *Engaging Minds, Fostering Global Citizenship*, and Canadian Crossroads International's mission statement, which reads: 'CCI's mission is to build a constituency of global citizens committed to voluntarism, international development and social action in the new millennium. This is accomplished by developing partnerships with countries from the South, organizing volunteer cooperative placements and internships, and by educating the public on development issues' (CCI, 2008).

A focus on youth in the global citizenship discourse and programs (whether through non-governmental volunteer sending programs or government policies and programs) is central to Canada's international activities. Youth play an important role in fostering Canada's image of good global citizenship abroad. Young people who participate in volunteer or study abroad programs generally benefit from the experience through skills development and employment experience and consider it both rewarding and life-changing. The benefits of these programs to the youth themselves have been widely documented by government agencies, volunteer sending organizations, and the youth themselves through on-line and documented testimonials or 'success stories'. Canada, as a country, also benefits from youth abroad programs as a form of Canadian public diplomacy and a means to project Canadian values abroad.

Youth Who Travelled Abroad: An Analysis

To understand youth abroad programs as a form of public diplomacy we must consider the experiences of young people who have participated in these programs. Here, I examine some of the youth's perspectives on their public diplomacy roles abroad, using on-line texts and information collected through interviews with young Canadians.[5] The first data set involved reviewing 'success stories' of International Youth Internship Program participants (interns) as summarized on the DFAIT website (www.dfait-maeci.gc.ca/ypi-jpi/success-en.asp). Summaries from a total of 70 participants from 2002–4 were available on this site. In this sample group of 70, 46 of the interns were women and 24 were men. More than half of these youth participants travelled to less developed countries for their internships.

The success stories offer some useful preliminary data for this research. It is important to point out that DFAIT has a vested interest in promoting a positive image of the program and, therefore, some of the potential negative experiences may have been omitted. In fact, of the 70 stories summarized in this document, only one mentioned an illness and even this illness did not prevent the intern from completing his work (even though he had to do so from home after leaving the country where he became ill). Furthermore, the summaries are brief and do not provide the detailed, rich information that interviews would offer. It is unclear what questions were asked, and thus it is difficult to know to what extent these summaries are biased in favour of the sending agency. Nonetheless, our interest here is self-reflection on global citizenship and diplomacy. Therefore, identity-related questions were not affected by the absence of negative impact stories. A second source for this research involved a review of on-line journal entries from 10 interns—three men and seven women—who participated in the CIDA International Youth Internship Program (IYIP). The journal entries were submitted by the youth and were likely subject to CIDA review before posting on-line. However, they are a first-hand account by the youth, lengthier than the 'success stories', and therefore allowed the youth to comment on the experience in greater depth and reflection. Journals were reviewed from the submissions available on-line in 2005 (www. acdi-cida.gc.ca/cida_ind.nsf/vall). This second data source shares some of the same challenges as the first because the host of the e-journals was responsible for delivering this particular program. Nonetheless, the direct quotes provided in these e-journals provide useful insights into the self-reflection and identities of young Canadians who went abroad for an internship experience. The final method employed for this research involved 10 intensive interviews (approximately two-hour interviews) with young Canadians who have returned from volunteer experiences and internships abroad.[6] The interview transcripts were coded using a discourse and content analysis similar to the analysis used for the on-line texts.

In total, then, information provided by 90 young Canadians was included in this study.

Reflections from Participants in Overseas Programs

Many of the youth who travel abroad reflect on their experience in terms of an opportunity for breaking down stereotypes and changing attitudes about the world. As one person notes: 'I'll admit it: I did not expect so many Peruvians to possess such a wealth of knowledge and skills.' In this comment, the intern is referring to the young, bright individuals who are developing software systems throughout the Amazon jungle. What is important about her comment is that on some level she realized that she held stereotypes about what a rural Peruvian would be like. Her findings shattered her stereotype. In the success stories several references were made to changing attitudes, being less judgemental, and being more open-minded. One intern writes, 'I learned how important it is not to judge the behaviour of others based on the context of your own life experiences.'

Breaking down stereotypes works both ways. The presence of Canadian youth in communities around the world can serve the same purpose of breaking down stereotypes for everyone. Assumptions about widespread affluence in Canada are often complicated by the presence of the young, debt-ridden students who receive volunteer stipends instead of salaries during their internships. Of course, such assumptions also take into account the fact that the opportunity to travel abroad remains a luxury that the majority of the world cannot afford, so poverty must be considered as a relative rather than absolute concept. More importantly, however, the presence of a diverse group of Canadians working abroad builds a better understanding, at least among participants, of diversity in Canada. One of the most interesting findings from the success stories is the perception among youth of the number of initiatives to place a diverse group of Canadians abroad, including people with visible minorities, people with disabilities, and indigenous youth. Enhanced cross-cultural understanding—within Canada upon their return—is therefore a crucial element in the learning/volunteer abroad programs. At the same time, it is not clear whether these programs promote global citizenship as outlined in several previous government initiatives.

As noted earlier, global citizenship has been part of Canada's foreign policy, and of the world view of many Canadians, for a long time, as famously depicted by Pierre Trudeau in his description of himself as a 'citizen of the world' (Gwyn, 1980: ch. 2). In the 2005 *International Policy Statement*, global citizenship refers to Canada's responsibilities to the world, the importance of public diplomacy, and the role that youth can play in promoting global citizenship. Global citizenship is difficult to measure and evaluate. For this research, I was interested, instead, in whether the youth consider themselves global citizens and what global citizenship means to them. For the purposes of my research, I define global citizenship as a way of understanding the world in which an individual's attitudes and behaviours reflect a compassion and concern for the marginalized and/or poor and for the relationship between poverty and wealth—within and between communities, countries, and regions. This definition may or may not reflect the perceptions of global citizenship held by the youth participants in the study.

While none of the youth in the two on-line data sets made an explicit reference to global citizenship, many of their comments reinforce some of the key elements of global citizenship, particularly related to attitudes, including cross-cultural awareness, being open-minded and less judgemental of other cultures, and seeing the world as interconnected. Global citizenship is therefore being encouraged in the youth internship programs through the cross-cultural awareness that happens while living outside of Canada. Even for those youth who are motivated to participate in the youth internship programs for less altruistic and more career-oriented goals, the intercultural exchange has an overwhelming impact in terms of breaking down cultural stereotypes and fostering an open-minded and more informed perspective of development challenges and opportunities.

The 10 interview participants were specifically asked if they considered themselves global citizens and half of the respondents said they did. One interview participant did not answer the question and one said that he definitely did not see himself as a global citizen. Three interviewees offered thoughtful responses reflecting their concern with the use of the term and the way in which it has been overused and become meaningless. For those who did consider themselves to be global citizens, the responses tended to highlight common responsibility based on an environmental perspective of shared resources. One individual was skeptical of the term, noting that it can be 'easily spun' by whoever adopts the term. He elaborates: 'I could work for Raytheon, or some weapons manufacturer and say I'm a global citizen.' Another interviewee sees the CIDA internship process as one of indoctrination into a certain kind of identity around global citizenship. She went on to comment on what she perceived as a hypocritical stance on global citizenship on the part of CIDA: 'we can't be a global citizen when our government policies are so totally hypocritical. . . . CIDA needs to give its interns a bit of a reality check about what Canadians are doing around the world, and integrate it with the rest of our foreign policy.' In this particular example, the youth participant was concerned with both the attitudes and actions of Canada and Canadians. As an extension of youth perceptions of global citizenship, the perceptions youth held of their public diplomacy or ambassadorial roles abroad are of special interest.

Youth Ambassadors Abroad?

And we were always so well received; it was almost as though we were some foreign diplomat as we came into a new area. So they would toast the Canadian government when we came, and pay honour to the Queen. It was quite surreal, because it was as though we were some great authority for Canada, even though we were just wee little interns. –'Rob', youth intern abroad participant describing his experience as a Canadian volunteering in another country

As the above quotation suggests, one participant felt quite strongly that he represented Canada in a diplomatic or ambassadorial way. Several of the youth participants (especially the DFAIT and CIDA participants) talked about their experiences in relationship to goodwill ambassadorship and highlighted diplomacy as a skill learned. The youth participants reflected on their experiences as acts of friendliness and kindness across borders. Emphasis was repeatedly placed on efforts to 'help' others, of making friendships in other places, and of promoting cross-cultural understanding.

Interesting reflections on identity and citizenship were also revealed. Some of the participants commented on the advantages of being Canadian abroad, noting that people were more likely to treat them kindly knowing they are from Canada rather than the United States. Other youth participants made reference to the fact that Canadians have had a presence in a specific community for a long time and therefore a positive reputation of Canadians was believed to have developed over the years. Some of the interview participants offered much more candid reflections on their perceptions of Canadians abroad. As one participant noted: 'Well, I don't think anyone cared if we were Americans or Canadians. We were "gringos" and we were from the North, and some folks saw that as us bringing our imperial minds and ways of organizing into their communities. And others saw that as a really great opportunity to connect with like-minded folks.' Another participant noted that host communities 'lump' all foreigners together: 'if you're white, you're considered a foreigner and you come from away.'

Perceptions of foreigners were determined, in part, by the amount of time spent in the country and ability to speak the local language. A young Canadian woman who travelled on a CIDA internship believed that American Peace Corps volunteers were much better integrated into the community because they live abroad for two years, are trained in advance of their placement, and are more likely to become fluent in the national language and to pick up local nuances. The Canadians, she argued, 'look ridiculous, like we were dropped in this place on the first day of Ramadan with no language and no idea where to get food, or where we were sleeping or anything.' The lack of preparedness on the part of the sending organization is reflected in nationalistic terms, and Canadians are perceived as less prepared (and perhaps less capable or qualified) than other foreigners. One individual who participated in the interview component of the research suggested that being from Canada was significant to his cross-cultural experience. The quotation at the beginning of this section reinforces the kind of image Canada aspires to project abroad. In Rob's experience, he found that his host country 'just loves Canada'. He attributed this positive relationship between the host community and Canada as a result of the large number of immigrants to Canada from his host country. Immigration policies are therefore an important factor in international diplomacy and how young Canadian internship participants are perceived in host countries. Most of the young Canadians interviewed recognized the importance of youth internships in projecting a particular image of Canada abroad, and the youth saw their own role abroad as one of goodwill ambassadorship.

Conclusion

In 2006, the Conservative government cut funding to DFAIT's Young Professionals International Internship Program (Adeba, 2006) and in 2008 threatened to cut CIDA's funding to the International Youth Internship Program (Berthiaume, 2008). In light of these policy shifts, it is crucial to examine the perceived and potential impact of youth abroad programs as a component of Canadian public diplomacy. It is important for Canada to project a positive image of itself and its citizens abroad for political and economic reasons. Youth who are open-minded and committed to learning about another culture reflect well on Canada and Canadians.

Many of the youth who have been abroad see their internship experiences as an opportunity to learn about the world, open their minds, and break down previously held stereotypes. Furthermore, youth who participate in internships abroad recognize that their actions overseas reflect on Canada as a country and they realize that they are, in some ways, youth ambassadors. The use of young Canadian interns in overseas programs is an important part of Canadian foreign policy, demonstrating Canada's commitment to democratic values, co-operation, peace, and poverty alleviation, among other values. Young Canadians live the rhetoric of Canadian foreign policy and thereby play a role in shaping Canada's image of good global citizenship.

Canada's public diplomacy mandate of good global citizenship and its efforts to project Canadian values abroad through 'soft power' or 'attractive causes' (Nye, 2004) include youth abroad programs. This form of public diplomacy is especially important for small and medium-sized states (middle powers) because it generates political clout and earns the nation a reputation as an influential or reputable player on the world stage. Canada's global influence, in addition to economic or military power, depends increasingly on public perceptions abroad of Canadian values (Potter, 2004). Evidence of Canada's commitments to the promotion of public diplomacy and the use of civil society groups and young volunteers abroad are found in the 2005 *International Policy Statement* and in the programs developed in recent years, such as the International Youth Internship Program and the Students for Development (formerly Canada Corps) program.

Canadian youth abroad programs constitute a large and growing component of Canada's public diplomacy. Youth abroad programs also help shape a particular image of Canada as a 'warm fuzzy' nation (Michaud, 2007). As such, these programs can divert the international community's attention away from Canada's other (less palatable) current and recent international activities and commitments, such as Talisman Energy's adventures in Sudan and the ongoing military presence in Afghanistan. Examples of Canada's broad failings include its lack of achievement and effort in reaching the United Nations recommended contribution of 0.7 per cent of gross national product in development assistance and its continued use of tied aid, whereby aid is linked to recipient country assurances to purchase donor services and/or supplies. Thus, the actions of young Canadians may not be enough to foster, maintain, and project an image of Canada as a good global citizen. More research is needed from host countries that receive young Canadians to determine what image is created.[7]

At the same time, Canadian foreign policy-makers need to take a closer look at the range of values Canada is projecting abroad and the (often contradictory) messages we send in development assistance programs and foreign policy more generally. Sending youth abroad as pseudo ambassadors may not be enough to establish an image of good global citizenship in the long run, nor should it be. Canada, therefore, needs to revisit some of the ways in which the promotion of Canadian values abroad, combined with Canada's other foreign policy mandates of economic prosperity and security, in fact diminish this country's image, and therefore influence, abroad.

Youth abroad programs are a small but important part of Canada's public diplomacy strategy because young Canadians volunteering abroad generally promote a positive image of Canada as a caring and giving nation. However, young Canadian interns abroad are not well trained for their mission of public diplomacy, so their ambassadorial roles tend to be haphazard and unintentional. Furthermore, they do not adequately compensate for the limited, and diminishing, international activities of the Canadian government and cannot be seen as a fallback plan for broader and more meaningful international engagement in the developing world. In the face of potential cuts to the CIDA youth internship programs, the strengths and benefits of youth abroad as part of Canada's public diplomacy and global citizenship mandate need to be revisited. At the same time, however, greater effort is needed to ensure that the Canadian government broadens its public diplomacy efforts and re-examines its international development commitments.

Notes

1. CUSO estimates that around 65,000 Canadians have volunteered overseas. CUSO alone accounts for approximately 11,000 of those volunteers, Canada World Youth boasts the return of 22,000 volunteers, and thousands of recent university graduates have gone abroad with government-funded international youth program placements (Kelly and Case, 2007).

2. 'Youth' is defined by the Canadian International Development Agency as young people between the ages of 18 and 30.

3. In August 2008, an article in *Embassy* magazine (Berthiaume, 2008) suggested that the future of CIDA internship programs was 'up in the air'. The article noted that the CIDA youth internship program was under review and funding had not been allocated beyond one year.

4. Canada World Youth (CWY) is one example of a volunteer-sending program for Canadians. CWY offers cross-cultural educational programs for youth (ages 17–24) in Canada and abroad, usually for three to six months in duration.

5. Previous attempts to evaluate youth internship programs have been carried out by HRDC (2000) and DFAIT (1999). In both of these documents, however, the emphasis was on job satisfaction and the number of youth who found employment as a result of the internship. These evaluations tell us little about how international youth internship programs promote a culture of global citizenship and what that means for youth.

6.   I would like to thank Anna Hunter for conducting these interviews in 2006 and for transcribing the material.

7.   Rebecca Tiessen and Barbara Heron are carrying out this research in a five-year study funded by the International Development Research Centre. Interviews are underway and no results are yet available.

Chapter Twelve

About Solitude, Divorce, and Neglect

The Linguistic Division in the Study of Canadian Foreign Policy

Stéphane Roussel

One of the lasting images in contemporary Canadian politics is the coexistence of 'two solitudes', a concept coined by novelist Hugh MacLennan (2003 [1945]) that depicts how English-speaking and French-speaking communities live their collective lives separately, usually ignoring each other. This cliché is also present in Canadian foreign policy (CFP), one of the many areas in which francophone and anglophone public opinion is said to diverge on the basis of different views, ideas, or values. Indeed, many authors support the idea that 'French-Canadians [are] more dovish, isolationist, and anti-militaristic than their Anglo-Canadians counterparts' (Rioux, 2005: 1; see also Granatstein, 2007: ch. 6). It has been demonstrated elsewhere that, with respect to public opinion at least, this claim is not supported by polls or political party programs (Roussel and Boucher, 2008; Roussel and Théorêt, 2004). But what about the attitude of these groups within the Canadian foreign policy research community? Any critical overview of the literature in Canadian foreign policy cannot ignore the potential dividing lines induced by linguistic division among the researchers.

The purpose of this chapter is to assess how this linguistic division affects the study of CFP. This task is critical because it reveals within the study of CFP a hidden French discourse, marginalized and ignored by the dominant English one. Of course, this relationship between the 'dominant' and 'dominated' discourses must be treated carefully. A francophone perspective on Canadian foreign policy is very much alive; articles and books written by French-speaking researchers on this topic are flourishing, and there is a growing demand for this literature beyond the francophone political and academic circles. Moreover, contrary to many other dominated discourses, such as feminism, this French perspective (if there is anything that could labelled as such) hasn't needed to fight to establish its credibility or to repel attacks from the dominant discourse.

But a problem remains. As we will see, the two languages don't have equal status and we cannot reduce this inequality to a simple 'communication issue', i.e., the fact that most anglophones don't speak French. The concept of 'two solitudes' carries first and foremost a feeling of mutual neglect and misunderstanding. One of the most persistent allegations by French-speaking researchers is of being ignored by their English-speaking counterparts. This applies not only to their work, but also to their concerns and values. French-speaking researchers are well connected to the English intellectual universe, while the reverse is absolutely not the case.

Being critical also means to reveal the political purpose of a discourse and the power relations produced and reproduced by it. If French-speaking members of the CFP research community are in fact being ignored by their anglophone colleagues, is this necessarily the expression of a power relationship? This question also calls for a nuanced answer. On the one hand, some alternative (and sometimes simpler) hypotheses exist. But on the other, some evidence does point towards the operation of a power relationship, especially when the debate touches on issues that could pitch the two linguistic communities against each other, such as national unity.

We will examine the impact of the linguistic division on the study of CFP from two separate angles. In the first section of the chapter, we will make a qualitative assessment of the interaction between English- and French-speaking researchers. We will present evidence supporting the impression, common among French-speaking researchers, that their intellectual contributions are almost completely ignored by their English-speaking counterparts. In the second section, we will assess how the English-speaking community deals with the most important challenge that the linguistic division creates in the realm of Canadian foreign policy, which is national unity. We will see that this so-called 'priority' is, in fact, largely neglected. In the conclusion, we will suggest an alternative hypothesis designed to explain the attitude of the English-speaking community towards the French-Canadian intellectual universe.

Studying Canadian Foreign Policy in English, and in English Only

The Absence of French in the Anglo-Canadian Intellectual Universe of Canadian Foreign Policy

Recently, two important research contributions have supported the claim, made by French-speaking political scientists, that their work is largely ignored by their English-Canadian colleagues. The first, conducted by François Rocher (2007), shows that Francophone researchers' work is almost absent in the intellectual universe of their English colleagues in the field of Canadian politics. Working with a sample of 84 books published between 1995 and 2005 by anglophone academics, Rocher and his team reviewed the works cited in these books and sorted them according to linguistic criterion (publication language and linguistic origin of the author of the cited work). The results indicate clearly a systematic and chronic under-representation or 'discrimination' against research contributions by French-speaking authors. Of the 26,040 references found in these 84 books, only 1,962 are from French authors—an average of 7.5 per cent, and a median of 4.9 per cent. The obvious task following from this study is to assess if the situation is the same in the field of Canadian foreign policy.

Some preliminary observations about the state of the literature in the field of Canadian foreign policy suggest that the situation is probably worse than in the area of Canadian politics. As we noted elsewhere, many literature overviews simply ignore the French contribution to this field (Nossal et al., 2007: 13–14). These observations were reinforced by a second major study, this one published by Claire Turenne Sjolander. Recalling the 'already noted difference between English Canadian and Québécois with respect to foreign policy', the author asked 'if the field of Canadian foreign policy, as taught in French, is the same as the field taught in English'. Using a sample of 30 syllabi from courses on Canadian foreign policy, the author made striking, while not surprising, observations regarding the intellectual universe of the English-speaking academics in this field:

> No matter where Francophone students are taking their French-language Canadian foreign policy courses, they confront the same reality: their professors, teaching in French, ask their students to read a lot, most commonly a significant majority, of assigned texts in Canada's other official language. Anglophone colleagues do not feel obliged, or practically able, to reciprocate— *not a single French language reading is included on the English language course outlines surveyed.* (Turenne Sjolander, 2007: 103; emphasis added)

The observations made by Rocher and Turenne Sjolander beg fascinating questions. Most importantly, is the impression that the French contribution to the study of CFP is systematically ignored by English-speaking authors supported by empirical data? In other words, would the findings by Rocher with respect to Canadian politics be duplicated in a study of the field of Canadian foreign policy?

Since 1945, the John Holmes Library of the Canadian Institute of International Affairs has produced a comprehensive bibliography of documents on Canadian foreign policy (see www.ciia.org). Setting aside official documents, this index contains a total of 40,400 texts, including 5,177 in French. On this basis, one can assess French-speaking researchers' contribution at 12.8 per cent of the overall production in the field. This figure does not include contributions made by francophones *in English*, but does include contributions *in French* made by English-speaking researchers. For this reason, this figure may look suspect, but it remains the most plausible one.[1] Based on this figure, we would expect that if they are fairly represented in the study of CFP, French-speaking researchers will appear in about 12.8 per cent of the references made by their English-speaking colleagues.

Table 12.1 The John Holmes Library Bibliography

Texts	Number	%
Texts in French	5,177	12.8
Texts in other languages than French	35,223	87.2
Total	40,400	100.0

Applying Rocher's methodology to a sample of recent publications on Canadian foreign policy reveals that the situation is indeed worse in CFP than in the broader study of Canadian politics. The sample includes 266 texts (gathered from 33 books, edited volumes, and journal issues) covering the period 1997–2006 (see Appendix to this chapter). All of these texts were written by English-speaking authors only.[2] Conference papers, research notes, and similar documents were left aside. Likewise, non-academic documents, such as official documents and popular magazines (e.g., *Saturday Night* and *Maclean's*) weren't considered. References in the sample are sorted according to two criteria: (1) the language of the document cited, and (2) the language of the author. In this sample, a total of 7,844 references (with a repeated reference in the same document being counted as one) can be found, excluding official documents, because they are usually available in the two languages. References made to French-speaking politicians were kept when these did not come from an official document.

The results are quite telling. Among these 7,844 references, a total of 61 references in French (including six texts in French written by English-speaking authors) were found, for an average of 0.78 per cent per document. If French-language publications account for just under 13 per cent of the total production in the field, this means that the works published in French are *cited 16 times less* than what one might expect. The picture is even worst if we consider the median, which drops to a pathetic 0.25 per cent.[3]

Table 12.2 References Made by English-speaking Authors

References	Number	%
a. Total number of references	7,844	100.0
b. Texts in French by French-speaking authors	55	0.70
c. Texts in French by English-speaking authors	6	0.08
d. Texts in French (b + c)	61	0.78
e. Texts in English by French-speaking authors	208	2.65
f. Texts written by French-speaking authors (b + c)	263	3.35
g. Texts from the French universe (b + c + e)	269	3.43

Is publishing in English the solution for French-speaking authors to gain more visibility among their English-speaking colleagues? Apparently, yes, but not enough to fill the gap. In the sample used here, references to works by French-speaking researchers published in English were found four times more than those published in French (208 against 55). English texts written by French-speaking researchers account for 2.65 per cent of the total number of references. Adding this number increases the general 'score' of the French researchers (for a total of 263 references), but by very little: they now account for an average of 3.35 per cent. In total, references made by English-speaking researchers to sources belonging in one way or another to the French intellectual universe account for 3.43 per cent. If one accepts that the overall contribution of francophones to the research in the field is at 12.8 per cent, then French-speaking researchers *are still cited four times less than what one can expect.*

Hence, these figures indicate that French-speaking researchers are correct in their impression that their work is largely ignored by their anglophone colleagues. This phenomenon deserves an explanation. But many hypotheses can be used here.

Competing Hypotheses over the Absence of French in the English Study of CFP

These figures indicate that the inattention to French-speaking scholars' contributions to the study of Canadian foreign policy is even more profound than it is in the field of Canadian politics. How can this be explained?

A first series of hypotheses are based on the state of the Canadian foreign policy field itself. To be sure, part of the explanation comes from the fact that a good share of the references in academic documents are made to works of a theoretical nature. In the discipline of International Relations, theory is largely dominated by English-speaking (or, more precisely, American) authors. Against this, French-speaking authors are almost completely absent and unknown to their English-speaking colleagues—Raymond Aron and Didier Bigo being among the rare exceptions here.

In the same vein, it is important to be aware that French contribution to the study of Canadian foreign policy is relatively recent, having emerged only in the 1960s or even 1970s. Until the mid-1960s, the number of academic documents published in French had been dramatically low. For example, the bibliography published by the John Holmes Library listed only 145 academic documents in French out of a total of 4,645 documents (3.1 per cent) published during the period 1945–65. Using other sources, Paul Painchaud (1977) reached the same conclusion. This could explain the relatively low number of references for the early period, but does not explain anything for the contemporary period.

Since 1965, the proportion of contributions to the field by French-speaking researchers has increased substantially and reached its current 'cruise altitude' of around 13 per cent of the total number of publications per year. But, as Claire Turenne Sjolander (2007: 104) reminds us, 'literature in French on Canadian foreign policy is often very difficult to find.' This is certainly true for those teaching undergraduate classes who need to find texts on a large variety of topics. But since

French-speaking authors occupy 13 per cent of the ground, why can they not achieve a breakthrough at least in certain areas?

This leads to the 'concentration' hypothesis, i.e., the idea that French-speaking scholars are concentrating their efforts in certain areas of CFP. As we will see in the second half of this chapter, there is some evidence supporting this hypothesis. If these areas are of limited interest to their English-speaking colleagues (such as Quebec's international activities, or the Canadian contribution to La Francophonie), it could explain their absence in reference lists. But French-speaking scholars have certainly made important contributions in other areas of more general interest, such as arms control, military industry reconversion, foreign aid, regional integration, peacekeeping operations, Canada–US relations, decision-making processes, etc. (Nossal et al., 2007: 15). While probably part of the answer, the concentration effect cannot explain the absence of French in the English work on CFP.

Another possibility is simply that there is no need to consult work by French-speaking scholars because everything is available in English. This hypothesis is certainly disturbing, because it assumes there is nothing original produced by French-speaking researchers, especially if it is read against the concentration hypothesis: not only are French-speakers concentrating their efforts in overly narrow areas, but what they are doing in these areas is not original and does not deserve to be reported. The opposite conclusion is also disturbing, albeit in a different way: if some of the work written by French-speaking authors is truly original, it means that English literature on Canadian foreign policy remains incomplete. This is a serious consequence.

The second category of hypotheses refers to the language barrier. If a majority of English-speaking researchers cannot read French (a proposition that is disturbing in itself), no one can expect them to quote French documents. But French-speaking researchers are also publishing in English. As has been demonstrated in another research study (Cornut and Roussel, 2009), this certainly helps, but a deficit remains.

A third category of hypothesis is related to cultural variables and refers to a form of discrimination. Involuntarily or not, and unconsciously or not, French researchers are left aside because the values and the vision they are promoting in their work do not reflect the dominant discourse in CFP. Put this way, the absence of French researchers' work reflects a power relationship whereby knowledge itself is patrolled and controlled. Can this hypothesis be sustained?

An indirect approach to test the cultural variable is to test the 'self-isolation' hypothesis. If French-speaking researchers are no better than their English-speaking counterparts in citing French work, this would indicate that the problem is related more to the field than the cultural background of the authors. The sample used— one book plus 19 chapters in other volumes (see Appendix)—is so small that all results must be received with great caution. Nevertheless, it gives an indication that the self-isolation hypothesis is unlikely. French-speaking authors make reference to sources belonging to the French intellectual universe (14 per cent) in almost the same proportion as their contribution to the field (13 per cent). Of course, much more research is necessary to validate that result. For example, it is possible that these figures are also a consequence of a 'concentration effect': if French-speaking researchers are all concentrating their efforts in the same narrow area, they are more likely to cite each other's work. Nevertheless, within the context of the small sample we used, there is no indication that a self-isolation process is at play.

Table 12.3 References Made by French-speaking Authors

References	Number	%
a. Total number of references	992	100.0
b. Texts in French by French-speaking authors	85	8.6
c. Texts in French by English-speaking authors	24	2.4
d. Texts in French (b + c)	109	10.9
e. Texts in English by French-speaking authors	30	3.0
f. Texts written by French-speaking authors (b + e)	115	11.6
g. Texts from the French universe (b + c + e)	139	14.0

This brief study regarding the place of French in the study of Canadian foreign policy addresses only the sociological issue raised by the linguistic division within the research community (how researchers from different cultural communities view each other). But it says nothing about the attitude of the English-speaking community towards the linguistic division as an *object of research* in the field of Canadian foreign policy.

Such an assessment is difficult to conduct, first and foremost because there are very few English studies on the impact of the linguistic division on foreign policy. While many authors recognize the fact that francophones were absent in the realm of foreign affairs and defence until the late 1960s and even 1970s (e.g., Granatstein, 1982: 4–6), the consequences of this situation are ignored. Contrary to this, French-speaking researchers perceive this discrimination as one of the factors that prompted the emergence of Quebec's independent paradiplomacy (Nossal et al., 2007: 570–1). Hence, it is hard to determine how the coexistence of two official languages could affect Canadian foreign policy—except with some very general comments (if not platitudes) about the distinctiveness of Canadian international identity, the mediation ability and tolerance of people used to dealing with linguistic difference on a daily basis, or the skills of fluent bilingual diplomats.

Another approach to assess the attitude of English-speaking researchers towards the dualistic nature of Canada could be to see what they have to say about the international activities of Quebec, the province where French-speakers are concentrated and, as a majority, control the state apparatus. The problem with such an approach is that, almost naturally, the vast majority of issues related to the international activities of the Quebec government present only a secondary interest for those concerned with Canadian foreign policy in general. Not surprisingly, the literature in English about Quebec's international involvement is minimal.

Is it nevertheless possible to find a specific issue related primarily to Quebec (or to the existence of a strong French community in Canada) and framed in a manner that it could be important or inescapable for *any* researchers in Canadian foreign policy? Actually, it is. As we will see in the next section, one issue in particular has systematically been described as 'central' to foreign policy by all Canadian governments since the 1940s, if not since World War I, and this issue—national unity—clearly involves a linguistic dimension.

National Unity: The Forgotten Priority

Our goal is to assess the impact of the linguistic division on the study of Canadian foreign policy. The first part of this chapter showed that the flow of knowledge between the two linguistic communities is essentially one way, with French-speaking academics receiving English knowledge, while the opposite is not true. Here we consider complementary information about that impact by examining the English literature regarding the most important challenge raised by the French majority in Quebec.

Surveying the literature on 'national unity and foreign policy' is much more promising than an examination of 'Quebec's international role', because (in theory) no researcher in Canadian foreign policy can ignore it, regardless of whether she or he developed a special interest in Quebec (or French). Actually, it remains difficult (though not impossible) to talk about national unity without making any reference to Quebec and to the linguistic division.

The remainder of this chapter explores the perception of an interesting contradiction in the literature on Canadian foreign policy. On the one hand, almost everybody accepts the idea that national unity is a priority in CFP, if not *the* priority. On the other hand, that so-called 'priority' does not receive, in the English literature on Canadian foreign policy, the importance that it commands.

A Very Important Issue . . . But . . .

National unity has interfered with foreign policy since Canada's early steps on the international stage. The debates surrounding the Canadian contribution to the South African War (1899) and the creation of a Canadian Navy in 1910 showed the first signs of a division between French-Canadian nationalists and Anglo-Canadian imperialists (Stacey, 1977). The real crisis took place in 1917–18, when conscription measures ignited a major clash between French Canadians and Ottawa's political class. The Conservative Party of Canada paid a high price for having managed the crisis so badly and was almost wiped off Quebec's electoral map—and then out of power—for the next 40 years (Cyr, 2008; Nossal et al., 2007: 293).

However, William Lyon Mackenzie King, Prime Minister for 22 years between 1921 and 1948, learned from this lesson. In 1937, Escott Reid, a future 'mandarin' in the Department of External Affairs, systematized the principles guiding King's foreign policy (Reid, 1989: 107). Reid, who identified seven principles, stated that:

The [first] guiding principle in the formulation of Canada's foreign policy should be the maintenance of the unity of Canada as a nation . . . . This means that a government should not adopt a policy on a matter of overwhelming importance, involving deep differences of opinion between Canadians, unless this policy is supported not merely by a substantial majority of Canadians but by substantial majorities in each important section of Canada. Otherwise, there will develop between different groups of the Canadian people cleavages so great that the continued existence of the dominion of Canada may be gravely endangered. . . . The maintenance of a substantial degree of Canadian unity is an essential prerequisite to the effective carrying out of any foreign policy. (Reid, 1986: 118–19)

Hence, national unity was the highest priority of the government. Ten years later, Louis St Laurent, recently appointed as Secretary of State for External Affairs, echoed King's concerns in his famous Gray Lecture of February 1947:

The first general principle . . . is that our external policies shall not destroy our unity. No policy can be regarded as wise which divides the people whose efforts and resources must put it into effect. . . . The role of this country in world affairs will prosper only as we maintain this principle, for a disunited Canada will be a powerless one.

In the mid-1960s, the national unity imperative in foreign policy took on another dimension. It was no longer simply a question of avoiding international (especially military) commitments that could lead to a clash between English and French Canada, but was also about countering foreign initiatives that could encourage Quebec's nationalism (such as the visit of French President Charles de Gaulle in 1967). More importantly, it was about balancing, controlling, or even countering Quebec City's growing presence on the international stage. With the election of the Parti Québécois (PQ) in 1976, this last task became even more urgent, since Quebec's international representation was perceived as a means to promote the sovereignist project.

Since then, no one has really contested the central nature of national unity as a priority in Canadian foreign policy. Indeed, it is difficult to find somebody saying that national unity is *not* a priority (although not impossible, as we will see later, but these exceptions remain implicit rather than explicit). After all, Quebec sovereignists represent the most direct threat against the integrity and identity of the Canadian state. As James McHugh (2006: 432) put it, 'any claim to self-determination, based upon a unilateral right to withdraw from a federal union as part of a previously established sovereign identity . . . presents potentially severe consequences for a federal state's foreign policy.'

Yet, a paradox emerges; while the threat to Canadian unity has intensified, the issue has never been presented as clearly and straightforwardly as it was by St Laurent. Of course, it is possible to find some trace or vague reference to the national unity imperative in subsequent white papers on foreign policy (Canada,

1970: 11; Clark, 1985: 3),[4] but nowhere as explicitly as in 1947. The most telling example is probably the 1995 white paper; published a few months before the referendum of October 1995, the notion of national unity is completely absent from the document.

Is the relative invisibility of the national unity issue in the white papers reflected in a similar absence in the academic literature? Many authors recall that national unity remains a central objective and a guiding principle of Canadian foreign policy. For example, Jennifer Welsh, outlining 'three operating principles to guide our policy-makers', suggests that the third one must be to 'approach the future of North America with Quebec in mind' (Welsh, 2005: 65). In the same vein, 'preserving national unity' is one of the priorities identified by political scientist Steven Kendall Holloway (2006: 177–92), along with sovereignty, security, political autonomy, economic and cultural autonomy, prosperity, and projection of Canadian identity. National unity is also viewed as a central consideration when Ottawa must decide how or if to recognize new states created as a result of a secession process, such as Biafra in 1968 (Nossal et al., 2007: 181), Croatia and Slovenia in 1991, and Kosovo in 2008.

But to what extent have these concerns percolated in the literature on Canadian foreign policy? What do we, as an academic community, know (and say) about this issue? And what are the differences, if any, between English and French-speaking authors?

National Unity: A Very Discrete Issue

To gather enough material to answer these questions, another sample was created with documents addressing any international or foreign policy dimension of the Canadian national unity issue. The term 'national unity' is defined in a broad sense to include all pre- or post-referendum political issues related to foreign and defence policy, to provinces' (and especially Quebec's) international relations, and federal actions or responses. Emphasis is put on policy analysis, political science (including political economy), and contemporary (post-1968) history, while pure historical research (pre-1968), as well as law and economics, is excluded. Unpublished manuscripts (including conference papers), official documents, magazines, theses, and dissertations are also excluded.

Again using the bibliography provided by the John Holmes Library, the sample was constituted through a search using key words such as 'separatism', 'nationalism', 'federalism', 'national unity', 'sovereignty', and 'Quebec' for the period 1968–2008. The resulting sample includes a total of 144 documents, including 92 written by English-speaking authors[5] and 52 written by French-speaking authors.[6] These results give a good sense of the state and scope of academic attention to the issue of national unity.

The analysis of this sample reveals many interesting facts. First, the total number is surprisingly low if one takes into account the (theoretical) importance of the issue—only 144 out of a pool of 40,400 documents published since 1945, or 0.36 per cent. Topics such as relations with the United States or Europe (notably Canada's contribution to NATO) received much more attention. The first observation is certainly that this 'priority' is, to say the least, a 'discrete' one.

Second, documents written by English-speaking researchers about national unity account for almost double those written by French-speaking authors (92 against 52). This ratio calls for some observations. On the one hand, it is expected that French-speaking researchers (a vast majority of whom are Québécois) take this question to heart, since the challenge to national unity comes first and foremost from the will of a substantial part of the Quebec population to see their province achieve sovereignty.[7] Hence, even if they contribute only 12.8 per cent of literature on Canadian foreign policy, there is nothing surprising in the fact that they account for 36 per cent of the academic writing on the specific question of national unity. This reinforces the 'concentration' hypothesis discussed earlier.

On the other hand, it is important to keep in mind that 38 of the 92 documents written by English-speaking authors were in fact written by scholars teaching outside Canada (the vast majority of these being located in the US), and 6 of the 52 documents were published by French-speaking authors teaching outside Canada (generally in France). Pulling out these documents reduces the sample to 100 documents: 54 in English and 46 in French. *This brings the ratio close to half for each linguistic group.* Hence, there is a clear under-representation of English-Canadian authors compared to French-Canadian ones if the latter are producing only 12.8 per cent of the overall literature in Canadian foreign policy. It can be said, then, that the debate over national unity is, relatively speaking, much more important for French researchers than it is for English researchers. While not necessarily surprising, this observation is significant since a national unity crisis affects both linguistic groups.

Table 12.4 Language and Origins of the Authors

Documents	Number	%	Sub-total	%
Total number	144	100	144	100
By English-speaking authors living in Canada	54	37.5	92	64
By English-speaking authors living outside Canada	38	26.4		
By French-speaking authors living in Canada	46	32.0	52	36
By French-speaking authors living outside Canada	6	4.1		

Considering the importance given to the issue of national unity and its relative absence from the literature on foreign policy, it is fair to conclude that this issue suffers from a clear 'deficit of attention' in English Canada. Obviously, this does not mean that English-speaking Canadians don't have anything to say about national unity. On the contrary, many academics have written about this topic over the last 40 years. Nevertheless, it is interesting to note that those who are talking about national unity rarely add a foreign policy dimension to their analysis; and those who are talking about Canadian foreign policy rarely talk about national unity![8]

Similarly, some authors in Canadian foreign policy suggest that national unity is crucial, but are not paying attention to this issue. A good example is Andrew

Cooper's important and substantial book on Canadian foreign policy, published just two years after the 'near death experience' of the 1995 referendum:

> As the sources of international opportunity swelled out [in the early 1990s], the foci of Canadian domestic politics became seriously circumscribed. The long-standing obsession of Canadian political life with national unity and the question of Quebec's constitutional status intensified with the failure of the Meech Lake and Charlottetown accords, the revival of the Quebec nationalist/ sovereignty movement under Lucien Bouchard and the events surrounding the 30 October 1995 referendum. *The repercussions on Canadian foreign policy emanating from this series of domestic crises have been enormous.* (Cooper, 1997: 2; emphasis added)

Having said this, Cooper never mentions the issue in the rest of the book. The same can be noticed in Jennifer Welsh's *At Home in the World*. Even if she suggests 'keeping Quebec in mind' as an 'operating principle' for the management of relations with the rest of the continent, and even if she presents her role during the referendum of 1995 as her first experience as 'warrior for Canada', the question of national unity is absent from the rest of the book (Welsh, 2005: 85, 235).

Quantitative observations from the sample of documents on national unity are underscored by other evidence pointing in the same direction. Using the empirical data gathered by Claire Turenne Sjolander about the teaching of CFP, it is possible to show that the important (if not vital) topic of Canadian unity is completely absent in classrooms. On 22 English-speaking syllabi, only four deal with national unity (and this includes two from the same lecturer). Even those addressing the question of domestic sources of Canadian foreign policy ignore this aspect.

The conclusion of this section is quite clear. Even if the issue of national unity is almost unanimously considered to be a priority in Canadian foreign policy, this topic is almost absent in the literature, both from quantitative and qualitative points of view. Before trying to explain the origin and nature of this inattention, it is worth considering more carefully the discourse of national unity in those documents that do address the issue.

Debating the Divorce

In the documents written by English-speaking researchers, what are the most prominent themes? Basically, three dimensions of the issue are covered. The first theme is that of the provinces as international actors, with special attention to Quebec. According to Michael Hawes's classical literature overview, the 'federalist perspective' is based on the assumption 'that the Canadian preoccupation with federalism (often cited as the key feature of Canadian politics) is mirrored in its external behaviour' (Hawes, 1984: 9–12). Hawes focused on the debate surrounding the provinces' roles in the international realm and established a clear relationship between provincial involvement in foreign policy and national unity. 'While provincial involvement in Canada's external relations can be traced back to the early years of Confederation, it was not until the 1960s that provincial international activity began to be perceived as a threat to the unity of the Canadian state' (ibid., 11).

This federalist perspective remains the most prominent approach to addressing the relationship between national unity and foreign policy. It is probably also the richest, because it provides an explanation for decisions made at both federal and provincial levels. It further helps to frame the nature of the problem, from both Ottawa's and Quebec City's perspective. This kind of analysis is common in documents providing a general overview of Canadian foreign policy (Nossal, 1997; Kirton, 2007; McHugh, 2006). While there are very few works from francophone authors on the impact of Quebec international politics on Canadian foreign policy, this absence is partly compensated by work on Quebec's international relations.

The second most common theme in the relevant documents is the effort to predict the future, i.e., what things will look like in the days, months, and years after a sovereignist triumph in a referendum. In 1976–80 period, numerous documents described a very dark future for Quebec and how its independence would imperil North American security, if not the whole Western alliance (Stethem, 1977–8; Lentner, 1978: 390–2; Starnes, 1977; Lisée, 1990: 148). These authors depicted a continent vulnerable to Soviet surprise attack, thanks to the gap left in the air defence system by Quebec's withdrawal from NORAD, or the possibility of violent confrontation between French-speaking sovereignists and English-speaking federalists. Other scenarios contemplate a 'Quebec imperialism' aimed at Labrador and the Maritime provinces. Of course, some exceptions provide a balanced and nuanced assessment of the political and strategic consequences of separation (Jockel, 1980; Stairs, 1977), but in general, alarmist scenarios dominate the discourse. While they received little credit in official circles,[9] it is likely that these documents were intended to minimize international support for Quebec sovereignists by depicting them as dangerous and irresponsible. It is interesting to note that the sovereignists didn't help their own cause by remaining almost silent on the security and defence dimensions of their project, and their rare initiatives on this issue were clumsy and naive (Roussel, with Robichaud, 2001). Very few academic documents in French were produced during that period, when International Relations and strategic studies were nascent in Quebec.

The period surrounding the second referendum (1992–8) was by far the most intellectually active one, with 58 of the 144 documents produced. In general, the tone was much more moderate and balanced, even while it remained pessimistic, depicting a dark future for Canada as well as for Quebec, and a very difficult time for the two communities if separation ever occurred (e.g., Morrison, 1992; Black, 1997–8; MacFarlane, 1997; Stairs, 1996). But contrary to the first referendum, French-speaking academics were present and ready to engage a debate on sensitive issues such as the future defence policy of a sovereign Quebec or the possibility for the new state to become a member of international institutions such as the North American Free Trade Agreement (NAFTA). Not surprisingly, the tone is much more optimistic, since they generally concluded that the risk of violence during the process was low, that the new state would be able to assume its own defence and also take over its share of Canadian defence commitments (NATO and NORAD), and, in general, that defence issues wouldn't be the most urgent problem (Coulon, 1991: 261–5; Brodeur, 1992; Roussel, 1999). In fact, the most intense debate was almost exclusively in French, with strategic studies experts squared off against pacifist activists (Roussel, with Robichaud, 2001).

The third prominent theme in the literature is foreign intervention in the process, mainly from France, which, needless to say, is viewed with very little sympathy (Holloway, 1992, 2006; Black, 1998; Bosher, 1998). Here, too, the tone is quite different from that in the French documentation, in which relations with France were celebrated and highly regarded (Bastien, 1998; Paquin, with Beaudoin, 2006; Comeau and Fornier, 2002; Portes, 2001; Poulin, 2002; and for a critical perspective, Légaré, 2003).

Interestingly, even if the prospect of a third referendum has not seemed likely since 1995, the issue of national unity remains, in relative terms, much more present than it was before 1992. But national unity is generally addressed as a part of a wider enterprise, such as an overview of Canadian (or Quebec) foreign policy (Fraser, 2005; Fry, 2002; Kirton, 2007; Paquin, with Beaudoin, 2006; McHugh, 2006; Vengroff and Rich, 2006), or in the context of specific events, such as the war in Iraq, Canadian participation in the American missile defence project, or the war in Afghanistan (Granatstein, 2007; Haglund, 2006). Only 7 of the 29 documents produced during this period address national unity as their central focus (Doran, 2001; Harvey et al., 2001; Mason, 2006; Piromalli, 2001; Thomsen and Hynek, 2006; Paquin, 2001; Roussel, with Robichaud, 2001).

The most interesting point is not what these sources are covering, but what they are *not* covering. Two related themes seem important here. The first is Ottawa's strategy designed to counter the Quebec sovereignist project. The agenda of the Parti Québécois government has been well studied by French-speaking authors,[10] but that of the federal government (or the federalist groups) has not. Ottawa is generally depicted as reactive, acting under constraints and doomed to manage the consequences of Quebec's separation.[11] A critical analysis of the diplomatic strategy used by Ottawa, especially before the 1995 referendum, remains to be written. In the same vein, while there was a good deal of speculation about what Ottawa should do if sovereignists ever win a referendum, there is no post-facto in-depth history of the contingency planning in Ottawa in 1995.

More important is the lack of research about the federal government as an actor engaged in nation-building efforts aimed not only at countering the sovereignist project, but also at reinforcing Canadian identity. While the domestic dimension of that effort is well covered in the area of Canadian politics, its international dimension remains to be studied, with the exceptions of Thomsen and Hynek (2006) and Massie and Roussel (2008). An interesting example of the connection between foreign policy and national identity-building can be found in Lloyd Axworthy's memoirs. According to the former Minister of Foreign Affairs, one of the motivations behind the adoption of the human security agenda was the potential attraction of such a concept among the young people of Quebec (Axworthy, 2003: 58–9). Many authors have raised the question of nation-building in the discussion over public diplomacy, promotion of values and culture, or identity-building, but it is worth noting that the words 'national unity' are rarely used in this literature. Of course, one can say that national unity is implicit throughout. But this simply displaces the problem. Why is it implicit? Why is the issue of national unity overwhelmingly hidden in the literature?

Things Better Left Unsaid?

How can we explain this surprising lack of attention to an issue described as fundamental to Canadian foreign policy? Several hypotheses can be proposed here.

The first possible explanation, simple but limited, is related to the definition of the field of Canadian foreign policy. If one defines 'foreign policy' as 'policy concerning the foreign', then issues related to domestic politics are thereby excluded. 'Realist' students in International Relations rely on this assumption. The state is a unitary actor and what happens inside the state is of a secondary interest, if of any interest at all. From this perspective, national unity, which is a domestic issue, simply is not relevant to the realm of Canadian *foreign* policy. Scholars of CFP must therefore leave this issue to their colleagues in Canadian politics. But this narrow statement contradicts not only Canadian leaders' discourses since 1947, but also the strong sense among many scholars that foreign policy is a continuation of domestic politics (Nossal et al., 2007: 28, 53–6).

The second possible explanation is also quite simple: contrary to other central issues in Canadian foreign policy (such as Canada–US relations), the importance of national unity is not constant. Since the danger of a third referendum is viewed as minimal, it should not be surprising that the attention devoted to it has waned, too. John Kirton's text on Canadian foreign policy offers a clear example of this attitude. Little attention is paid to the national unity issue, largely because the author considers the issue to be fading away. Moreover, the threat of foreign intervention in Canadian politics has also disappeared, even if the competition has moved onto other battlefields, such as the recent debate over Quebec's representation in UNESCO. According to Kirton (2007: 230), 'International actors are now entirely on a united Canada's side.' The same could be said about Jennifer Welsh (2005: 156), who notes that 'national cohesion is more robust' in the post-9/11 era. Hence, the sense of emergency seems to have disappeared and this issue is not important any more. To reinforce this argument, one can add that since the *cause* of the threat to national unity is, to some, not relevant to the area of foreign policy, there is no need for those studying CFP to pay attention to this question as long as there is no *consequence* for foreign policy. This makes sense, but this line of argument leads us to ignore all of Ottawa's efforts to prevent a new unity crisis or to build a stronger national identity.

This second hypothesis could be considered in relation to a third one. For some authors, Canadians must stop wasting time and energy on this 'counterproductive' issue, especially if there is no crisis on the horizon. Discussion about national unity is nothing but an obstacle or distraction in the pursuit of the Canadian national interest, and must be treated accordingly. Moreover, any concession to Quebec nationalists' efforts to get more power will only weaken Canada. This is the position of some 'realists' (or hard-liners, from Quebec federalists' perspective), who advocate letting the Québécois leave the federation if this is what they want, while maintaining a very firm position in the subsequent negotiations. This would include sensitive issues like the borders of the new state, which could be reduced to a small enclave on the shores of the St Lawrence River.[12] Authors defending this approach could be ranked among the very small group of those who argue that national unity is *not* a priority of Canadian foreign policy. But this approach to the problem is naturally unacceptable for those who still believe in the importance of keeping Canada united.

The examination of the 'deficit of attention' phenomenon results in different kinds of explanations from those used to explain the absence of French-speaking academics in the intellectual universe of their English-speaking colleagues. But is there any relation between the two phenomena? Or, more precisely, is there an intersection in their cause? There is a possible common explanation, as we will see in the conclusion.

Conclusion: The Cultural Misunderstanding

This chapter provided some evidence supporting the claim that French-speaking authors are dramatically under-represented in English literature on Canadian foreign policy. Moreover, it showed that national unity, one of the most important priorities involving a linguistic dimension is, relatively speaking, largely ignored by English-speaking researchers. There is a clear 'deficit of attention' paid to these two dimensions of the study of Canadian foreign policy.

We examined various explanations for these two attitudes. The absence of French-speaking authors in English documents can be explained by some distinctive characteristics of CFP as a research field (such as a concentration effect), or by the linguistic barrier. In the same vein, the deficit of attention towards national unity issues can be explained by the nature of the problem and the way it is framed. While none of these explanations are really convincing in and of themselves, their cumulative effect can provide a more satisfactory explanation.

Is it nevertheless possible to find a common interpretation of these two phenomena? After all, they share some characteristics, the most important one being that both are directly related to the linguistic duality of Canada and the CFP academic community. Moreover, the contributions by Rocher and Turenne Sjolander indicate that the observations provided in this chapter are not isolated cases. These hints indicate that, beyond the limited or ad hoc explanation, there could be a common and more comprehensive interpretation. This brings us back to the critical dimension of this chapter.

François Rocher's interpretation of his own data provides an interesting starting point. The author concluded his study by pointing to the existence of a 'systemic discrimination' in the field of Canadian politics, a discrimination that 'is likely anchored in a form of cultural imperialism that is pernicious precisely and especially because it ignores the process at play. This study clearly demonstrates that power relations are . . . exercised in the field of science' (Rocher, 2007: 849). What is the nature of these power relations?

> The fact of ignoring, or worse, excluding a significant portion of scholarly works in the analysis and understanding of the Canadian reality is problematic in many regards; it produces biased representation of social reality, and leads to tendencies to universalize the research questions of the dominant group, thereby marginalizing a group of scholars systematically discriminated against, while contributing to a disproportional increase of the influence of scholars who already serve as the social actors through which public authorities define both problems and solutions before them, even if their influence might be indirect or diffuse. In short, this phenomenon illustrates the manner in which representations of social and political reality are constructed in Canada, as the point of view of francophone scholars is only rarely taken in consideration. (Ibid.)

Rocher's view can be applied to the field of Canadian foreign policy. But it is possible to extend the argument further.

As noted in the introduction to this chapter, there is a very common belief, in both French and English Canada, that the two linguistic communities nurture distinct views about foreign policy. According to that common wisdom, French-speaking Canadians (or Québécois—and the difference between the two is rarely acknowledged) are more pacifist than their English-speaking co-citizens. In its most malign incarnation, this distinction has led to accusations that Quebecers' foreign policy attitudes are anti-Semitic or proto-terrorist, as was the case in the summer of 2006 during the Israeli bombing in Lebanon.[13]

This kind of idea (false, from this author's perspective) could also be part of a cultural explanation. Since it is widely believed that French-speakers have different views about foreign policy, and that these views can be disturbing, a sort of cultural barrier could dissuade researchers from looking at the French literature if they have no obligation to. Hence, the perception of a difference in values and visions leads to discrimination, which in turn reinforces that perception of difference because it deprives researchers of the occasion to change their minds.

This cultural misunderstanding may have various consequences. One of the most important is probably that English-speaking researchers are deprived of a large and potentially rich pool of ideas and data. Another is the fact that this lack of knowledge is a real problem when the time comes to address some delicate issue, such as the Quebec–Ottawa relationship on the international stage or the future of the federation itself. But the worst consequence is probably that the cultural misunderstanding nourishes false perceptions that make prejudices and extreme positions possible.

Acknowledgements
The author would like to express his gratitude to Jérémie Cornut (Ph.D. candidate, Political Science, UQAM) and Jean-Christophe Boucher (Ph.D. candidate, Political

Science, Université Laval) for data-gathering and interpretation. A special thanks to Dr Samantha Arnold (University of Winnipeg) for her comments and advice, and to Dr Kim Richard Nossal (Queen's University) and Dr Bruno Charbonneau (Laurentian University) for their remarks.

Notes

1. Rocher (2007: 841–2) assessed the contribution of French-speaking authors in his field as 20 per cent of the total, but this figure is based on the percentage of SSHRC grants received by French-speaking authors and the percentage of French-speaking academics among those who identify themselves as participating in the field of 'Canadian Studies'. Thus, this figure does not reflect their real contribution in terms of publications.

2. In order to avoid 'interferences', books authored or co-authored by French-speakers were left out. In the case of edited volumes, chapters written by French-speaking authors were also left out. For example, chapters by Michaud (1, 17, and 19), Tessier and Fortmann (8), Bernier (9), Mace (10), and Turenne Sjolander (15) in Nossal and Michaud, *Diplomatic Departures: The Conservative Era in Canadian Foreign Policy, 1984–93* (2001), were not surveyed. Edited volumes including even one francophone co-editor and using a single final bibliography were left out.

3. As a comparison, Rocher (2007: 842–3) got an average of 7.5 per cent and a median of 4.9 per cent. The reader must also keep in mind that the median is calculated on the basis of N = 33 (number of books/issues). A calculation with N = 244 is simply too close to zero!

4. In the latter document (Clark, 1985), national unity ranked first among the six priorities, but the issue is not addressed anywhere in the document.

5. Including 38 documents authored by scholars teaching outside Canada, mainly in the US.

6. Including six documents by scholars teaching outside of Canada and 17 written in English.

7. An easy counter-argument here could be that English Canadians are also deeply concerned by the consequences of any weakening of national unity.

8. A good example of this is the book published by Harder and Patten on *The Chrétien Legacy* (2006). One chapter, written by Robert Young, deals with the national unity issue but does not talk about foreign policy, and the chapter dedicated to foreign policy, written by Tom Keating, does not address national unity. For an example of the opposite, see Fraser (2005).

9. For the American reaction, see Lisée (1990: 335–9).

10. The sovereignist strategy to get international recognition after a 'yes' in the 1995 referendum is described in detail in Duchesne (2006). See also Cardinal (2005); Nossal et al. (2007: 593–7).

11. Among the rare exceptions in this regard is Lisée (1990).

12. The classic statement of this can be found in Bercuson and Cooper (1991). For a more international perspective, see Black (1997–8).

13. On this episode, see Boucher and Roussel (2007). In this case, the most important point is not that some columnists made accusations of anti-Semitism, but the fact that very few voices were raised in English Canada to oppose them.

Appendix: Sample on Canadian Foreign Policy (1997–2007)

1. Journals
Canadian Foreign Policy: volumes 6 (1998–9), 9 (2001–2), and 13 (2006) = 9 issues
International Journal: volumes 53 (1997–8), 57 (2001–2), and 61 (2005–6) = 12 issues

2. Monographs
Clarkson, S. 2002. *Uncle Sam and Us: Globalization, Neoconservatism, and the Canadian State*. Toronto and Washington: University of Toronto Press and Woodrow Wilson Center Press.

Cohen, A. 2003. *While Canada Slept: How We Lost Our Place in the World*. Toronto: McClelland & Stewart.

Cooper, A.F. 2004. *Tests of Global Governance: Canadian Diplomacy and United Nations World Conferences*. New York: United Nations University Press.

English, A.D. 2004. *Understanding Military Culture: A Canadian Perspective*. Montreal and Kingston: McGill-Queen's University Press.

Gammer, N. 2001. *From Peacekeeping to Peacemaking: Canada's Response to the Yugoslav Crisis*. Montreal and Kingston: McGill-Queen's University Press.

Haglund, D.G. 2000. *The North Atlantic Triangle Revisited: Canadian Grand Strategy at Century's End*. Toronto: CIIA.

Inwood, G.J. 2005. *Continentalizing Canada: The Politics and Legacy of the Macdonald Royal Commission*. Toronto: University of Toronto Press.

Mahant, E., and G.S. Mount. 1999. *Invisible and Inaudible in Washington: American Policies toward Canada*. Vancouver: University of British Columbia Press.

Melakopides, C. 1998. *Pragmatic Idealism: Canadian Foreign Policy, 1945–1995*. Montreal and Kingston: McGill-Queen's University Press.

Simpson, E. 2001. *NATO and the Bomb: Canadian Defenders Confront Critics*. Montreal and Kingston: McGill-Queen's University Press.

Sloan, E. 2002. *The Revolution in Military Affairs: Implications for Canada and NATO*. Montreal and Kingston: McGill-Queen's University Press.

Stevenson, B.J.R. 2000. *Canada, Latin America and the New Internationalism*. Montreal and Kingston: McGill-Queen's University Press.

Welsh, J. 2005. *At Home in the World: Canada's Global Vision for the 21st Century*. Toronto: Harper Collins.

3. Edited volumes
Cooper, A.F., and G. Hayes, eds. 2000. *Worthwhile Initiatives? Canadian Mission-Oriented Diplomacy*. Toronto: Irwin. (8 chapters, 1 left aside)

Irwin, R., ed. 2001. *Ethics and Security in Canadian Foreign Policy*. Vancouver: University of British Columbia Press. (14 chapters)

McRae, R., and D. Hubert, eds. 2001. *Human Security and the New Diplomacy*. Montreal and Kingston: McGill-Queen's University Press.

Michaud, N., and K.R. Nossal, eds. 2001. *Diplomatic Departures: The Conservative Era in Canadian Foreign Policy, 1984–93*. Vancouver: University of British Columbia Press. (12 chapters, 7 left aside)

4. Canada Among Nations: 1997 to 2006 (10 volumes)
Totals:
• 13 books
• 195 chapters in edited volumes (including 137 from *Canada Among Nations*)
• 58 journal articles
Sample includes 266 different texts. Number of references = 7,844

5. Books and chapters from French-speaking authors added for comparison
Michaud, N., and K.R. Nossal, eds. 2001. *Diplomatic Departures: The Conservative Era in Canadian Foreign Policy, 1984–93*. Vancouver: University of British Columbia Press. (7 chapters by French-speaking authors)
Roussel, S. 2004. *The North American Democratic Peace: Absence of War and Security Institution-Building in Canada–US Relations, 1867–1958*. Montreal and Kingston: McGill-Queen's University Press.
Roussel, S., ed. 2007. *Culture stratégique et politique de défense. L'expérience canadienne*. Montréal: Athéna.
Plus 9 chapters from *Canada Among Nations*.
Total: 1 book plus 19 chapters

Chapter Thirteen

At Home on Native Land

Canada and the United Nations Declaration on the Rights of Indigenous Peoples

J. Marshall Beier

A recurrent theme of this volume has been a critique of the very project of foreign policy analysis itself. This is not to say that foreign policy analysis—that is, the examination of the details, sources, and determinants of the diplomacies performed by states—is not important or that it should be abandoned. Rather, the point, as it emerges from the various contributions to this volume, is that a preoccupation with foreign policy alone gives us only one part of a much bigger picture. Of course, this can fairly be said of anything we might ever care to study, all of which will necessarily be nested in still broader contexts, and so it is unavoidable that lines must eventually be drawn. The question, then, is not whether it is reasonable to have drawn lines but whether the lines thus drawn are reasonable. Seeking an answer to this question suggests still others. Do the boundaries we have set for ourselves cause us to miss seeing things that bear directly and in meaningful ways on that which we have singled out for investigation? Are the things excluded so significant in their own right that a strong case can be made to include them? To what extent do the lines we have drawn appear as arbitrary once we take account of what lies beyond them? And, perhaps most important of all for students of politics, what circulations of power account for these lines and whose interests do they serve?

This chapter pursues these questions through an area of inquiry more often treated as domestic politics and seldom taken up in the study of Canada's presence and position in the international sphere: Indigenous peoples' politics. This is also an area, however, where the sub-field of foreign policy analysis cannot fairly be said to lag significantly behind the rest of International Relations since an awareness of the importance of Indigenous politics has only recently begun to take root in the field. What this nascent area of inquiry has begun to reveal is something of the arbitrariness of our traditional preoccupation with the state and the persistent centring of state politics even when a somewhat broader understanding of 'the international' is adopted. The challenge here turns out to be one that speaks not only to the traditional realist and liberal approaches, but also to critical ones in a variety of ways (Beier, 2005). Among other things, it suggests that critical scholars have erred in ceding the ground of foreign policy analysis to the conceptual mainstream and that this lapse arises from the failure to imagine diplomacy as something much more varied and multi-sited than what pertains to the interactions of states alone. A focus on foreign policy—the preserve of states—may be one way to think about international diplomacies, but it need not be the only one. Still, this is a volume centrally concerned with Canadian foreign policy, and so, the questions above are posed by way of a major change in Canada's position on the historic United Nations Declaration on the Rights of Indigenous Peoples. As we shall see, the past, present, and imaginable future of Indigenous peoples' international political engagements stand as a formidable challenge to the very fundamentals of our accustomed understanding of diplomacy itself, revealing it to be arbitrary and contingent. In regard to our field of study, they enjoin us to think about how we imagine the limits of global diplomacy when we privilege foreign policy, and why.

Continuity and Change

On 29 June 2006, at the first session of the recently renamed United Nations Human Rights Council, Canada adopted a position that would have seemed almost unthinkable just months earlier. On that day, Canada joined Russia in voting against the UN Draft Declaration on the Rights of Indigenous Peoples. Little over a year later, when the Declaration was adopted in September 2007 by the UN General Assembly by a vote of 143–4, with 11 abstentions, Canada was joined by New Zealand, Australia, and the United States in casting the only negative votes (Russia was among the abstentions). With this move, Canada placed itself in a tiny minority of countries opposed to a historic current that has been gaining considerable momentum. It also signalled the sum and substance of its evolving foreign policy position with respect to Indigenous peoples worldwide. The decision by Stephen Harper's Conservative government to reverse Canada's stance of many years followed, somewhat ironically, on the steady growth of Indigenous voices in global politics since at least the early 1990s. Increasingly, the global political initiatives enacted by Indigenous peoples have affected outcomes on a range of important issues and in a manner without historical precedent. In just one of many examples with a particular relevance to Canada, the international diplomatic campaign begun by the Labrador Innu in the late 1980s in an effort to halt NATO low-level flight training over northern Labrador and Quebec marked something of a triumph when it began to draw the support even of NATO governments. The significance of this can scarcely be gainsaid, given the long history of often outright refusals by states to take seriously and engage Indigenous diplomacies. The global ascendancy of these and other diplomatic practices and initiatives has also come at a time when a number of important treaty-related issues have been before the Canadian courts and, importantly, emerges amid the enduring echoes of a call in the 1996 *Report of the Royal Commission on Aboriginal Peoples* for a 'restructured relationship' between Canada and its First Nations—one to be founded upon 'recognition of Aboriginal nationhood'.

It is important to acknowledge, however, that the developments of the last couple of decades do not bespeak a new move by Indigenous peoples to assert a presence as global political actors. It is not just in the present context that the inter-national diplomacies of Indigenous peoples have been conceived and enacted. Much to the contrary, Indigenous peoples the world over have complex and comprehensive diplomatic traditions that long predate the arrival of outside colonial powers in their environs. From time immemorial, Indigenous societies in Africa, the Americas, and elsewhere interacted to establish and sustain trade relations, to manage and resolve conflict, to ensure access to resources, and so forth. In short, they performed diplomacies that gave shape and content to fully functioning inter-national systems. Though they operated without the particular form of organized political community we know as the state, they nevertheless proved through the colonial era to be quite amenable to opening and sustaining relations with states, limited only by the ebb and flow of the European states' willingness to recognize them across different sites and moments of the colonial encounter. Drawing on unique and decidedly non-Western philosophical and cosmological traditions, Indigenous diplomacies are more than mere artifacts of a bygone historical era. Rather, they and the possibilities they embody remain inextricably a part of traditional knowledges and lifeways that, though not unaffected by colonialism, endure to greater or lesser extents for many Indigenous peoples. They are very much parts of the present global political landscape, even if marginalized ones, and they shape contemporary inter-national political interactions both with states and between Indigenous peoples themselves.

It is also not the case that those systems of interaction and diplomacy have only recently reached beyond their immediate or traditional environs to interface more globally. In pre-colonial Australia, Indigenous networks of exchange extended over thousands of kilometres and, with circuits reaching even into Southeast Asia, also served to activate and sustain social networks between distant peoples (de Costa, 2007). Throughout the period of European global colonial expansion, Indigenous peoples sent delegations to the royal courts of Europe both to plead particular cases and to formalize relations. In the Americas in particular, states responded with formalizations of their own by concluding treaties with Indigenous peoples—a practice otherwise reserved to the management of relationships between states and empires. In the early 1920s the traditionalist Iroquois leader Levi General, who was known by the title Deskaheh, on behalf of the Six Nations of Grand

River Territory sought sovereignty and recognition for his people and travelled to Europe on an Iroquois passport to gain backing for his people's cause at the League of Nations. In this he succeeded, and a number of nations, including Ireland, Panama, Persia, the Netherlands, and Norway, supported his diplomatic efforts, which were explicitly founded on established practices and precedents of Indigenous–European diplomatic interaction. The British and Canadians, however, were less than enthusiastic about Deskaheh's diplomatic mission, effectively quashing it by claiming this to be a domestic matter, and on his return after more than a year of overseas diplomacy, Deskaheh was denied re-entry to Canada: the Six Nations leader spent the last months of his life on a reservation near Niagara Falls, New York, where he died in 1925 (Belanger, 2007; Dickason, with McNab, 2009: 337–8). Indigenous diplomacies such as this, in many and varied ways, have been performed globally over many centuries.

And this begins to suggest an answer to the questions posed above concerning the boundaries we have set for ourselves in the study of Canadian foreign policy and in the field of foreign policy analysis more generally. The almost complete neglect of Indigenous diplomacies by mainstream and critical scholars alike has left out an important part of the bigger picture, even if the focus remains confined to the diplomatic histories of states alone. But before turning more directly to the case for revisiting the boundaries that have wrought this exclusion, it is necessary to say something more about the developments of recent years, which seem certainly to have captured the attention of states themselves, even if scholars have not been quite as quick to acknowledge them.

From Indigenous Globalism to Global Indigenism

An implicit assumption of much realist- and liberal-inspired International Relations scholarship is that the state is the guarantor of security for those who reside within. This assumption underwrites the moral basis for legitimacy in treating the state as not only the central unit of analysis but also the referent object of security—i.e., as that which is to be secured. The state is thus made a bearer of rights and of interests and, in turn, must be able to sustain a persuasive claim to guarantee the rights and advance the interests of those over whom it exercises dominion if this legitimacy is to be upheld. In order that it can fulfill this duty, the state itself must be secured from threat. This much, at least, seems quite obvious, and so the logic giving rise to the preoccupation with the state makes a great deal of sense on its own terms. If the state is the guarantor of rights and security, it stands to reason that the predations of other states are the foremost threat to be addressed in safeguarding these. To the extent that this logic prevails, the interface between states would certainly appear to be the point at which the problematic of security is most fruitfully addressed. The fly in the ointment, however, is that all of this is premised on what is ultimately an abstraction that presumes the rights and interests of the state to be, if not always congruent with, at least compatible with those of the people(s) in whose name it would proclaim its sovereignty. What, then, of instances where the state can be characterized as the problem and not the solution?

Where there is significant disenfranchisement, it can be said that there is also a challenge to the authority and sovereign legitimacy of the state. This is especially so when the state itself is in some essence understandable as a threat to the security and well-being of those who are disenfranchised. This possibility has occasioned much rethinking of the central preoccupation with the state in the field of security studies since the early 1990s. Indeed, one of the first major shifts giving rise to what has since come to be categorized under the increasingly broad rubric of 'critical security studies' (see, e.g., Krause and Williams, 1997) was a near wholesale abandonment of the state as the referent object of security. As Charles Tilly (1985) has suggested, the very logic of the state as protector is immediately suspect since no other human endeavour expends more blood and treasure than that most extreme measure by which states seek to ensure security: war. More particularly, however, there has been no shortage of examples of states directly and purposively menacing the security and well-being of specific groups and even large populations within their borders. In these instances, to privilege the security of the state is to hide from view the often profound insecurity of disenfranchised groups within. And this is a key reason why self-consciously critical scholarship in International Relations has moved beyond the preoccupation with the state and has worked to populate our understanding of global politics with a much wider range of subjects, including individuals and non-state groups, even if, as noted in the Introduction to this volume, the field of foreign policy analysis has been somewhat slower to embrace the change.

Interestingly, in the world of actual international diplomatic practice, some of the most significant developments of recent years do seem to recognize that when the state becomes the threat, that which ensures its security works contrary to the security of those who are imperilled. This has come to include even sovereignty. The human security vision championed by Canada and made central to expressions of the country's foreign policy, especially under Foreign Minister Lloyd Axworthy through the latter half of the 1990s, already reflected a move towards a broader conception of the referent objects of security. But even more extraordinary has been the increasing willingness of states to override the sovereign right of other members of the states system—sacrosanct for centuries—and intervene in defence of human rights where the state in question is deemed unwilling or unable to do so itself. Now famously cast as the 'Responsibility to Protect', this, too, has owed much to Canadian international diplomatic efforts. These developments, which have tended to place more emphasis on the liberal notion of corresponding obligations as the flip side of rights where states are concerned, bespeak a recognition that the idea of the state as the guarantor of rights and interests is no longer as uncritically accepted as it once was. And this, in turn, suggests a moment of historic opportunity for those with a case to press against the status quo of state power and who are able to make their presence felt in global political forums to do just that.

As to the first of these two criteria, Indigenous peoples have long historical grievances originating in the European conquest and colonial domination of the non-European world. Even with formal 'decolonization' of parts of Asia and Africa, institutions (not least of all the state) and legacies of colonialism have remained very much intact, often continuing to frustrate hopes for Indigenous self-determination and in ways contrary to traditional forms of social and political life. This is all the more so where the advanced European settler state is firmly entrenched as, for example, in North America and Australia. At the same time, Indigenous peoples typically do not find their interests well represented by the state inasmuch as the aim of self-determination characteristic of so many Indigenous political struggles conflicts with states' monopoly on sovereignty and, again, the state form of political organization is often itself anathema to traditional lifeways. There is also a case to be made that, in human security terms at least, the status quo of ongoing subjugation by states constitutes a palpable material threat to Indigenous peoples the world over, who suffer significantly higher than average rates of poverty, disease, and suicide (Stidsen and Dahl, 2006). In many places, including Canada, they are over-represented among victims of violence, including political violence, and are incarcerated in numbers disproportionate to their share of overall populations. Even where recognized and officially guaranteed, Indigenous peoples' rights to land, resources, and distinct cultural and spiritual practices are all too often abridged, assailed, or ignored altogether (ibid.).

Though they may manifest in new ways, these are not new problems. Rather, they all have their historical antecedents dating to the earliest days of colonial conquest and domination. As noted above, Indigenous peoples' inter-national diplomacies also are not new. What is new is the considerable degree of success they have enjoyed in gaining a legitimate speaking position to press their own rights and interests in global political fora since the latter part of the twentieth century. Here there is what can be described as a significant historical rupture of the near-complete refusal by states since at least the late nineteenth century to take Indigenous peoples seriously as bona fide global political actors. Though the history of treaty-making (again, an exercise that involves mutual recognition by two sovereign entities) stands as an important historical precedent supporting Indigenous peoples' contemporary claims, the ultimate failure to honour so many treaty obligations invites the charge that they were more in the way of an expedient cynically conceived by the settler societies. In Canada, for example, it made economic, political, and military sense to expropriate land through the treaty process rather to engage in costly armed adventures such as the 'Indian Wars' south of the border. In many instances, however, a resort to force seems to have been preferred by states because it existed as a viable alternative. For its part, the United States Congress passed legislation in 1871 banning treaty-making with Indigenous peoples—not coincidentally, this was followed in short order by the climactic and, it turned out, decisive years of the much mythologized 'Indian Wars' on the Great Plains. Decades later, the attempt by Indigenous peoples to gain standing at the League of Nations was opposed and blocked by states (Niezen, 2003: 31–6). Indeed, though it constitutes only one (albeit crucial) dimension of their many and varied diplomatic histories, the centuries-long record of Indigenous peoples' efforts to engage states in international diplomatic liaison has met mostly with disappointment, failure, and even outright treachery.

By the middle of the twentieth century, the seeds of change were planted as the host of ills suffered by Indigenous peoples began to figure more prominently on the agenda at the United Nations. The first hints of a recognition of 'group rights' in the emergent UN human rights regime following World War II opened a space for this. However, the emphasis was still strongly on individual rights and, through instruments such as the 1966 Covenant on Civil and Political Rights, could accommodate discussion of Indigenous peoples only as racial, linguistic, or religious minorities. Importantly, this preserved the notion of the singular state as the guarantor of rights and security inasmuch as it affirmed the duty of each signatory state to ensure rights on behalf of such groups within areas of its sovereign control. It did not entail or imply the possibility that such groups constituted inter-national or global political subjects. Indigenous peoples could be conceived as an 'issue area', but not as global political actors in their own right.

In the summer of 1982, something of a qualitative break with this history became discernible as Indigenous peoples' delegations from around the world arrived in Geneva to take part in the first meeting of the United Nations Working Group on Indigenous Populations. Lacking the material resources that sustain the usual conventions and, no less, the trappings of state diplomacies, many of the delegates might have seemed unlikely diplomats. Tony Black Feather and Garfield Grass Rope of the Tetuwan Oyate, or Lakota Nation, for example, did not enjoy grand hotels, fine restaurants, or chauffeured transportation during their stay—able to attend on only small private donations, they stayed in a homeless shelter, ate at a soup kitchen, and travelled on foot to the UN meetings. But however modest their means, they were the first to have standing at the UN on behalf of the Teton Sioux Nation Treaty Council, which was first established in 1895 to carry forward the international diplomacies of the Tetuwan Oyate.

Taking this longer view of things, the pace of change was something less than glacial, having taken nearly a century before the Teton Sioux Nation Treaty Council could begin to fulfill its founding vision. But little more than a decade after Tony Black Feather and Garfield Grass Rope first arrived in Geneva, the UN General Assembly endorsed a 'Decade of the World's Indigenous Peoples' (1995–2004) and, just eight months after that endorsement, the Sub-Commission on Prevention of Discrimination and Protection of Minorities adopted a Draft Declaration on the Rights of Indigenous Peoples (forerunner to the text eventually opposed by the Harper government in 2006). All of this remained under the auspices of the UN Economic and Social Council and thus decidedly subordinate to the sovereign right of states. Indigenous peoples had nevertheless achieved an important degree of standing at the UN, which, by 2000, was formalized in the Permanent United Nations Forum on Indigenous Issues; remarkably, states and Indigenous peoples have been apportioned equal voting weight in this forum. Although still not free of the tethers of their initial construction as a human rights 'issue area', Indigenous peoples had broken the state monopoly on the speaking position through which their rights and interests could be engaged at the UN.

As all of this was unfolding, Canada was initially at the forefront among states in terms of institutional readiness to engage Indigenous diplomacies. Already in the mid-1980s, a desk was set up at External Affairs Canada (now DFAIT) by career diplomat Wayne Lord to deal with international Indigenous issues. Lord then served as Departmental Coordinator for International Aboriginal Affairs in the Human Rights Division of DFAIT through the mid-1990s and, in 1998, became Director of a new eight-person Division of Aboriginal and Circumpolar Affairs. Only in New Zealand was anything like this Division established as part of a foreign ministry, and there its mission was largely confined to cultural activities. The Canadian unit, by way of contrast, grew out of the Human Rights Division and was consequently much more explicitly amenable to engaging Indigenous diplomacies for which space had been opening by way of the UN human rights regime. Without overstating the case—states, including Canada, still worked to contain the extent and implications of an Indigenous role in global politics short of anything like a sovereign right (Niezen, 2003: 164–5; Beier, 2007: 124–5)—there is no disputing that a historic change has been marked by the unprecedented extent to which Indigenous peoples have come to be recognized as global political actors not only at the UN, but also by the International Labour Organization, the World Bank, the Inter-American Development Bank, the Arctic Council, the Organization of American States, and others. It is the achievement of this audible speaking position that is the change of truly historic importance.

Recalling the long history of denial and exclusion of Indigenous peoples from the hegemonic circuits of diplomacy, what accounts for the change of fortune in recent years? If Indigenous diplomacies and the resolve to carry them to the states system are not new, how has their unprecedented global reach and audibility been achieved in recent years? Franke Wilmer (1993) suggests that its sources lie in changes in the normative basis of the international system itself, from *realpolitik* to self-determination as a fundamental ordering principle. This, according to Wilmer, has resulted in an overall climate more agreeable to the essentially normative claims of Indigenous peoples on issues such as autonomy, historical birthright, and redress of the legacies of colonialism. The fact that the point of entry for Indigenous diplomacies has been through the UN human rights regime would certainly seem to lend support to this view. It is also noteworthy in this regard that Canada's response comes nested in DFAIT's Human Rights Division. Karena Shaw (2002), however, cautions against fashioning an account that, in effect, writes Indigenous peoples out of this history by locating the important sources of change in the *sui generis* evolution of a European idea: sovereignty. To do so is, ironically, to re-centre the state and to miss seeing Indigenous people as authors of what has been achieved in recent years.

Following Shaw, an evolving international system is only part of the story and seems to be more in the way of a necessary than a sufficient condition—that is, attenuating some barriers to change, but not the historical motor force per se. Rather, the change of historic proportions issues from the global political agency of Indigenous peoples themselves. In this sense, it is a change *reflected* in the establishment of an international Indigenous affairs desk at External Affairs Canada in 1990s, but was first signalled by the arrival of Tony Black Feather, Garfield Grass Rope, and others in Geneva in August 1982. This is not to say that Indigenous global political agency dawned at that point. As discussed above, Indigenous peoples have long, varied, and rich diplomatic histories. Even through the colonial encounter, this agency was actively exercised despite having been so rebuffed by states for centuries. Through most of this history, however, these efforts have constituted what might be best described as 'Indigenous globalism'. That is, the many diplomatic initiatives mounted by Indigenous peoples certainly evinced a global outlook, but these initiatives tended to be in the manner of relatively separate appeals to state power and the hegemonic institutions of global governance without any significant degree of co-ordination among them. In this sense, they can be thought of as disaggregated vertical insertions into a dominant power structure that was not inclined, and could not be impelled, to recognize them.

What has taken hold during the last several decades, however, is better described as 'global indigenism' and is distinguished from 'Indigenous globalism' in that it arises out of complex networks of horizontal connections among Indigenous peoples. For example, the American Indian Movement in the US was influential in politicizing Canadian Aboriginal leaders in the late 1960s, which led to their overwhelmingly negative response to the government's 1969 White Paper on Indian policy, and in 1999 the leaders of Canada's Assembly of First Nations and the National Congress of American Indians signed a far-reaching protocol for co-operation on political, trade, and human rights issues (Dickason, with McNab, 2009: 371–2; Dickason, 2006: 294). These are contemporary expressions of the rich traditions of Indigenous diplomacies with origins long predating the onset of colonialism. But global indigenism is also much more than the sum of its parts. It inheres in networks of interaction and exchange renewed between Indigenous peoples themselves and developed to the point where a truly global network of networks has emerged and is institutionalized in transnational organizations including, but not limited to, the International Indian Treaty Council, the Indigenous Peoples of Africa Coordinating Committee, and the Inuit Circumpolar Council. In combination with more localized organizations like the Assembly of First Nations or the Teton Sioux Nation Treaty Council, these complex networks have enabled the breakthroughs of recent years because they have made it impossible to maintain denial of the authentic and well-functioning political communities and bona fide global political agency in which they are rooted. They also constitute a sophisticated and dynamic world of inter-national diplomatic interaction almost entirely overlooked by both mainstream and critical scholarship in the field of foreign policy analysis.

Whose Diplomacy?

It should come as no surprise that state-centric approaches to the study of International Relations have paid little attention to non-state forms of political community and their place in global politics. As noted at the outset of this chapter, lines have to be drawn somewhere and the conceptual mainstream of our discipline has elected to confine its focus in such a way as to privilege the state. If one accepts the assumptions that inform this choice, it is not necessarily more problematic than any other set of exclusions we might make. As Robert Cox (1986: 207) has famously observed, 'theory is always for someone and for some purpose', and the problem-solving approaches of the mainstream are concerned first and foremost with the global political status quo, its own particular features, and, variously, how to survive (realism) or live well (liberalism) in it. But critical approaches, as described in the Introduction to this volume, do not, to paraphrase Cox (ibid., 208), take the world as they find it. Instead, they seek to unsettle our comfortable assumptions and to reveal how power works through those assumptions in ways that make us its accomplice. It is therefore a startling omission indeed for critical approaches to have paid so little attention to Indigenous diplomacies. That they have not owes much to having so widely opted to quit the field of foreign policy analysis and to direct their gaze elsewhere in the realms of global politics where the state is perhaps less centrally at issue. But I would like to suggest that something of a critical lapse in this move deserves a bit more comment.

Critical scholars have tended to see a global political terrain populated by many more kinds of actors than state-centric models have allowed. Accordingly, a host of alternative foci have been seen in critical scholarship, many residing in what has come to be called 'global civil society'. At the same time, the line between the global and the local is blurred as critical scholars urge us to see that, for example, hegemonic global power depends vitally on sources as seemingly remote from the 'high politics' of international relations as prostitution or migrant domestic workers (Enloe, 1989). For many, disrupting the status quo of power relations does not mean merely to seize and reapportion that power but to seek for the empowerment of those who have been marginalized or excluded. Something similar can be said of Indigenous peoples' claims for autonomy and self-determination, which typically do not amount to a call for sovereign statehood. Even where it has taken place, decolonization and the proliferation of statehood have not been synonymous with an end to domination over Indigenous peoples. At the same time, though it has certain affinities with all of them, global indigenism is not comfortably subsumed under global civil society, emergent global forms of protest and resistance (such as the anti-globalization movement), or other issue-oriented movements, however complex and integrated their networks.

Residing in what Kevin Bruyneel (2007) has described as a 'third space of sovereignty', a notion signifying that the politics of indigeneity is located neither wholly within nor wholly without the state, Indigenous peoples' claims are simultaneously addressed to and against the state. Unlike other activist networks and movements, they are also characterized by a visceral connection to land in the sense of a relationship between a people and a place that is felt to be inviolable. Though inextricably bound up in the political systems of the states that have come to exercise suzerainty over them, they nevertheless may not be beholden to the state in the same manner as other citizens. Rather, they assert a position of at least relative autonomy backed by historical claims to nationhood, international law, and sometimes varying circumstances and degrees of recognition by the state itself. This sits uneasily with an international human rights regime wherein states are the guarantors of rights to, principally, individuals since the 'rights' at issue are often fundamentally collective ones and the foremost barrier to their ultimate fulfillment is the imposition of the colonial state itself. In this sense, the state may rightly be regarded less as a guarantor of rights than as a bearer of opposing rights. Many Indigenous peoples consequently resist colonial domination over their lives in ways that mark out the state as object of resistance. It is not difficult to see, therefore, why the global political engagements of Indigenous peoples stand somewhat apart from those of other non-state actors for whom the state is more likely to be invested with hope that it might serve as a vehicle to advance their cause or aspirations.

For all of these reasons, it is important to engage global indigenism as diplomacies, albeit of a qualitatively different sort from those practised by states. This involves more than populating global politics with more actors. It is a belated recognition that the world of inter-national diplomacies already includes more actors and a wider array of practices than our disciplinary conventions have left us inclined to acknowledge. It is also a consciously counter-hegemonic move inasmuch as it recognizes diplomacy as a privileged practice taking place in a well-resourced and privileged sphere. To cede this ground to states is simultaneously to reaffirm the kind of power that for so long rendered Indigenous diplomacies inaudible. It is also to allow one very particular set of human diplomatic practices originating in Europe to define other historical trajectories out of existence in much the same manner as discourses of 'civilization' and 'savagery' once worked to affirm the state as the only viable form of political community. Global indigenism, in contrast, calls into question the mainstream conceptions of what diplomacy is and whom it can be for, whose interests it can speak, and whose voices may legitimately speak them.

The position adopted by Canada in June 2006 was indicative of a status quo politics that not only resists Indigenous peoples' claims but also resists taking them seriously as global political actors, even within the relatively safe discursive confines of the UN Human Rights Council. P. Whitney Lackenbauer and Andrew F. Cooper (2007) have gone so far as to characterize this as the 'Achilles heel of Canadian good international citizenship'—a strong claim indeed, and one that brings clearly into relief the significance of global indigenism not only for Canadian foreign policy in its many particulars, but also, and in the most fundamental sense, for the role Canada has long sought to cultivate for itself in the world. Though there have been some more recent signs that the fraught relations between Indigenous peoples and the Harper government could see some improvement, such as the historic formal apology given by Prime Minister Harper in June 2008 for the cultural and personal damage caused by residential schools in Canada, the position taken in June 2006 and September 2007 will have enduring significance for having placed Canada in the company of a small minority of states resisting what can fairly be characterized as a current of historic change. And if the image of good international citizenship on which Canadian foreign policy has long traded is called into question by this, it seems most profoundly to be so because the Canadian state is here seen to place its conception of its own self-interest ahead of what seems a growing international consensus on vindication of the rights of a very broad category of marginalized peoples. Although government officials claimed that the Canadian state had to vote against the non-binding Declaration for constitutional reasons, the Aboriginal peoples in Canada clearly understood that this refusal to 'do the right thing' was based on a fear of losing some state control over natural resources (Dickason, with McNab, 2009: 431–2).

A further consequence of all of this is that it treats as settled those questions regarding who or what count as legitimate actors in global politics and what may constitute meaningful diplomatic practices. In fact, these are not at all settled questions. Moreover, the failure to engage them in the field of foreign policy analysis is consistent with this same status quo politics. And this proposes an answer to the question posed at the beginning of this chapter concerning which circulations of power and whose interests are served by the boundaries we continue to draw for the field. But it is not just the conceptual mainstream that reproduces these boundaries. Implicit in the critical rejection of foreign policy analysis as a field is an acceptance of the dominant conception of diplomacy that has come to define it. This both allies foreign policy analysis with a conservative politics (and, therefore, also with status quo circulations of power that might be quite inequitable) and simultaneously impoverishes it as a field of study by cutting it off from an important and instructive set of diplomacies understood on much broader terms than within the narrow confines of state-to-state interaction alone.

This chapter, then, ends with a call for a critical refusal to surrender the fuller range of diplomatic possibilities and practices to a narrow state-centric conception of foreign policy alone. As critical scholars have done in security studies and elsewhere, the field of foreign policy analysis itself and of Canadian foreign policy in particular can be revealed to be enclosed spaces whose boundaries may obscure more than they bring into view, but this is not most fruitfully accomplished by taking the status quo at its word that diplomacy is the exclusive preserve of states. Rejecting this premise, as opposed to a wholesale rejection of the field, is imperative both to encourage critical scholarship and to address what otherwise amounts to critical complicity with the denials and erasures of Indigenous diplomacies. Though distinct from those of states, these diplomacies are every bit as meaningful.

Acknowledgements
Research for this chapter was supported by a grant from the Social Sciences and Humanities Research Council of Canada. For their generosity with their time, the author gratefully acknowledges the invaluable input of Charmaine White Face and members of the Aboriginal and Circumpolar Affairs Division of Foreign Affairs Canada.

Chapter Fourteen

Critical Conclusions about Canadian Foreign Policy

Lana Wylie

Introduction

Students of Canadian foreign policy often begin their academic careers in large lecture halls overflowing with other undergraduates, some of them eager to learn about Canadian actions on the world stage. For over 70 years, students in these courses have been told about Canada's role in World Wars I and II, how Canada has managed relations with the superpower to the South, about their government's proud history of peacekeeping and similar topics that frequently highlight how Canadian policy has made a difference in the world. In most cases, Canadian foreign policy has been presented unproblematically. Yet, though many undergraduates today might begin their university careers with unproblematic visions of Canadian foreign policy they do not always leave with the same views. What has changed? Certainly, large university classrooms look the same as they did 30 or 40 years ago (with the addition of an LCD screen or two), but the content has shifted. While students still learn the basic history and 'facts' about Canadian actions on the world stage, the teaching of these events is now increasingly infused with questions that ask students to problematize Canada's position internationally. Many courses not only add a week or two of critical analysis, but in some cases the entire course may be positioned so students learn to critically evaluate the whole of Canadian history in international affairs. Thus, though Canadian foreign policy is still being 'taught' in the traditional ways, students of the twenty-first century are also being taught to understand Canada's place in the world through an increasingly critical lens. This book reflects this evolution in the understanding and teaching of Canadian foreign policy.

This movement away from an exclusive focus on mainstream understandings in the classroom is also reflected in the academic literature. In the field of Canadian foreign policy we stand on the cusp of change. While we see that many scholars remain wedded to mainstream approaches that completely dominated the discipline in the not-so-distant past we can also see that the edges of the mainstream are being eroded. It is increasingly common for newer scholars to problematize the field in their research and writing. As such, in the last 10 years especially, there have been numerous very good journal articles, single-authored monographs, and one edited collection (on feminist approaches to Canadian foreign policy) that have attempted to expand our understanding of the field in this way. Yet, as evidence of the continued power of the mainstream, teachers of Canadian foreign policy did not have one book that looked at the field from a broadly critical perspective. This volume has attempted to fill this void by drawing on the work of many of the leading critical scholars in the field of Canadian foreign policy.

Disciplining and the Study of Canadian Foreign Policy

In Chapter 1, Heather Smith reflected on the disciplining nature of Canadian foreign policy. She asked us to consider whether we have ever been disciplined as we studied Canadian foreign policy. Have we been taught that there was one way or a limited number of correct ways to understand Canadian actions on the world stage? Her sense is that many of us, critical and mainstream scholars alike, have been disciplined in this way.

I would add that, too often when we have been taught a certain way over our academic careers, we don't realize we are being disciplined. We are simply being 'good' students, following the standards of evidence, methods, and good writing set down by our learned superiors. When we are rejected for thinking differently, we often fail to challenge the prevailing view and instead adapt our work based on the feedback. I did not begin my career by asking critical questions. I first learned Canadian foreign policy in the late 1980s and early 1990s from some very fine scholars who, because they were not exposed to critical analysis, did not ask us to ask the 'how possible' questions. I was effectively disciplined.

To this day my scholarship continues to be informed by these experiences. I admittedly have trouble not following the standards set forth over my career. That is not to say that I think now that I must always challenge those standards. I believe, as I expect do many in this volume, that there is incredible value in the 'mainstream' and in the 'traditional' ways of asking questions and studying a problem. Yet, I now realize that by not asking other kinds of questions I was seeing the world through a narrow lens.

Oddly enough, I came to critical approaches by following the standards of evidence and research set down by the mainstream. My Ph.D. dissertation research began with a typical mainstream research question. I set out to explain why the United States continued to isolate Cuba while Canada instead followed a policy of engagement. I began by looking in the traditional spaces of mainstream research. Perhaps, I thought, electoral politics explains the difference. Cuban-Americans hold immense influence over elections in Florida, and Florida is, after all, a swing state in presidential elections. Canada, on the other hand, does not have a significant Cuban immigrant population. In most of the scholarly literature on Cuban–US relations this explanation is well accepted and is even considered to be common sense (for more on the role of common sense in IR theory, see Kyle Grayson in this volume; Smith, 1996).

Yet, once I began to conduct my interviews in Washington, Ottawa, and Havana, I was amazed by the differences in the way Canadians and Americans saw the same issues, events, and people in Cuba and even understood the country itself. Here we had American and Canadian diplomats in Havana, often living close to each other, using the same grocery stores, visiting the same restaurants, and going to the same parties (having a good time isn't difficult in the diplomatic community in Havana), yet they told me very different stories about life in Havana and politics and society in Cuba.[1] Electoral politics could not explain these different perceptions, these different ideas of the 'truth'. I asked myself 'how is it possible' that the two accounts were so different. I thus opened the door to critical studies, though admittedly it was the back door and I wasn't sure what building I was entering when I did so. When my research revealed identity differences I had entered further into this unknown territory. I had discovered that Canadian and American perceptions of Cuba and their relationship with the Cuban state reflected their understandings of what it meant to be 'Canadian' or 'American'; or, in other words, their perceptions reflected their beliefs about 'the United States' and 'Canada' as international actors. Yet, when I explained my findings to many of my mainstream advisers and colleagues I was challenged. How could I 'prove' identity was the answer? Where were the empirical findings? I struggled. I drew on opinion polls and other 'legitimate' sources of evidence, and I kept trying to fit what I knew was my understanding of the 'answer' to my research question into traditional research boxes.

As I rewrite my dissertation manuscript for publication I continue to struggle with these questions. How do I speak to everyone (critical and mainstream scholars and students alike) and remain true to my understanding of the process at work? Thus, I write this concluding chapter as someone still not fully undisciplined, someone searching for answers to both the 'how possible' questions asked by critical scholarship and the other questions posed primarily by the mainstream. This also comes across in how I attempt to fulfill my role as co-editor of this volume. I find myself asking my co-editor, 'Can't this author be more forceful in her opinions?' or 'Shouldn't there be more empirical evidence to support his assertion?' I am then gently reminded that this is a critical volume and by reviewing the submissions in this way I am essentially trying to discipline these authors into the mainstream.

Critical Approaches and Their Critics

It is an uneasy task to group critical theorists together because there are significant differences between feminists, Marxists, post-colonialists, and others. There isn't one critical way of looking at any issue, problem, or case in foreign policy analysis. For example, Marxists and neo-Gramscians might highlight the capitalist or class underpinnings whereas feminists would reveal the gendered nature of the issue at hand. These and other critical approaches, however, share important characteristics. The chapters in this book remind us that critical scholars question the taken-for-granted assumptions of mainstream theorizing and political discourse. Ann Denholm Crosby, in Chapter 3, argues that the claims that realism and liberalism 'make about states and markets reflecting external, objective laws that govern social, political, and economic organization can only be made from inside those theoretical constructs themselves.' Critical perspectives help us see alternatives that are hidden within the narratives sketched by mainstream perspectives. By reformulating the idea of public diplomacy as foreign policy, rather than as a tool of foreign policy, Samantha Arnold, in Chapter 2, brings attention to practices that would otherwise go unnoticed. She demonstrates that public diplomacy is not just about projecting an already created identity abroad but also works to create the national identity at home. Thus, understanding public diplomacy as operating to produce a national brand for consumption at home as well as abroad contributes to a greater understanding of the range of strategies undertaken by the government. Thus, by seeing past these mainstream perspectives we begin to remove some of the limitations on our ability to imagine alternative ways of understanding and even doing foreign policy.

Likewise, rather than accepting the political discourse as it is presented, critical scholars question the assumptions underlying the practice of foreign policy. In Chapter 7, Kyle Grayson points out that the questions posed by the Department of Foreign Affairs and International Trade's 2003 *Dialogue on Foreign Policy* were based on the assumption that the three pillars of Canadian foreign policy outlined in *Canada in the World* had been guiding Canadian international behavior since they were articulated in 1995. Grayson reveals how this assumption implicitly narrowed the dialogue over Canadian foreign policy. Similarly, in Chapter 10 Mark Neufeld brings our attention to the way elites use myths in political discourse in an attempt to garner public support for their agendas. In particular, he shows how the myth of Lester B. Pearson has been employed in the debate about Canada's involvement in Afghanistan. Likewise, Claire Turenne Sjolander and Kathryn Trevenen, in Chapter 4, reveal that through evoking an image of Canada as a moral actor striving to protect the women and children of Afghanistan, the Canadian government effectively paints those opposing Canada's involvement in the conflict as content to ignore the suffering of these groups. Turenne Sjolander and Trevenen show that '[i]n the context of this moral outrage, critics of the war become the "real" enemy.' Critical voices thus help us recognize the silencing produced by these narratives. Critical approaches offer new and interesting ways of seeing the world, widening our understanding of the issue at hand and revealing the power structures that perpetuate inequalities. Thus, despite their significant differences, each approach turns our attention away from an exclusive focus on the state to the possibility that other actors, processes, or power relations might be involved in the formulation of foreign policy, and at the same time asks us to question the common-sense assumptions and practices.

Although academics are increasingly aware of the value of critical approaches to the field of International Relations and the analysis of foreign policy, in many circles these approaches are not only wildly misunderstood but dismissed as unworthy of serious scholars. Oxford University Press publishes a series of 'very short introductions' to many academic fields. Each volume summarizes a field in a 'Coles Notes' formula. In the 2007 *International Relations: A Very Short Introduction*, Paul Wilkinson spends less than one page (in his 144-page manual) to tell new IR scholars about critical approaches to the field. Under the label 'Postmodern deconstructionism' he writes:

> They claim to be able to 'deconstruct' the writings and discourse of academics and policy makers who interpret the world, including, of course, international relations. They believe that they are able, by the process of 'deconstruction', to uncover the underlying 'subjective' meanings and intentions of the texts in light of the social and cultural climate in which they were produced. Their depressing conclusion is that there is no objective international truth or reality we can discover. Hence instead of studying the real world of international relations they spend their time trying to reveal what they believe to be the 'distortions', 'subtexts', and 'deceptive' use of language in the texts in the 'conventional' literature. Paradoxically, the critical theorists who claim to use these methods spend all their time criticizing the authors of the texts, and have little or nothing to offer by way of independent criticism of the actual policies and actions of policy makers, either in their own countries or internationally—a clear case of self-destruction? (Wilkinson, 2007: 5)

Clearly, this is written by someone who has read very little, if any, of the critical scholarship available. This description is off base on many fronts. Critical scholars certainly engage with what Wilkinson would describe as 'the actual policies and actions of policy makers'. In this volume alone—to list only a few—the contributors tackle Canada's policy on nuclear weapons (Mutimer); the war in Afghanistan (Turenne Sjolander and Trevenen; Bell); Canadian border policy (Salter); circumpolar policies (Arnold); defence relations (Denholm Crosby). I am quite confident that Wilkinson himself would also consider these topics to be within his definition of the 'real world of international relations'.

Critical scholarship is also sometimes accused of ignoring questions of security or material well-being while overly focusing on normative issues, that is, the moral dimension of international relations, for example, the ethical behaviour of actors in the global arena. Indeed, normative concerns are central to much critical theorizing since many critical scholars, such as David Campbell (1993: 92), argue that 'ethics is indispensable to the very being of [a] subject.' Not only how we choose to study but the choice of what to study is value-laden. As such, all research is normative. Theories cannot be value-neutral. As Ann Denholm Crosby writes in Chapter 3:

> the dominant International Relations (IR) theoretical perspectives, realism and neo-liberalism, are culturally specific narratives about deeply rooted Western practices and knowledges rather than generic theories involving exogenously

given universals. As such, they provide rationales for the reproduction of Western relations of social, economic, and political power on a global basis. . . . these relations of power *inherently* produce vast insecurities for vast numbers of peoples. Directions for addressing these insecurities, then, do not, and cannot, reside in the theories that support their reproduction.

Critical theorists draw our attention to the often obscured normative aspects of our research and our theoretical perspectives.

However, that does not limit the topics that are studied by critical theorists. Those subjects considered by mainstream theorists to be the stuff of hard-power politics are well within the scope of critical scholarship. In fact, because critical scholars believe that all subjects are normative their scholarship reveals elements of hard-power politics that are obscured by the assumptions of mainstream research. These hidden elements, critical scholars point out, can be dangerous. In this volume Ann Denholm Crosby examines Canada–US defence relations. She argues that Canada's involvement in military co-operation that legitimates the US military's systems of mass control harms both North American and global security. She explains we must resist these systems and the military initiatives they facilitate on two levels, empirical and perspectival, which involves challenging recommendations and actions based in world views that also must be challenged. Thus, critical theory does not ignore questions of security but in many cases reveals the normative implications of the security issue under study. It provides an invaluable service in revealing the hidden dangers in seemingly benign policy choices and research practices.

Similarly, critical scholarship is accused of minimizing or even ignoring the role of the state. Rather than ignoring the state, critical scholarship points out that the mainstream has not given the state much, if any, sustained or effective thought. R.B.J. Walker's point on this is familiar to many of us. He writes:

> The worst caricatures of it [the state] are well known: the billiard ball or black box operating within a determinist mechanical system. . . . At the other extreme, there are finely detailed analyses of the foreign-policy making processes of individual states in which the state, as state, is dissolved in particularities. Even apart from these extremes, it would be difficult to argue that international political theory possesses anything like an adequate account of the nature of the state. (Walker, 1984: 531)

In these two mainstream caricatures, the state is accepted unproblematically. Far from not addressing the state, critical scholarship seeks greater understanding by problematizing the state. Even though Mark Salter, in Chapter 6, does not centre on the state as such, his examination of border policy first had to problematize the state in order to perceive the delocalization of the border into the domestic realm. Similarly, questioning the existence of the state as it is understood in the mainstream allows David Mutimer, in Chapter 8, to investigate the multiple Canadas in relation to nuclear weapons. Moreover, the traditional privileging of the state also results in the neglect of other kinds of global actors. In Chapter 13, J. Marshall Beier elucidates how our traditional preoccupation with the state and state politics limits our ability to imagine diplomacy as something that pertains not just to relations among states. He points out that although Indigenous peoples have long and varied *sui generis* diplomatic traditions, IR scholars have neglected Indigenous diplomacies. Thus, Beier shows us how our focus on the state has made us overlook a notable and sophisticated example of inter-national diplomatic interaction.

Likewise, why questioning the perceived truths and taken-for-granted assumptions of policy-makers and analysts of international relations is depressing, as Wilkinson has claimed, remains unclear. It is accurate to say that critical scholars often strive for epistemological self-awareness and therefore question the impact of their own and other scholars' theoretical starting points and personal views on their research and conclusions. Yet, that does not mean that the research or the conclusions are 'depressing'. For example, Kyle Grayson tackles the assumption of the mainstream that the debates over human security represent clear differences among scholars and policy-makers over the fundamental shape of Canadian foreign policy. He reveals that these debates reinforce commonalities in the ways in which scholars and practitioners of foreign policy view Canada's international role. He shows how both the soft-power and hard-power advocates share similar understandings; how the foreign policy approach taken by the Conservative government under Stephen Harper is not a drastic departure from the foreign policy of the Liberals steered by Foreign Minister Lloyd Axworthy in the late 1990s. The idea of human security fits nicely into the status quo of Canadian foreign policy and thus is easily adopted by both parties. He shows that Canadian foreign policy must move away from the current understandings of common sense to make a real difference in the world. While Grayson admits that changing Canadian foreign policy in this way is not a simple or easy task, his conclusions offer the possibility that we can implement the necessary changes and thereby make an important difference in the international arena. His conclusions are thus far from depressing—they offer hope for a better future for Canadians and the world. Rather than being depressing, critical research often offers alternatives and possibilities for a different and perhaps improved world.

Critical approaches not only address the same kinds of problems, issues, and cases as mainstream approaches, but also address issues outside of the terrain of mainstream scholarship. They open the spaces for unconventional subjects and methods. In Chapter 9, Alison Howell examines the prevalence of post-traumatic stress disorder in the Canadian Forces. She addresses the politics of this important issue, which is most often considered a social or medical problem, by asking why a neglected painting featuring a soldier suffering from shell shock became the centrepiece of military publications and displays after 80 years in storage. Howell argues that this medicalization of trauma obscures the politics of militarization and reinforces a structure that allows soldiers to be redeployed. Rebecca Tiessen, in Chapter 11, also addresses a neglected topic: the role of youth internships in Canadian foreign policy. She argues that these programs are designed to project an identity of Canada as a 'good global citizen' and divert attention from the less palatable aspects of Canada's foreign policy.

Critical theorists are also reproached for being 'unscientific'. Critical approaches have answered that complaint by pointing out the shortcomings of positivism, most importantly, the inability of positivism to address the full role of the social realm and the problems associated with its commitment to finding universal truths. Relying solely on empirical observation is a recipe, at best, for incomplete narratives of international relations, and, at worst, for misleading narratives.

In general, critical theorists reject positivism. But this does not have to be the case. A research program can borrow from positivism but be ontologically critical in the sense that it highlights how the social and political world is divided into various categories of inclusion and exclusion. Stéphane Roussel, in Chapter 12, most clearly represents this position. Applying quantitative research methods, Roussel examines the under-representation of French-speaking authors in the English literature on Canadian foreign policy. The privileging of English-language research results in a lack of attention to the issue of national unity. Roussel highlights the possible implications of this neglect for both the research and the foreign policy communities.

The above discussion is not meant to imply that critical approaches are above reproach but to point out the ways in which they have been unfairly and widely criticized by those who have given the various approaches only a cursory glance. Critical theorists of many stripes have been accused of dismissing the mainstream theories and other approaches. In my view this is often, though by no means always, a fair criticism. This is sometimes done by caricaturing other approaches and then dismissing them based on the caricatures. As Tony Porter pointed out in his effective critique of postmodernism, within this critical approach there is a '[j]uxtaposition of a professed acceptance of diversity with a brutal simplification of other approaches' (Porter, 1994: 116–17). Certainly this is a criticism that could be directed at the field as a whole. Without a doubt, critical theories are routinely dismissed by the mainstream. Furthermore, given the important emphasis some critical scholars place on pointing out the dangers inherent in mainstream approaches, it might be even more difficult for them to address this issue. Yet, engaging another theoretical tradition does not necessarily mean accepting all or any part of the theory or its assumptions uncritically. At a minimum, more dialogue should occur around these issues and more effort should be given to addressing this contradiction within the critical literature.

The Discipline of Canadian Foreign Policy

How could this book change the way we teach Canadian foreign policy? What does it mean for our thinking about the field as scholars? How do these novel cases and uncommon approaches to the subject upset the discipline?

As the first broadly critical survey of Canadian foreign policy, this volume has the potential to change the way we might study foreign policy in Canadian classrooms. Although many of us recognize the value in critical scholarship, teaching it in our foreign policy courses has not always been easy. Instead of assigning a single textbook supplemented by articles, we have had to do much of the legwork ourselves, pulling articles from many different journals to compile a reading list that made sense to us as teachers and to our students. This volume, though making no claim to representing all the critical voices in Canadian foreign policy scholarship, does provide a cross-section of the main approaches and topics and is thus easily adopted for use in the classroom.

This book also offers something new to us as researchers of Canadian foreign policy. It provides a coherent framework for investigating foreign policy questions via a critical lens. The approaches covered offer alternative narratives and opportunities to think differently about Canada's actions on the world stage. Yet, thinking 'differently' has a long history in the academic study of IR in Canada. Despite being in many ways part of a broad 'North American' university system (and by that I mean we conduct our classrooms in the same way as the Americans, often hire American scholars, publish in American journals, attend American conferences),[2] Canadians study International Relations and foreign policy in a way that is quite distinctive from their American colleagues. As Kim Nossal (2000) explains, there are considerable differences in the study of these topics on either side of the Canadian–American border. First, Canadians are perennially concerned with marking Canada's place in the world, and this is reflected in the relatively large literature on 'middle powers' or on topics considered to be reflective of Canadian foreign policy priorities (peacekeeping, human security, etc.). Likewise, Nossal points out that the differences are also methodological. Although Canadian scholars did not reject the behaviouralist turn that swept through American political science in the 1970s, Canadian scholars did not wholeheartedly jump on that bandwagon and gave it up almost entirely by the early 1980s while it remained the dominant methodology used by their American colleagues. Nossal notes that the last Canadian IR book to explicitly set out 'to construct scientific theories of foreign policy' was published in 1978 (Tomlin, 1978, quoted ibid.). Consequently, Canadian scholars did not adopt the systemic focus that was influenced by this 'scientific turn'. In the United States the emphasis on structural and rationalistic approaches at this time led to the development and embrace of neo-realism and, with it, a focus on the international system (ibid.). Although recognizing the influence of domestic- and individual-level variables on international relations is not uniquely Canadian, it is suggestive that Canadians have chosen this course of research despite their being so thoroughly intertwined with the academic environment just south of the border. In essence, then, though this book is the first comprehensively critical volume on Canadian foreign policy, it is not surprising that the critical methods and theories it expounds are beginning to establish a footing in Canadian political science departments.

The Practice of Canadian Foreign Policy

One of the tenets of many critical approaches is the idea that the researcher and the subject of the research are not isolated from one another. Critical approaches recognize that researchers themselves have a crucial role in the creation and validation of knowledge. As such, one cannot separate the ideas circulating in the ivory tower from the day-to-day practices of policy-makers.

This phenomenon is perhaps even exaggerated in Canada because of the relatively small size of both the academic environment and the foreign policy community. Interactions between individuals with shared interests in the two groups are common. Even more interesting is the opportunity for academics to spend some time in the policy-making community. Recent examples would include Lloyd Axworthy (the former Minister of Foreign Affairs has been employed at the Lui Centre for International Affairs at University of British Columbia and is the current President of the University of Winnipeg) and Michael Ignatieff (the former professor at the University of Toronto, who most recently had been the director of the Carr Center for Human Rights Policy at Harvard University, returned to Canada and entered federal politics in 2006, and then became the leader of the Liberal Party in December 2008).

Thus, we would expect that the adoption of more critical approaches in the study of foreign policy in Canada will influence how we practise Canadian foreign policy. We need to think about the implications of our own research. For example, by pointing out the inherent contradictions in the practice of Canadian foreign policy, how are we influencing Canada's engagement with the world? My hope is that critical scholarship is leading to a broader understanding within the Canadian government of how Canada's actions abroad affect all types of people in other countries and in Canada in ways we had not realized before.

This is already apparent in some areas. For example, the influence of feminist scholarship is visible in Canadian development policy. Although the Canadian International Development Agency's programs and determination lag behind the current academic thinking on issues, evidence indicates that the policy-making community has been listening to feminist researchers. Beginning in the early 1980s, CIDA began to explicitly target women in its development projects, based on the 'Women in Development' and later 'Gender and Development' frameworks developed in the academic literature. According to the CIDA website 'the Canadian International Development Agency (CIDA) has been a world leader in integrating gender equality analysis into its programming' (CIDA, 2008).

Before I began my Ph.D., I had the opportunity to work on one of these CIDA projects that targeted women's participation in development. The project co-ordinators were genuinely committed to empowering women through this project. Though success was mixed, overall the project did empower many of the women in the targeted community. Other reports of CIDA-funded gender-directed projects have also been positive. In her study of CIDA's policies on gender and development in the Philippines, Leonora Angeles recognizes the uneven results of CIDA's approach but applauds the organization's efforts to 'integrate gender concerns in all its programs and activities' (Angeles, 2003: 284). Despite these instances of what one might describe as 'success', the record is also troublesome. For example, the recent trend for aid agencies, including CIDA, to advocate gender mainstreaming[3] has come under criticism on a number of fronts. For example, Rebecca Tiessen (2004) points out that while the concept appears in aid agency reports, the implementation of the process has been 'watered down' (see also Rao et al., 1999; Parpart and Marchand, 1995). After participating in a CIDA project, Collette Oseen wrote, 'The principle which CIDA itself states as its second priority after basic human needs: "the full participation of women as equal partners in the sustainable development of their societies" was routinely ignored' (Oseen, 1999: 102).

However, most troubling is the realization that feminist scholarship has been both misunderstood and (mis)used in ways not consistent with its objectives. Incidents of such misuse are not uncommon. The blatant perversion of feminist scholarship to justify the American and Canadian military presence in Afghanistan is a case in point. Thus, though the incorporation of feminist scholarship in developmental policy-making is a progressive step, the problems associated with this in practice should serve as a cautionary tale.

This volume has sought to encourage researchers to take leaps into the unknown, investigate new ways of understanding, and push the limits of the current research and practice of Canadian foreign policy. Such a project entails risks, both to the researcher and to the subject of the research. A researcher pushing beyond the conventional limits of scholarly practice puts her or his career in jeopardy, as does one who shrugs off the false cloak of neutrality to engage in activist work. And although we all are more comfortable in putting ourselves at risk than we are in risking those we study, we must acknowledge that our research (like the research of our mainstream colleagues) does not exist in isolation. In most cases it will have an effect, and we can certainly do our best to take care that the effect is positive. Yet, whether through misuse of our ideas, our own mistakes, or simple happenstance, some of our research will bring about unfortunate outcomes for us or others that were neither planned nor foreseen. This does not mean that we should be afraid to try new methodologies or engage with ideas in innovative ways. Research that pushes the limits of scholarly boundaries is necessary for greater understanding. This volume is committed to this mission.

Notes

1. Although the United States lacks formal diplomatic relations with Cuba and thus does not have an embassy in Havana, there is a large US Interests Section in Havana that acts as a de facto embassy, providing consular services and the like. The Interests Section is formally a division of the Swiss embassy but in reality operates independently and is staffed by Americans.

2. In fact, a new faculty member at my own institution recently remarked that one can make the transition from an American institution to a Canadian university rather seamlessly. The only thing that had him confused was the different meaning of the term 'faculty meeting'. In the United States this implies a meeting of the faculty members in a department. In Canada it implies a meeting of the members of a Faculty (e.g., Social Sciences or Humanities).

3. Gender mainstreaming involves bringing gender concerns into the mainstream of society, or in the case of aid agencies, to incorporate gender equality into their programming.

References

Abrahamsen, Rita. 2005. 'Blair's Africa: The Politics of Securitization and Fear', *Alternatives* 30, 1: 55–80.

Adeba, Brian. 2006. 'Treasury Board Axes International Youth Programs', *Embassy*, 27 Sept. At: <embassymag.ca/page/view/.2006.september.27.programs>. (31 Mar. 2009)

Agamben, Giorgio. 1998. *Homo Sacer: Sovereign Power and Bare Life*, trans. D. Heller-Roazen. Stanford, Calif.: Stanford University Press.

Allison, Graham T. 1971. *Essence of Decision: Explaining the Cuban Missile Crisis*. Boston: Little, Brown.

Amoore, L. 2006. 'Biometric Borders: Governing Mobilities in the War on Terror', *Political Geography* 25, 3: 336–51.

Andreas, P. 2000. *Border Games: Policing the U.S.–Mexico Divide*. Ithaca, NY: Cornell University Press.

———. 2003a. 'A Tale of Two Borders: The U.S.–Canada Border and U.S.–Mexico Lines after 9-11', in P. Andreas and T.J. Biersteker, eds, *The Rebordering of North America: Integration and Exclusion in a New Security Context*. London: Routledge, 1–23.

———. 2003b. 'Redrawing the Line: Borders and Security in the Twenty-First Century', *International Security* 28, 2: 78–111.

———. 2005. 'The Mexicanization of the US–Canada border', *International Journal* 60, 2: 449–62.

Angeles, Leonora C. 2003. 'Creating Social Spaces for Transnational Feminist Advocacy: The Canadian International Development Agency, the National Commission on the Role of Filipino Women and Philippine Women's NGOs', *Canadian Geographer* 47, 3: 283–302.

Anholt, Simon. 2006. 'Public Diplomacy and Place Branding: Where's the Link?', *Place Branding and Public Diplomacy* 2, 4: 271–5.

Anker, Lane. 2005. 'Peacekeeping and Public Opinion,' *Canadian Military Journal* 6, 2: 23–32.

Arnold, Samantha. 2008. 'Nelvana of the North, Traditional Knowledge, and the Northern Dimension of Canadian Foreign Policy', *Canadian Foreign Policy Journal* 14, 2: 95–107.

Ashley, Richard K. 1987. 'Foreign Policy as Political Performance', *International Studies Notes* 13, 2: 51–4.

——— and R.B.J. Walker. 1990. 'Speaking the Language of Exile: Dissident Thought in International Studies', *International Studies Quarterly* 34, 3: 259–68.

Association of Universities and Colleges in Canada (AUCC). 2008. 'Students for Development'. At: <www.aucc.ca/programs/intprograms/sfd/sfd_e.html>. (7 Feb. 2008)

Atomic Energy Canada Ltd (AECL). 2008a. AECL Company Profile. At: <www.aecl.ca/Assets/Publications/Fact+Sheets/Profile.pdf>. (7 Nov. 2008)

———. 2008b. Projects: CANDU Projects. At: <www.aecl.ca/Projects/CANDU-P.htm>. (7 Nov. 2008)

————. 2008c. CANDU Country: Best Option for Canada. At: <www.aecl.ca/CANDU-Country.htm>. (7 Nov. 2008)

Atran, Scott. 2006. 'Moral Logic and Growth of Suicide Terrorism', *Washington Quarterly* 29, 2 (Spring): 127–47.

Augelli, Enrico, and Craig Murphy. 1996. 'Consciousness, Myth and Collective Action: Gramsci, Sorel, and the Ethical State', in Stephen Gill and James H. Mittelman, eds, *Innovation and Transformation in International Studies*. Cambridge: Cambridge University Press, 25–38.

Axworthy, Lloyd. 1997. 'Canada and Human Security: The Need for Leadership', *International Journal* 52, 2: 183–96.

————.1999. 'NATO's New Security Vocation', *NATO Review* 47, 4: 8–11.

————. 1999. 'Message from the Honorable Lloyd Axworthy, Minister of Foreign Affairs, to the Hague Appeal for Peace', Hague Appeal for Peace Conference, The Hague, Netherlands, 13 May. At: <w01,international.gc.ca/MinPub/Publication.aspx?isRedirect=True&Publication_id=37499&Language=E&docnumber=99/35>.

————. 2001. 'Human Security and Global Governance: Putting People First', *Global Governance* 7, 3: 19–23.

————. 2003. *Navigating a New World: Canada's Global Future*. Toronto: Knopf.

———— and Sarah Taylor. 1998. 'A Ban for All Seasons: The Landmines Convention and Its Implications for Canadian Diplomacy', *International Journal* 53, 1: 189–203.

Ayres, Jeffrey M. 2006. 'Civil Society Participation in Canadian Foreign Policy: Expanded Consultation in the Chrétien Years', in James et al. (2006: 491–512).

Bain, William. 1999. 'Against Crusading: The Ethic of Human Security and Canadian Foreign Policy', *Canadian Foreign Policy* 6, 3: 85–98.

Balibar, É. 2002. 'What Is a Border?' in Balibar, *Politics and the Other Scene*. London: Verso, 75–86.

Barnaby, Frank. 1994. *How Nuclear Weapons Spread: Nuclear Weapons Proliferation in the 1990s*. London: Routledge.

Bastien, Frédéric. 1998. 'À la demande du Québec: la diplomatie québécoise de la France de 1969 à 1980', *Études internationales* 29 (Sept.).

Bátora, J. 2005. 'Multistakeholder Public Diplomacy of Small and Medium-Sized States: Norway and Canada Compared', presentation to the International Conference on Multistakeholder Diplomacy, 11–13 Feb. At: <www.diplomacy.edu/Conferences/MSD/papers/batora.pdf>. (16 Nov. 2008)

————. 2005. 'Public Diplomacy in Small and Medium-Sized States: Norway and Canada', *Discussion Papers in Diplomacy* No. 97. The Hague: Netherlands Institute of International Relations Clingendael, Mar.: 1–29.

————. 2006. 'Emerging Tenets of Responsive Foreign Policymaking?', *International Journal* 61, 4: 929–42.

Beier, J. Marshall. 2005. *International Relations in Uncommon Places: Indigeneity, Cosmology, and the Limits of International Theory*. New York: Palgrave Macmillan.

————. 2007. 'Inter-National Affairs: Indigenity, Globality and the Canadian State', *Canadian Foreign Policy* 13, 3: 121–31.

———— and Samantha Arnold. 2005. 'Becoming Undisciplined: Toward the Supradisciplinary Study of Security', *International Studies Review* 7, 1: 41–61.

———— and Ann Denholm Crosby. 1998. 'Harnessing Change for Continuity: The Play of Political and Economic Forces behind the Ottawa Process', *Canadian Foreign Policy* 5, 3: 85–103.

Belanger, Yale D. 2007. 'Six Nations of Grand River Territory's Attempts at Renewing International Political Relationships, 1921–1924', *Canadian Foreign Policy* 13, 3: 29–43.

Belelieu, A. 2003. 'The Smart Border Process at Two: Losing Momentum?', *Hemisphere Focus* 11, 31: 1–8.

Bell, Colleen. 2006a. 'Subject to Exception: Security Certificates, National Security and Canada's Role in the "War on Terror"', *Canadian Journal of Law and Society* 21, 1: 63–83.

————. 2006b. 'Surveillance Strategies and Populations at Risk: Biopolitical Governance in Canada's National Security Policy', *Security Dialogue* 37, 2: 147–65.

Bennett, C. 2008. 'Comparative Politics of No-Fly Lists in the United States and Canada', in M. Salter, ed., *Politics at the Airport*. Minneapolis: University of Minnesota Press, 88–122.

Bennett, Tony. 2000. 'Acting on the Social: Art, Culture, and Government', *American Behavioral Scientist* 43, 9: 1412–28.

Bercuson, David, and Barry Cooper. 1991. *Deconfederation*. Toronto: Key Porter.

Bernier, Maxime. 2007. 'Notes for an Address by the Honourable Minister of Foreign Affairs, to the International Conference on Canada's Mission in Afghanistan', Montreal, 19 Sept. At: <www.canadainternational.gc.ca/canada-afghanistan/speeches-discours/sp_mfa_190907.aspx>.

Berthiaume, Lee. 2008. 'Future of CIDA Internship Program Up in the Air', *Embassy*, 20 Aug. At: <embassymag.ca/page/printpage/cida-8-20-2008>.

Bigo, D. 1996. *Polices en réseaux: l'expérience européenne*. Paris: Presses de Sciences Po.

————. 2001. 'The Mobius Ribbon of Internal and External Security(ies)', in M. Albert, D. Jacobson, and Y. Lapid, eds, *Identities, Borders, Orders: Rethinking International Relations Theory*. Minneapolis: University of Minnesota Press, 91–116.

————. 2002. 'Security and Immigration: Toward a Critique of the Governmentality of Unease', *Alternatives* 27, 1: 63–92.

Bi-National Planning Group. 2006. *Final Report on Canada and the United States (CANUS) Enhanced Military Cooperation*. Colorado Springs, Colo.: Peterson Air Force Base.

Black, Conrad. 1997–8. 'Taking Canada Seriously', *International Journal* 53 (Winter): 1–16.

Black, David. 2007. 'Leader or Laggard? Canada's Enduring Engagement with Africa', in Bratt and Kukucha (2007: 379–94).

———— and Heather A. Smith. 1993. 'Notable Exceptions? New and Arrested Developments in Canadian Foreign Policy Literature', *Canadian Journal of Political Science* 26, 4: 745–74.

Black, Eldon. 1998. *Direct Intervention: Canada–France Relations, 1967–1974*. Ottawa: Carleton University Press.

Blanchfield, Mike. 2007. 'PM shines light on "Canada at its best"; Harper touts rebuilding of Afghanistan, *Calgary Herald*, 23 May, 23.

Booth, Ken. 1991. 'Security and Emancipation', *Review of International Studies* 17, 4: 313–26.

————. 2007. 'The Writing on the Wall', *International Relations* 21, 3: 360–6.

Bosher, John. 1998. *The Gaullist Attack on Canada, 1967–1997*. Montreal and Kingston: McGill-Queen's University Press.

Boucher, Jean-Christophe, and Stéphane Roussel. 2007. 'From Afghanistan to "Quebecistan": Quebec as the Pharmakon of Canadian Foreign and Defence Policy', in Jean Daudelin and Daniel Schwanen, eds, *Canada Among Nations 2007: What Room for Manoeuvre?* Montreal and Kingston: McGill-Queen's University Press, 128–56.

Bratt, Duane, and Christopher J. Kukucha, eds. 2007. *Readings in Canadian Foreign Policy: Classic Debates and New Ideas.* Toronto: Oxford University Press.

Brecht, Bertolt. 1966. *Leben des Galilei.* Berlin: Suhrkamp Verlag.

British Columbia Civil Liberties Association. 2004. 'Submission of the British Columbia Civil Liberties Association to the Information and Privacy Commissioner for British Columbia on Implications of the USA Patriot Act on Government Outsourcing', 6 Aug. At: < www.bccla.org/othercontent/04patriot%20Act.htm>.

Brodeur, Jean-Paul. 1992. 'L'obstacle des troubles intérieurs', in Alain-G. Gagnon and François Rocher, eds, *Réplique aux détracteurs de la souveraineté du Québec.* Montreal: VLB, 103–19.

Brown, Chris, 2007. 'The Future of the Discipline', *International Relations* 21, 3: 347–50.

Bruyneel, Kevin. 2007. *The Third Space of Sovereignty: The Postcolonial Politics of U.S.– Indigenous Relations.* Minneapolis: University of Minnesota Press.

Burges, Sean W. 2006. 'Canada's Postcolonial Problem: The United States and Canada's International Policy Review', *Canadian Foreign Policy* 13, 1: 97–111.

Bush, George W. 2004. 'Remarks by President Bush at Pier 21. Halifax, Nova Scotia, Canada', 1 Dec. Washington: Office of the Press Secretary.

———. 2005. 'President Discusses War on Terror at National Endowment for Democracy', 6 Oct., Washington, DC. At: <www.whitehouse.gov/news/releases/2005/10/20051006-3.html>. (20 Jan. 2008)

Busumtwi-Sam, James. 2002. 'Development and Human Security', *International Journal* 58, 2: 253–72.

Butler, Judith. 1990. *Gender Trouble: Feminism and the Subversion of Identity.* London: Routledge.

———. 1993. *Bodies That Matter: On the Discursive Limits of 'Sex'.* London: Routledge.

Buzan, Barry. 1991. *People, States, and Fear: An Agenda for International Security Studies in the Post-Cold War Era*, 2nd edn. Boulder, Colo.: Lynne Rienner.

———, O. Wæver, and J. de Wilde. 1998. *Security: A New Framework for Analysis.* Boulder, Colo.: Lynne Rienner.

Calgary Herald. 2006. 'Our resolve honours soldier', 19 May.

Campbell, David. 1992. *Writing Security: United States Foreign Policy and the Politics of Identity.* Manchester: Manchester University Press.

———. 1993. *Politics without Principle: Sovereignty, Ethics, and the Narratives of the Gulf War.* Boulder, Colo.: Lynne Rienner.

———. 1998. *Writing Security: United States Foreign Policy and the Politics of Identity*, 2nd edn. Minnesota: University of Minnesota Press.

Canada. 1970. *Politique étrangère au service des Canadiens.* Ottawa: Secrétariat d'État aux Affaires extérieures du Canada.

———. 2005a. *Defence Policy Statement.* At: <www.forces.gc.ca/site/reports/dps/main/05_e.asp#1_1_2>. (14 Nov. 2007)

————. 2005b. *A Role of Pride and Influence in the World: Overview*. Ottawa: Department of Foreign Affairs and International Trade.

————. 2005c. *International Policy Statement: Development*. Ottawa: Canadian International Development Agency.

————. 2006. *Canadians Making a Difference in the World: Afghanistan*. Pamphlet. Ottawa.

————. 2007a. Speech from the Throne, 17 Oct. At: <www.sft-ddt.gc.ca/eng/media. asp?id=1364>. (22 Oct. 2007)

Canada, *Hansard*. 2006. Section 1845, The House of Commons Debate on the NORAD Agreement Renewal, 3 May. At: <www2.parl.gc.ca/HousePublications/Publication.aspx ?DocId=2174969&Language=E&Mode=1&Parl=38&Ses=1>.

Canada, Office of the Prime Minister. 2007. 'Prime Minister Stephen Harper announces additional funding for aid in Afghanistan', 26 Feb. At: <pm.gc.ca/eng/media. asp?id=1555>.

————. 2009. 'PM joins world leaders in supporting NATO's commitment to Afghanistan', 4 Apr. At: <pm.gc.ca/eng/media.asp?category=1&id=2509>.

Canada, Treaty Series. 1996. *Exchange of Notes between the Government of Canada and the Government of the United States of America constituting an Agreement relating to the North American Aerospace Defense Command (NORAD)*, 28 Mar. At: <www.treaty-accord. gc.ca>.

————. 2004. *Exchange of Notes between the Government of Canada and the Government of the United States of America concerning Missile Warning and constituting an Agreement to amend the North American Aerospace Defense Command Agreement (NORAD)*, 5 Aug. At: <www.treaty-accord.gc.ca/>.

————. 2006. *Agreement between the Government of Canada and the Government of the United States of America on the North American Aerospace Defense Command*, 12 May. At: <www.treaty-accord.gc.ca/>.

Canadian Crossroads International (CCI). 2008. 'Volunteer Opportunities'. At: <www. cciorg.ca/volunteer.html>. (7 Feb. 2008)

Canadian International Development Agency (CIDA). 2004a. 'Minister Carroll sends off first Canada Corps mission', news release, 21 Dec. At: <www.acdi-cida.gc.ca/cida_ind. nsf/0/46E3AD804E649C9485256F7100596BA5?OpenDocument>. (12 May 2005)

————. 2004b. 'CIDA Youth Action: Canada's International Youth Internship Program— IYIP'. At: <www.acdi-cida.gc.ca/youth/internships>. (12 May 2005)

————. 2005. 'Journal Library'. At: <www.acdi-cida.gc.ca/cida_ind.nsf/AllDocIds/ 616BD2AD8315A4A085256F390048B8DF?OpenDocument>. (12 May 2005)

————. 2007. At: <www.acdi-cida.gc.ca/index-e.htm>. (31 Oct. 2007)

————. 2008. At: <www.acdi-cida.gc.ca/cidaweb/acdicida.nsf/En/JUD-829101441-JQC>.

CANDU Operators Group (COG). 2008. 'COG Organization'. At: <www.candu.org/ organization.html>. (7 Nov. 2008)

Cardinal, Mario. 2005. *Point de rupture. Québec/Canada Le référendum de 1995*. Montreal: Société Radio-Canada, Bayard.

Care International and the Centre on International Cooperation. 2003. *Afghanistan Policy Brief: Good Intentions Will Not Pave the Road to Peace*, 15 Sept.

c.a.s.e. Collective. 2006. 'Critical Approaches to Security in Europe: A Networked Manifesto', *Security Dialogue* 37, 4: 443–87.

CBC. 2004. 'Canadian peacekeeping mission comes under fire at home', 24 Jan. At: <www.cbc.ca/news/background/afghanistan/peacekeeping.html>. (2 Nov. 2008)

CBC News. 2007. 'Canadian delegation meets with anti-sealing Europeans', 26 Mar. At: <www.cbc.ca/canada/north/story/2007/03/26/seal-tour.html>. (16 Nov. 2008)

Chandler, David. 2003. 'Rhetoric without Responsibility: The Attraction of Ethical Foreign Policy', *British Journal of Politics and International Relations* 5, 3: 295–316.

Chilton, P. 1996. *Security Metaphors: Cold War Discourse from Containment to Common House*. New York: Lang.

Chomsky, Noam. 1975. 'The Meaning of Vietnam', *New York Review of Books*, 12 June.

Cirincione, Joseph. 2005. 'The Declining Ballistic Missile Threat, 2005'. Washington: Carnegie Endowment Policy Outlook, Feb. At: <www.carnegieendowment.org/publications/index.cfm?fa=view&id=16439&proj=znpp>.

Clark, Joe. 1985. *Compétitivité et sécurité: Orientations pour les relations extérieures du Canada*. Ottawa: Approvisionnements et Services Canada.

Clark, Mary E. 2002. *In Search of Human Nature*. London: Routledge.

Clearwater, John. 1998. *Canadian Nuclear Weapons*. Toronto: Dundurn Press.

———. 1999. *US Nuclear Weapons in Canada*. Toronto: Dundurn Press.

———. 2007. *Just Dummies: Cruise Missile Testing in Canada*. Calgary: University of Calgary Press.

CNN. 2009. 'Canada's Harper doubts Afghan insurgency can be defeated', 2 Mar. At: <www.cnn.com/2009/WORLD/asiapcf/03/02/canada.afghanistan/index.html>.

Cohn, Marjorie. 2008. 'Afghanistan: The Other Illegal War', 1 Aug. At: <www.alternet.org/waroniraq/93473/afghanistan%3A_the_other_illegal_war/>.

Comeau, Paul-André, and Jean-Pierre Fournier. 2002. *Le Lobby du Québec à Paris: Les précurseurs du général de Gaulle*. Montréal: Québec Amérique.

Cooper, Andrew F. 1997. *Canadian Foreign Policy: Old Habits and New Directions*. Toronto: Prentice-Hall.

———. 1998. 'Diplomatic Puzzles: A Review of the Literature', in Robert Wolfe, ed., *Diplomatic Missions: The Ambassador in Canadian Foreign Policy*. Kingston, Ont.: School of Policy Studies, Queen's University, 27–41.

Copeland, Daryl. 2004. 'Guerrilla Diplomacy: Delivering International Policy in a Digital World', *Canadian Foreign Policy* 11, 2: 165–76.

———. 2005. 'New Rabbits, Old Hats: International Policy and Canada's Foreign Service in an Era of Reduced Diplomatic Resources', *International Journal* 60, 3: 743–62.

Cornut, Jérémie, and Stéphane Roussel. 2009. 'Does It Help for French-speaking Scholars in Canadian Foreign Policy to Publish in English?', paper presented at annual meeting of the Canadian Political Science Association, Ottawa, 24 May.

Côté-Boucher, Karine. 2008. 'The Diffuse Border: Intelligence-Sharing, Control and Confinement along Canada's Smart Border', *Surveillance and Society* 5, 2: 142–65.

Coulon, Jocelyn. 1991. *En première ligne: Grandeurs et misères du système militaire canadien*. Montréal: Le Jour.

Cox, Robert W. 1972. 'The Pearson and Jackson Reports in the Context of Development Ideologies', *Year Book of World Affairs 1972*: 187–202.

————. 1986. 'Social Forces, States and World Orders: Beyond International Relations Theory', in Robert O. Keohane, ed., *Neorealism and Its Critics*. New York: Columbia University Press, 204–54.

————. 1994. 'The Crisis in World Order and the Challenge to International Organization', *Cooperation and Conflict* 29, 2: 99–113.

————. 1996. 'Social Forces, States and World Orders: Beyond International Relations Theory', in Robert W. Cox, with Timothy J. Sinclair, *Approaches to World Order*. Cambridge: Cambridge University Press, 85–123.

Cowan, Geoffrey, and Nicholas J. Cull. 2008. 'Public Diplomacy in a Changing World', *Annals, American Academy of Political and Social Science* 616, 1: 6–8.

CTV. 2002. 'Ex-Soldier Trial Spotlights Post-Trauma Stress'. At: <www.ctv.ca>. (11 Mar. 2006)

Cyr, Marc-André. 2008. 'De l'engagement à la révolte. Les Canadiens français et les guerres mondiales', *Arguments* 10, 2: 10–22.

Dallaire, Roméo. 2003. *Shake Hands with the Devil: The Failure of Humanity in Rwanda.* Toronto: Random House Canada.

Davies, Norman. 1997. *Europe: A History*. Oxford: Oxford University Press.

de Costa, Ravi. 2007. 'Cosmology, Mobility and Exchange: Indigenous Diplomacies before the Nation-State', *Canadian Foreign Policy* 13, 3: 13–28.

Deleuze, Gilles. 1986. *Foucault*. Minneapolis: University of Minnesota Press.

Denholm Crosby, Ann. 1998. *Dilemmas in Defence Decision-Making: Constructing Canada's Role in NORAD, 1958–96.* London: Macmillan Press.

Department of Foreign Affairs and International Trade (DFAIT). 1995. *Canada in the World: Canadian Foreign Policy Review 1995.* Ottawa: DFAIT. At: <www.dfait-maeci.gc.ca/ foreign_policy/cnd-world/menu-en.asp>.

————. 1998a. *The Lysøen Declaration.* Lysøen, Norway: Government of Norway and Government of Canada.

————. 1998b. 'Toward a Northern Foreign Policy for Canada'. At: <www.international. gc.ca/polar-polaire/final4.aspx?lang=en>. (16 Nov. 2008)

————. 1999a. *Human Security: Safety for People in a Changing World.* Ottawa: Government of Canada.

————. 1999b. *A Perspective on Human Security.* Lysøen, Norway: Government of Norway and Government of Canada.

————. 2000. 'The Northern Dimension of Canada's Foreign Policy'. At: <www. international.gc.ca/polar-polaire/ndfp-vnpe2.aspx?lang=en>. (16 Nov. 2008)

————. 2003a. *Freedom From Fear: Canada's Foreign Policy for Human Security.* Ottawa: Government of Canada.

————. 2003b. *A Dialogue on Foreign Policy: A Report to Canadians.* Ottawa: Government of Canada.

————. 2004. '2003–2004 Success Stories'. At: <www.dfait-maeci.gc.ca/ypi-jpi/success-en.asp>. (11 May 2005)

————. 2005. *Canada's International Policy Statement: A Role of Pride and Influence in the World.* Ottawa: Government of Canada, 19 Apr.

————. 2007. 'Nuclear Disarmament and Non-Proliferation: Canadian Policy'. At: <www. dfait-maeci.gc.ca/arms/nuclear2-en.asp>. (12 Nov. 2007)

Department of National Defence Canada (DND). 1999. 'Overview: A System Approach'. The Board of Inquiry: Croatia. At: <www.forces.gc.ca/hr/boi/engraph/overview_e.asp>. (13 Feb. 2006)

———. 2007. *Canada's Approach: The Kandahar Provincial Reconstruction Team*. Ottawa: Department of National Defence.

Der Derian, James. 1989. 'The Boundaries of Knowledge and Power in International Relations', in James Der Derian and Michael J. Shapiro, eds, *International/Intertextual Relations: Postmodern Readings of World Politics*. Lexington, Mass.: Lexington Books, 1–10.

Dickason, Olive Patricia. 2006. *A Concise History of Canada's First Nations*, adapted by Moira Jean Calder. Toronto: Oxford University Press.

———, with David T. McNab. 2009. *Canada's First Nations: A History of Founding Peoples from Earliest Times*, 4th edn. Toronto: Oxford University Press.

Doran, Charles F. 2001. *Why Canadian Unity Matters and Why Americans Care: Democratic Pluralism at Risk*. Toronto: University of Toronto Press.

Doty, Roxanne. 1993. 'Foreign Policy as Social Construction: A Post-Positivist Analysis of U.S. Counterinsurgency Policy in the Philippines', *International Studies Quarterly* 37, 3: 297–320.

———. 1996. *Imperial Encounters: The Politics of Representation in North–South Relations*. Minneapolis: University of Minnesota Press.

———. 2001. 'Desert Tracts: Statecraft in Remote Places', *Alternatives* 26, 4: 523–43.

Drache, D. 2004. *Borders Matter: Homeland Security and the Search for North America*. Halifax: Fernwood.

Duffield, Mark. 2001. *Global Governance and the New Wars: The Merger of Development and Security*. London: Zed Books.

———. 2002. 'Social Reconstruction and the Radicalization of Development: Aid as a Relation of Global Liberal Governance', *Development and Change* 33, 5: 1049–71.

———. 2007. *Development, Security and Unending War: Governing the World of Peoples*. Cambridge: Polity.

Duchesne, Pierre. 2006. 'Diplomatie préréférendaire', in Paquin, with Beaudoin (2006: 194–206).

Edkins, Jenny. 1999. *Poststructuralism and International Relations: Bringing the Political Back In*. Boulder, Colo.: Lynne Rienner.

———. 2003. *Trauma and the Memory of Politics*. Cambridge: Cambridge University Press.

Edwards, Gordon. 1983. 'Canada's Nuclear Industry and the Myth of the Peaceful Atom', in Ernie Regehr and Simon Rosenblum, eds, *Canada and the Nuclear Arms Race*. Toronto: James Lorimer, 122–70.

Enloe, Cynthia. 1989. *Bananas, Beaches, and Bases: Making Feminist Sense of International Politics*. Berkeley: University of California Press.

———. 1996. 'Margins, Silences and Bottom Rungs: How to Overcome the Underestimation of Power in the Study of International Relations', in Steve Smith, Ken Booth, and Marysia Zalewski, eds, *International Theory: Positivism and Beyond*. Cambridge: Cambridge University Press, 186–202.

———. 2000. *Manoeuvres: The International Politics of Militarizing Women's Lives*. Berkeley: University of California Press.

Epprecht, Marc. 2004. 'Work-Study Abroad Courses in International Development Studies: Some Ethical and Pedagogical Issues', *Canadian Journal of Development Studies* 25, 4: 687–706.

Escobales, Roxanne. 2008. 'Afghanistan risks becoming "failed state", report warns', 31 Jan. *Guardian Unlimited*. At: <www.guardian.co.uk/print/0,,332319438-108920,00.html>. (31 Jan. 2008)

Farish, M. 2006. 'Frontier Engineering: From the Globe to the Body in the Cold War Arctic', *Canadian Geographer* 50, 2: 177–96.

Fortman, Michel, and Albert Legault. 1992. *A Diplomacy of Hope: Canada and Disarmament, 1945–1988*. Montreal and Kingston: McGill-Queen's University Press.

Foucault, Michel. 1990. *The History of Sexuality: An Introduction*, vol. 1. New York: Random House.

———. 1991. 'Governmentality', in Graham Burchell, Colin Gordon, and Peter Miller, eds, *The Foucault Effect: Studies in Governmentality*. Chicago: University of Chicago Press.

———. 2003. *Society Must Be Defended: Lectures at the College de France*, trans. David Macey. New York: Picador.

———. 2007. *Security, Territory, Population: Lectures at the Collège de France 1977–1978*, ed. A. Davidson, trans. G. Burchell. London: Palgrave Macmillan.

Fowler, Robert. 2008. 'Alice in Afghanistan: A Review of Stein and Lang, *The Unexpected War*', *Literary Review of Canada* 16, 1: 3–5.

Fraser, Graham. 2005. 'Liberal Continuities: Jean Chrétien's Foreign Policy, 1993–2003', in David Carment, Fen Osler Hampson, and Norman Hillmer, eds, *Canada Among Nations 2004. Setting Priorities Straight*. Montreal and Kingston: McGill-Queen's University Press, 171–86.

Fraser, Whit, and John Harker. 1994–5. 'A Northern Foreign Policy for Canada', *CARC— Northern Perspectives* 22, 4. At: <www.carc.org/pubs/v22no4/policy.htm>. (16 Nov. 2008)

Freeman, Alan. 2007. 'Change tune on war, PM told', *Globe and Mail*, 13 July.

Friedman, Thomas. 1999. 'From Supercharged Financial Markets to Osama bin Laden, the Emerging Global Order Demands an Enforcer', *New York Times Magazine*, 28 Mar.

Fry, Earl H. 2002. 'Quebec's Relations with the United States', *American Review of Canadian Studies* 32 (Summer).

Gagnon, Georgette, Audry Macklin, and Penelope Simons. 2003. *Deconstructing Engagement: Corporate Self-Regulation in Conflict Zones—Implications for Human Rights and Canadian Public Policy*. Toronto: Relations in Transition, A Strategic Joint Initiative of the Social Sciences and Humanities Research Council and the Law Commission of Canada.

Gee, Marcus. 2008. 'Show the world, Canadians tell country', *Globe and Mail*, 5 Feb.

Gibb, Gordon R. 2006. *Lester B. Pearson: The Geek Who Made Canada Proud*. Toronto: Jackfruit Press.

Globe and Mail. 2006. 'Harper's ringing words on the Afghanistan mission', 14 Mar.

Grace, Sherrill E. 2001. *Canada and the Idea of North*. Montreal and Kingston: McGill-Queen's University Press.

Granatstein, J.L. 1982. *The Ottawa Men: The Civil Service Mandarins, 1935–1957*. Toronto: Oxford University Press.

———. 1992.'Peacekeeping: Did Canada Make a Difference? And What Difference Did

Peacekeeping Make to Canada?', in John English and Norman Hillmer, eds, *Making a Difference: Canada's Foreign Policy in a Changing World Order*. Toronto: Lester, 222–36.

———. 1993. 'Canada and Peacekeeping: Image and Reality', in J.L. Granatstein, ed., *Canadian Foreign Policy: Historical Readings*, rev. edn. Toronto: Copp Clark Pitman, 276–85.

———. 2007. *Whose War Is It? How Canada Can Survive in the Post-9/11 World*. Toronto: HarperCollins.

———. 2008. 'Mike Pearson's true heir: Stephen Harper', *National Post*, 2 Feb.

Grayson, Kyle. 2004. 'Branding Transformation in Canadian Foreign Policy: Human Security', *Canadian Foreign Policy* 11, 2: 41–68.

———. 2006. 'Promoting Responsibility and Accountability: Human Security and Canadian Corporate Conduct', *International Journal* 56, 1: 479–95.

———. 2008. 'Human Security as Power-Knowledge: The Biopolitics of a Definitional Debate', *Cambridge Review of International Affairs* 21, 3: 383–401.

———. Forthcoming 2009. 'Dangerous Liaisons: Human Security, Neoliberalism, and Corporate (Mis)Conduct in Canada', *International Politics*.

Gregory, Bruce. 2008. 'Public Diplomacy: Sunrise of an Academic Field', *Annals, American Academy of Political and Social Science* 616, 1: 274–90.

Grenier, Major Stephane. 2005. *Operational Stress Injuries (OSI): A New Way to Look at an Old Problem*, 21 June. At: <www.cfpsa.com/en>. (11 Mar. 2006)

Gusterson, Hugh. 1999. 'Missing the End of the Cold War in International Security', in Jutta Weldes, Mark Laffey, Hugh Gusterson, and Raymond Duvall, eds, *Cultures of Insecurity: States, Communities, and the Production of Danger*. Minneapolis: University of Minnesota Press, 319–46.

Gwyn, Richard. 1980. *The Northern Magus: Pierre Trudeau and Canadians*. Toronto: McClelland & Stewart.

Hacking, Ian. 1995. *Rewriting the Soul: Multiple Personality and the Sciences of Memory*. Princeton, NJ: Princeton University Press.

Haglund, David G. 2006. 'Québec's "America Problem": Differential Threat Perception in the North American Security Community', *American Review of Canadian Studies* 36 (Winter): 552–67.

Halperin, Morton H., with Priscilla Clapp and Arnold Kanter. 1974. *Bureaucratic Politics and Foreign Policy*. Washington: Brookings Institution Press.

Hamelin, Louis-Edmond. 1978. *Canadian Nordicity: It's Your North Too*, trans. William Barr. Montreal: Harvest House.

Hampson, Fen Osler, with Jean Daudelin, John B. Hay, Todd Martin, and Holly Reid. 2002. *Madness in the Multitude: Human Security and World Disorder*. Toronto:: Oxford University Press.

——— and Dean Oliver. 1998. 'Pulpit Diplomacy: A Critical Assessment of the Axworthy Doctrine', *International Journal* 54, 2: 379–406.

Hansen, Lene. 2006. *Security as Practice: Discourse Analysis and the Bosnian War*. London: Routledge.

Harder, Lois, and Steve Patten, eds. 2006. *The Chrétien Legacy: Politics and Public Policy in Canada*. Montreal and Kingston: McGill-Queen's University Press.

Harker, John. 2000. *Human Security in Sudan: The Report of a Canadian Assessment Mission.* Ottawa: Government of Canada.

Harper, Stephen. 2006a. 'Prime Minister Stands by Canada's Commitment to Afghanistan', 17 May. At: <pm.gc.ca/eng/media.asp?id=1165>.

———. 2006b. 'Address by the Prime Minister at the Canada–UK Chamber of Commerce. London, UK', 14 July. At: <pm.gc.ca/eng/media.asp?id=1247>. (20 Sept. 2007)

———. 2007a. 'Announcement of additional funding for aid in Afghanistan', Office of the Prime Minister, 26 Feb. At: <www.pm.gc.ca>. (3 June 2007)

———. 2007b. 'Prime Minister Stephen Harper speaks to Canadian troops during visit to Afghanistan, Khandahar, Afghanistan', 23 May. At: <pm.gc.ca/eng/media.asp?id=1667>.

Harvey, Frank, David Carment, and John Stack, eds. 2001. *The International Politics of Quebec Secession: State-Making and State-Breaking in North America.* New York: Praeger.

Hataley, T.S., and Kim Richard Nossal. 2004. 'The Limits of the Human Security Agenda: The Case of Canada's Response to the Timor Crisis', *Global Change, Peace & Security* 16, 1: 5–17.

Heininen, Lassi, and Heather N. Nicol. 2007. 'The Importance of Northern Dimension Foreign Policies in the Geopolitics of the Circumpolar North', *Geopolitics* 12, 1: 133–65.

Hemming, Jon. 2007. 'Too much aid to Afghanistan wasted: Oxfam', 20 Nov. Reuters: Rawa News. At: <www.rawa.org/temp/runews/2007/11/20/too-much-aid-to-afghanistan-wasted-oxfam.html>. (28 Jan. 2008)

Heron, Barbara. 2004. 'Canada's Changing Presence in Developing Countries: Findings and Implications of a Study into Short-Term vs Long-Term International Placements', paper presented at the 2004 Canadian Association for the Study of International Development conference, Winnipeg.

Holloway, Steven K. 1992. 'Canada without Québec', *Orbis* 36 (Fall): 531–43.

———. 2006. *Canadian Foreign Policy: Defining the National Interest.* Peterborough, Ont.: Broadview Press.

Howard, Ben A. Strategic Joint Staff. 2006. 'Operation Athena Afghanistan,' 12 Dec., Afghanistan Briefing. Ottawa: Department of National Defence.

Howell, Alison. 2005. 'Peaceful, Tolerant and Orderly? A Feminist Analysis of Discourses of "Canadian Values" in Canadian Foreign Policy', *Canadian Foreign Policy* 12, 1: 49–69.

Hughes, Susan. 2004. *Lester B. Pearson.* Markham, Ont.: Fitzhenry & Whiteside.

Human Rights Watch. 2002. 'Afghanistan: "We want to live as humans"', *Repression of Women and Girls in Western Afghanistan* 14, 11 (Dec.).

———. 2003. *In the Name of Counter-Terrorism: Human Rights Abuses Worldwide.* New York: Human Rights Watch.

Husymans, J. 1998. 'Security! What Do You Mean? From Concept to Thick Signifier', *European Journal of International Relations* 4, 2: 226–55.

———. 2006. *The Politics of Insecurity: Fear, Migration and Asylum in the EU.* London: Routledge.

Ignatieff, Michael. 2003. 'The Burden', *New York Times Magazine*, 5 Jan., 1–10. At: <www.mtholyoke.edu/acad/intrel/bush/burden.htm>. (11 Jan. 2006)

International Boundary Commission. 2007. 'Who Are We and What Do We Do?' At: <www.internationalboundarycommission.org/ibcpg2.htm>.

Ivison, John. 2008. 'Manley report invokes the spirit of Pearson', *National Post*, 23 Jan..

Jackson, Andrew. 2000. *Taxes, Growth, and Inequality*. Ottawa: Canadian Centre for Policy Alternatives.

———. 2004. 'Income Inequality and Poverty: The Liberal Record', *CanadaWatch* 9, 3 and 4: 42.

Jaeger, Brigadier General Hilary. 2006. 'Mental Health Care in the Canadian Forces', *On Track* (Conference of Defence Associations Institute) 1, 11: 30–2.

Jaimet, Kate. 2006. 'Canada's military does more harm than good in Afghanistan: CARE', CanWest News Service (electronic version), 13 Sept.

James, Patrick, Nelson Michaud, and Marc J. O'Reilly, eds. 2006. *Handbook of Canadian Foreign Policy*. Lexington, Mass., and Toronto: Lexington Books.

Jeffrey, Leslie Ann. 2005. 'Canada and Migrant Sex Work: Challenging the "Foreign" in Foreign Policy', *Canadian Foreign Policy* 12, 1: 33–48.

Jockel, Joseph T. 1980. 'Un Québec souverain et la Défense de l'Amérique du Nord contre une attaque nucléaire', *Études internationales* 11 (June): 303–16.

Keating, Tom. 2002. *Canada and World Order: The Multilateralist Tradition in Canadian Foreign Policy*, 2nd edn. Oxford: Oxford University Press.

Keck, Margaret, and Kathryn Sikkink. 1998. *Activists beyond Borders*. Ithaca, NY: Cornell University Press.

Keegan, John. 1999. *The First World War: An Illustrated History*. New York: Knopf.

Kelly, Sean, and Peter Case. 2007. *The Overseas Experience: A Passport to Improved Volunteerism—A Research Report*. Toronto: Image Canada.

Keskitalo, E.C.H. 2004. *Negotiating the Arctic: The Construction of an International Regime*. New York and London: Routledge.

Khoong, Yuen Foong. 2001. 'Human Security: A Shotgun Approach to Alleviating Human Misery?', *Global Governance* 7, 3: 231–6.

Kilgour, David. 1999. 'Youth Leadership and Development', Notes for an address by Honourable David Kilgour, MP, Edmonton Southeast, Secretary of State (Latin America and Africa) to Canada World Youth, Edmonton House Suite Hotel, Edmonton, Mar. At: <www.david-kilgour.com/secstate/youthdev.htm>. (27 Nov. 2008)

Kirton, John. 2007. *Canadian Foreign Policy in a Changing World*. Toronto: Thompson Nelson.

Kitchen, V. 2004. 'Smarter Cooperation in Canada–US Relations', *International Journal* 59, 3: 693–710.

Klein, Naomi. 2000. *No Logo: Taking Aim at the Brand Bullies*. Toronto: Vintage Canada.

———. 2005. 'The Rise of Disaster Capitalism', *The Nation*, 14 Apr.

———. 2007. *The Shock Doctrine: The Rise of Disaster Capitalism*. New York: Allen Lane.

Krause, Keith, and Michael C. Williams, eds. 1997. *Critical Security Studies: Concepts and Cases*. Minneapolis: University of Minnesota Press.

Lackenbauer, P. Whitney, and Andrew F. Cooper. 2007. 'The Achilles Heel of Canadian Good International Citizenship: Indigenous Diplomacies and State Responses in the Twentieth Century', *Canadian Foreign Policy* 13, 3: 99–119.

——— and M. Farish. 2007. 'The Cold War on Canadian Soil: Militarizing a Northern Environment', *Environmental History* 12, 4: 920–50.

Laxer, J. 2003. *The Border: Canada, the U.S. and Dispatches from the 49th Parallel.* Toronto: Doubleday Canada.

———. 2007. *Mission of Folly: Why Canada Should Bring the Troops Home from Afghanistan.* At: <www.jameslaxer.com/>. (18 Feb. 2007)

Légaré, Anne. 2003. *Le Québec otage de ses allies: Les relations du Québec avec la France et les Etats-Unis.* Montréal: VLB.

Lentner, Howard H. 1978. 'Canadian Separatism and Its Implication for the United States', *Orbis* (Summer): 375–93.

Levi, Werner. 1991. *Contemporary International Law: A Concise Introduction*, 2nd edn. Boulder, Colo.: Westview Press.

Linklater, Andrew. 1996. 'The Achievements of Critical Theory', in Steve Smith, Ken Booth, and Marysia Zalewski, eds, *International Theory: Positivism and Beyond.* Cambridge: Cambridge University Press, 279–98.

Lipschutz, Ronnie. 1997. 'From Place to Planet: Local Knowledge and Global Environmental Governance', *Global Governance* 3: 83–102.

——— and Judith Mayer. 1996. *Global Civil Society and Global Environmental Governance: The Politics of Nature from Place to Planet.* Albany: State University of New York Press.

Lisée, Jean-François. 1990. *Dans l'oeil de l'aigle: Washington face au Québec.* Montréal: Boréal.

Lord, Kristin M. 2005. 'Linking Theory and Practice: What Academics (Should Have to) Say about Public Diplomacy', paper presented at the APSA Conference on International Communication and Conflict, Washington, DC, 31 Aug. At: <www8.georgetown.edu/cct/apsa/papers.cfm>. (16 Nov. 2008)

Loyn, David. 2007. 'Afghan optimism for future fading', BBC News (Kabul), 3 Dec. At: <news.bbc.co.uk/2/hi/south_asia/7124294.stm>.

McDonald, Laura. 2003. 'Gender and Canadian Trade Policy: Women's Strategies for Access and Transformation', in Turenne Sjolander et al. (2003: 40–54).

MacDonald, Norine. 2007. 'Losing Hearts and Minds: The Empty Shell of Human Security in Southern Afghanistan', *Human Security Bulletin* (Canadian Consortium on Human Security) (Jan.–Feb.).

MacFarlane, S. Neil. 1997. *Sovereignty and Stability: The Domestic and Regional Security Implications of Québec Separation.* Hanover, NH: John Sloan Dickey Center for International Understanding, Dartmouth College.

McHugh, James. 2006. 'The Foundations of Canadian Foreign Policy: Federalism, Confederalism, International Law, and the Quebec Precedent', in James et al. (2006).

MacKay, Peter. 2007a. 'Notes for an address by the Honourable Peter MacKay, Minister of Foreign Affairs and Minister of the Atlantic Canada Opportunities Agency, to the Standing Committee on Foreign Affairs and International Development', 20 Mar.

———. 2007b. 'Notes for an address by the Honourable Peter MacKay, Minister of Foreign Affairs and Minister of the Atlantic Canada Opportunities Agency, to the Vancouver Board of Trade, Vancouver, British Columbia', 11 Apr.

———. 2007c. 'Notes for an Address by the Honourable Peter MacKay, Minister of Foreign Affairs and Minister of the Atlantic Canada Opportunities Agency, to the Pugwash Conference', 7 July. At: <w01.international.gc.ca/minpub/Publication.aspx?isRedirect=True&publication_id=385287&Language=E&docnumber=2007/27>. (7 Nov. 2008)

————. 2007d. 'Speaking Notes for the Honourable Peter G. MacKay, PC, MP, Minister of National Defence, for the Diplomatic Forum, St. Andrews-on-the-Sea, New Brunswick', 10 Sept.

————. 2007e. 'Address by the Honourable Peter Gordon MacKay, Minister of National Defence, to the Chateauguay Chamber of Commerce: "The Hard Questions", Chateauguay, Quebec', 17 Oct.

MacKenzie, Major-General Lewis. 2002. 'Attack the Causes of Soldiers' Stress', National Post, 8 Feb., A14.

————. 2003. 'Protect Us from "Touchy-Feely" Soldiers', National Post, 10 Mar., A14.

MacLean, George. 2002. '(Re)Defining International Security Policy: Canada and the New Policy of Human Security', in David Mutimer, ed., Canadian International Security Policy: Reflections for a New Era. Toronto: York Centre for International and Security Studies, 11–24.

MacLennan, Hugh. 2003 [1945]. Two Solitudes. Toronto: McClelland & Stewart.

McNally, David. 2002. Another World Is Possible: Globalization and Anti-capitalism. Winnipeg: Arbeiter Ring Publishing.

McQuaig, Linda. 2008. 'Canadian "Peacekeeping" Troops in Afghanistan: Keep Pearson Out of It', Toronto Star, 20 Feb.

McRae, Robert, and Don Hubert, eds. 2001. Human Security and the New Diplomacy: Protecting People, Promoting Peace. Montreal and Kingston: McGill-Queen's University Press.

Manley, John. 2008. Report of the Independent Panel on Canada's Future Role in Afghanistan (Manley Report). Ottawa.

Marchand, Marianne, and Jane L. Parpart, eds. 1995. Feminism/Postmodernism/Development. London: Routledge.

Maslow, Abraham. 1966. The Psychology of Science: A Reconnaissance. New York: Harper and Row.

Mason, Dwight N. 2006. The Foreign and Defense Policies of an Independent Québec. Washington: Canada Institute Occasional Paper Series, Woodrow Wilson International Center for Scholars, Jan.

Massie, Justin, and Stéphane Roussel. 2008. 'Unité nationale et construction sociale des mythes en politique étrangère canadienne: Une perspective constructiviste-libérale', Canadian Foreign Policy 14, 2: 67–93.

Meyers, D.W. 2003. 'Does "Smarter" Lead to Safer? An Assessment of the US Border Accords with Canada and Mexico', International Migration 41, 1: 5–44.

Michaud, Nelson. 2007. 'Values and Canadian Foreign Policy-making: Inspiration or Hindrance', in Bratt and Kukucha (2007: 337–57).

Miller, Lynne. 1990. Global Order: Values and Power in International Relations. Boulder, Colo.: Westview Press.

Missile Defense Agency. At: <www.mda.mil/>.

Mohanty, Chandra. 1991. 'Cartographies of Struggle: Third World Women and the Politics of Feminism', in Chandra Talpade Mohanty, Ann Russo, and Lourdes Torres, eds, Third World Women and the Politics of Feminism. Bloomington: Indiana University Press, 1–47.

————. 1997. 'Under Western Eyes: Feminist Scholarship and Colonial Discourses', in Padmini Mongia, ed., Contemporary Postcolonial Theory: A Reader. London: Arnold, 172–97.

Morrison, Alex, ed. 1992. *The Canadian Strategic Forecast 1992, Divided We Fall: The National Security Implications of Canadian Constitutional Issues.* Toronto: CISS.

Murphy, Craig, and Roger Tooze. 1991. 'Getting Beyond the Common-Sense of the "IPE" Orthodoxy', in Roger Tooze and Craig Murphy, eds, *The New International Political Economy.* Boulder, Colo.: Lynne Rienner, 11–32.

Mutimer, David. 2000. *The Weapon State: Proliferation and Framing of Security.* Boulder, Colo.: Lynne Rienner.

Netcorps. 2007. At: <www.netcorps-cyberjeunes.org>. (31 Oct. 2007)

Neufeld, Mark. 1995. 'Hegemony and Foreign Policy Analysis: The Case of Canada as Middle Power', *Studies in Political Economy* 48 (Autumn): 7–29.

———. 1999a. Contribution to Maxwell Cameron, ed., 'Round Table on Canadian Foreign Policy', *Canadian Foreign Policy* 6, 3: 1–24.

———. 1999b. 'Democratization in/of Canadian Foreign Policy: Critical Reflections', *Studies in Political Economy* 58 (Spring): 97–119.

———. 1999c. 'The Pitfalls of Emancipation and Discourses of Security: Reflections on Canada's "Security with a Human Face"', in Samantha Arnold and J. Marshall Beier, eds, *(Dis)Placing Security: Critical Re-evaluations of the Boundaries of Security Studies.* Toronto: York Centre for International and Security Studies, 19–34.

———. 2004. 'Pitfalls of Emancipation and Discourses of Security: Reflections on Canada's "Security with a Human Face"', *International Relations* 18, 1: 109–23.

———. 2007. 'Hegemony and Foreign Policy Analysis: The Case of Canada as a Middle Power', in Bratt and Kukucha (2007: 94–107).

New, W.L. 1998. *Borderlands: How We Talk about Canada.* Vancouver: University of British Columbia Press.

Newman, D. 2003. 'On Borders and Power: A Theoretical Approach', *Journal of Borderland Studies* 18, 1: 13–25.

Niezen, Ronald. 2003. *The Origins of Indigenism: Human Rights and the Politics of Identity.* Berkeley: University of California Press.

Nimijean, Richard. 2006. 'The Politics of Branding Canada: The International–Domestic Nexus and the Rethinking of Canada's Place in the World', *Revista Mexicana de Estudios Canadienses (nueva época)* 11: 67–85.

Nord, Douglas C. 2006. 'Canada as a Northern Nation: Finding a Role for the Arctic Council', in James et al. (2006: 289–315).

North Atlantic Treaty Organization (NATO). 1991. 'The Alliance's Strategic Concept Agreed by the Heads of State and Government Participating in the Meeting of the North Atlantic Council, Rome, 8 November 1991'. At: <www.nato.int/docu/basictxt/b911108a.htm>. (7 Nov. 2008)

———. 1999. 'The Alliance's Strategic Concept: Approved by the Heads of State and Government Participating in the Meeting of the North Atlantic Council in Washington D.C. on 23rd and 24th April 1999'. At: <www.nato.int/docu/pr/1999/p99-065e.htm>. (7 Nov. 2008)

Norton-Taylor, Richard. 2008. 'Peace hopes in Afghanistan hit by aid shortfall', *The Guardian*, 25 Mar., 23.

Nossal, Kim Richard. 1997. *The Politics of Canadian Foreign Policy*, 3rd edn. Scarborough, Ont.: Prentice-Hall.

———. 1998. 'Pinchpenny Diplomacy: The Decline of "Good International Citizenship" in Canadian Foreign Policy', *International Journal* 54, 1: 88–105.

———. 1999. Contribution to Maxwell Cameron, ed., 'Round Table on Canadian Foreign Policy', *Canadian Foreign Policy* 6, 3: 1–24.

———. 2000. 'Home-Grown IR: The Canadianization of International Relations', *Journal of Canadian Studies* 35, 1: 95–114.

———. 2006. 'A Question of Balance: The Cult of Research Intensivity and the Professing of Political Science in Canada', *Canadian Journal of Political Science* 39, 4: 735–54.

———. 2007. 'Analyzing Domestic Sources of Canadian Foreign Policy', in Bratt and Kukucha (2007: 163–76).

———, Stéphane Roussel et Stéphane Paquin. 2007. *Politique internationale et défense au Canada et au Québec*. Montréal: Les Presses de l'Université de Montréal.

NPT. 1970. *The Treaty on the Non-Proliferation of Nuclear Weapons*, UN Department of Disarmament Affairs. At: <disarmament.un.org/wmd/npt/npttext.html>. (7 Nov. 2008)

Nye, Joseph. 2004. *Soft Power: The Means to Success in World Politics*. New York: Public Affairs.

Nyers, P. 2003. 'Abject Cosmopolitanism: The Politics of Protection in the Anti-Deportation Movement', *Third World Quarterly* 24, 6: 1069–93.

O'Connor, Gordon. 2006. 'Speaking Notes for the Honourable Gordon J. O'Connor, PC, MP, Minister of National Defence at the Conference of Defence Associations Institute Annual General Meeting', 23 Feb. Ottawa. At: <www.dnd.ca/site/newsroom/view_news_e.asp?id=1860>. (25 Nov. 2006)

———. 2006. 'Speaking Notes for the Honourable Gordon J. O'Connor, PC, MP, Minister of National Defence for NATO Parliamentary Association Meeting. Quebec City, Quebec', 17 Nov. At: <www.forces.gc.ca/site/newsroom/view_news_e.asp?id=2145>. (15 Dec. 2006)

Ombudsman, Department of National Defence/Canadian Forces. 2002a. *Special Report: Systemic Treatment of CF Members with PTSD*. Ottawa: Department of National Defence, Office of the Ombudsman, Feb.

———.2002b. *Follow-up Report: Review of DND/CF Actions on Operational Stress Injuries*. Ottawa: Department of National Defence, Office of the Ombudsman, Dec.

———.2003. *Off the Rails: Crazy Train Float Mocks Operational Stress Injury Sufferers*. Ottawa: Department of National Defence, Office of the Ombudsman, 6 Mar.

Oseen, Colette. 1999. 'Women Organizing for Change: Transformational Organizing as a Strategy for Feminist Development', in Marilyn Porter and Ellen Judd, eds, *Feminists Doing Development: A Practical Critique*. London: Zed Books, 101–11.

Owens, Heather, and Barbara Arneil. 1999. 'The Human Security Paradigm Shift: A New Lens on Canadian Foreign Policy (A Report of the University of British Columbia Symposium on Human Security)', *Canadian Foreign Policy* 7, 1: 1–12.

Oxfam International. 2006. 'Kicking the Habit: How the World Bank and the IMF Are Still Addicted to Attaching Economic Policy Conditions to Aid', *Oxfam Briefing Paper* 96, Nov.

Pape, Robert. 2005. *Dying to Win: The Strategic Logic of Suicide Terrorism*. New York: Random House.

Paquin, Stéphane. 2001. 'Les relations internationales du Québec et l'unité nationale: Le prolongement international des conflits internes?', *Bulletin d'histoire politique* 10: 85–98.

————, with Louise Beaudoin, eds. 2006. *Histoire des relations internationales du Québec.* Montreal: VLB.

Paris, Roland. 2001. 'Human Security: Paradigm Shift or Hot Air?', *International Security* 26, 2: 87–102.

————. 2007. 'Trilateral Mishmash', *Globe and Mail*, 26 Feb.

Peabody, David. 2005. 'The Challenges of Doing Good Work: The Development of Canadian Forces CIMIC Capability and NGOs', Conference of Defence Associations Institute, Oct. (electronic version).

Pearson, Lester B. 1969. *Partners in Development: Report of the Commission on International Development.* New York: Praeger.

————. 1975. *Mike: The Memoirs of The Right Honourable Lester B. Pearson, Volume 3 1957–1968.* Toronto: University of Toronto Press.

Peterson, V.S. 1992. 'Security and Sovereign States: What Is at Stake in Taking Feminism Seriously?', in V.S. Peterson, ed., *Gendered States.* Boulder, Colo.: Lynne Rienner, 31–64.

Piromalli, Michelle. 2001. *Canada's Domestic Security: The Role of the Canadian Forces in the Event of Quebec Separation.* Halifax: Dalhousie University Press.

Porter, Tony. 1994. 'Postmodern Political Realism and International Relations Third Theory's Third Debate', in Claire Turenne Sjolander and Wayne S. Cox, eds, *Beyond Positivism: Critical Reflections on International Relations.* Boulder, Colo.: Lynne Rienner.

Portes, Jacques. 2001. 'L'émergence de l'histoire du Québec dans le monde?', *Globe* 4: 291–303.

Potter, Evan H. 2002. 'Canada and the New Public Diplomacy', *Discussion Papers in Diplomacy* No. 81. The Hague: Netherlands Institute of International Relations Clingendael, July: 1–19.

————. 2002–3. 'Canada and the New Public Diplomacy', *International Journal* 58, 1: 43–65.

————. 2004. 'Branding Canada: The New Public Face of Canadian Diplomacy', paper presented at the annual meeting of the International Studies Association, Le Centre Sheraton Hotel, Montreal, 17 Mar. At: <www.allacademic.com/meta/p72344_index. html>. (27 Nov. 2008)

Poulin, Philippe. 2002. 'France–Québec: Quarante ans de relations directes et privilégiées', *Bulletin d'histoire politique* 10 (Winter): 144–9.

Pratt, Cranford. 2000–1. 'Ethical Values and Canadian Foreign Policy', *International Journal* 56, 1: 37–53.

————. 2007. 'Dominant Class Theory and Canadian Foreign Policy: The Case of the Counter-Consensus', in Bratt and Kukucha (2007: 176–96).

Preston, Andrew. 2003. 'Balancing War and Peace: Canadian Foreign Policy and the Vietnam War, 1961–1965', *Diplomatic History* 27, 1: 73–111.

Proliferation Security Initiative (PSI). 2008. 'Introduction'. At: <www.proliferationsecurity. info/introduction.html>. (7 Nov. 2008)

Random House Unabridged Dictionary. 2006. At: <dictionary.reference.com/browse/ discipline>. (21 Nov. 2008)

Rao, Aruna, R. Stuart, and D. Kelleher. 1999. 'Roots of Gender Inequality in Organisations', in Aruna Rao, Rieky Stuart, and David Kelleher, eds, *Gender at Work: Organizational Change for Equality.* West Hartford, Conn.: Kumarian.

Rawi, Mariam. 2006. 'Women in Afghanistan Today: Hopes, Achievements and Challenges,' speech delivered to the University of South Australia by a member of the Revolutionary Association of the Women of Afghanistan (RAWA), 27 Apr. At: <www.rawa.org/rawi-speech.htm>. (11 Aug. 2008)

Razack, Sherene. 2004. *Dark Threats and White Knights: The Somalia Affair, Peacekeeping and the New Imperialism*. Toronto: University of Toronto Press.

Reford, Robert. 1992. 'Peacekeeping at Suez, 1956', in Don Munton and John Kirton, eds, *Canadian Foreign Policy: Selected Cases*. Scarborough, Ont.: Prentice-Hall, 58–77.

Regehr, Ernie. 2004a. 'Space and Missile Defence: Sorting Fact from Controversy', *Briefing* 04/3 (Mar.). Waterloo, Ont.: Project Ploughshares. At: <www.ploughshares.ca>.

———. 2004b. 'BMD, NORAD, and Canada–US Security Relations', *Briefing* 04/4 (Mar.). Waterloo, Ont.: Project Ploughshares.

———. 2006. 'NORAD Renewal: Considerations for the Parliamentary Debate', Project Ploughshares, *Briefing* 06/4 (May). Waterloo, Ont.: Project Ploughshares.

Reid, Escott. 1986. 'Canada and the Threat of War', in J.L. Granatstein, ed., *Canadian Foreign Policy: Historical Readings*. Toronto: Copp Clark Pitman, 118–19.

———. 1989. *Radical Mandarin: The Memoirs of Escott Reid*. Toronto: University of Toronto Press.

Rioux, Jean-Sébastien. 2005. *Two Solitudes: Quebecers' Attitudes Regarding Canadian Security and Defence Policy*. Calgary: CDFAI.

Rocher, François. 2007. 'The End of the "Two Solitudes"? The Presence (or Absence) of the Works of French-speaking Scholars in Canadian Politics', *Canadian Journal of Political Science* 40 (Dec.): 833–57.

Rose, Nikolas. 1998. *Inventing Our Selves: Psychology, Power, and Personhood*. Cambridge: Cambridge University Press.

———. 1999. *Powers of Freedom: Reframing Political Thought*. Cambridge: Cambridge University Press.

———. n.d. *Power in Therapy: Techne and Ethos*. At: <www.academyanalyticarts.org/rose2.html>. (1 Mar. 2004)

Rosenberg, Justin. 1994. *The Empire of Civil Society: A Critique of the Realist Theory of International Relations*. London: Verso.

Ross, Jennifer. 2001. 'Is Canada's Human Security Policy Really the "Axworthy Doctrine"?', *Canadian Foreign Policy* 8, 2: 75–93.

Roussel, Stéphane. 1999. 'Velvet Divorce or Violent Breakup? Political Violence in Quebec: Looking Ahead to the Next Referendum', *Strategic Datalink* (Canadian Institute of Strategic Studies) 78 (Apr.).

——— and Jean-Christophe Boucher. 2008. 'The Myth of the Pacific Society: Quebec's Contemporary Strategic Culture', *American Review of Canadian Studies* 38.

———, with Chantal Robichaud. 2001. 'L'élargissement virtuel: un Québec souverain face à l'OTAN (1968–1995)', *Les cahiers d'histoire* 20 (Winter): 147–93.

——— and Charles-Alexandre Théorêt. 2004. 'A "Distinct Strategy"? The Use of Canadian Strategic Culture by the Sovereigntist Movement in Quebec, 1968–1996', *International Journal* 59: 557–77.

Ruggie, Gerard. 1993, 'Territoriality and Beyond: Problematizing Modernity in International Relations', *International Organization* 47, 1: 139–74.

Said, Edward W. 1979. *Orientalism*. London: Vintage Books.

Salter, M.B. 2006. 'The Global Visa Regime and Political Technologies of the International Self', *Alternatives* 31, 2: 167–89.

———. 2007a. 'Governmentalities of the Airport', *International Political Sociology* 1, 1: 49–66.

———. 2007b. 'Canadian Post-9/11 Border Policy and Spill-over Securitization: Smart, Safe, Sovereign?', in M. Orsini and M. Smith, eds, *Critical Policy Studies*. Vancouver: University of British Columbia Press, 299–319.

Sands, Christopher. 2006. 'The Rising Importance of Third-Country Issues in Canada's Relations with the United States', in Andrew Cooper and Dane Rowlands, eds, *Canada Among Nations 2006: Minorities and Priorities*. Montreal and Kingston: McGill-Queen's Press, 125–44.

Saunders, Doug. 2007. 'Ottawa sends Inuit to take on the Hague', *Globe and Mail*, 15 Mar.

Schneider, C.P. 2004. 'Culture Communicates: US Diplomacy That Works', *Discussion Papers in Diplomacy* No. 94. The Hague: Netherlands Institute of International Relations Clingendael. At: <www.clingendael.nl/publications/2004/20040300_cli_paper_dip_issue94.pdf>. (27 Nov. 2008)

Schneider, S., with M. Beare and J. Hill. 2000. *Alternative Approaches to Combating Transnational Crime*, Final Report of the Federal Transnational Crime Working Group (Ottawa). At: <ww2.ps-sp.gc.ca/Publications/Policing/TransCrime_e.pdf >.

Segal, Hugh, ed. 2005. *Geopolitical Integrity*. Montreal: Institute for Research on Public Policy.

Senlis Council. 2006a. *Afghanistan Five Years Later: The Return of the Taliban*. Spring–Summer.

———. 2006b. *An Assessment of the Hearts and Minds Campaign in Afghanistan*. Autumn (electronic version).

———. 2007. *Recommendations to the Independent Panel on Canada's Future Role in Afghanistan*. 1 Dec.

Shani, Giorgio, Makoto Sato, and Mustapha Kamal Pasha, eds. 2007. *Protecting Human Security in a Post 9/11 World*. Basingstoke, UK: Palgrave Macmillan.

Shaw, Karena. 2002. 'Indigeneity and the International', *Millennium: Journal of International Studies* 31, 1: 55–81.

Smith, Gordon. 2007. *Canada in Afghanistan: Is It Working?* Calgary: Canadian Defence and Foreign Affairs Institute, Mar.

Smith, Heather A. 2003. 'Disrupting Internationalism and Finding the Others', in Turenne Sjolander et al. (2003: 24–39).

———. 2005. 'Of Faultlines and Homefronts: A Letter to the Prime Minister', *Canadian Foreign Policy* 12, 1: 3–18.

Smith, Sandy. 1986. 'The Peace Corps: Benign Development?' *The Peace Corps* 7, 13 (Sept.). At: <multinationalmonitor.org/hyper/issues/1986/09/smith.html>. (27 Nov. 2008).

Smith, Steve. 1996. 'Positivism and Beyond', in Ken Booth, Steve Smith, and Marysia Zalewski, eds, *International Theory: Positivism and Beyond*. Cambridge: Cambridge University Press, 1–44.

———. 1997. 'Power and Truth: A Reply to William Wallace', *Review of International Studies* 23, 4: 507–16.

————. 2004. 'Singing Our World into Existence: International Relations Theory and September 11', *International Studies Quarterly* 48, 3: 499–515.

Sokolsky, Joel. 2005. 'Between a Rock and a Soft Place: The Geopolitics of Canada–US Security Relations', in Hugh Segal, ed., *Geopolitical Integrity*. Montreal: Institute for Research on Public Policy, 299–331.

———— and Joseph Jockel. 2000–1. 'Lloyd Axworthy's Legacy: Human Security and the Rescue of Canadian Defence Policy', *International Journal* 56, 1: 1–18.

Spivak, Gayatri Chakravorty. 1999. *A Critique of Postcolonial Reason: Toward a History of the Vanishing Present*. Cambridge, Mass.: Harvard University Press.

Stacey, C.P. 1977. *Canada and the Age of Conflict: A History of Canadian External Policies*, vol. 1: *1867–1921*. Toronto: Macmillan Canada.

Stairs, Denis. 1977. 'Devolution and Foreign Policy: Prospects and Possibilities', in *Options: Proceedings of the Conference on the Future of the Canadian Federation*. Toronto: University of Toronto, Oct., 116–43.

————. 1996. *Canada and Québec after Québécois Secession: 'Realist' Reflections*. Halifax: Centre for Foreign Policy Studies, Dalhousie University.

————. 1999. 'Canada and the Security Problem', *International Journal* 54, 3: 386–403.

Standing Committee on Foreign Affairs and International Trade. 1997. 'Canada and the Circumpolar North: Meeting the Challenges of Co-operation into the Twenty-First Century'. At: <www.parl.gc.ca/35/Archives/committees352/fore/reports/07_1997-04/fore-07-cov-e.html>. (16 Nov. 2008)

Staples, Steven, and Bill Robinson. 2007. 'More Than the Cold War: Canada's Military Spending 2007–08', Canadian Centre for Policy Alternatives, *Foreign Policy Series* 3, 2 (Oct.).

Starnes, John. 1977. 'Québec, Canada and the Alliance', *Survival* 19 (Sept.–Oct.): 212–15.

Statistics Canada. 2003. *Canadian Community Health Survey Cycle 1.2—Mental Health and Well-Being—Canadian Forces (CCHS)*. Ottawa: Statistics Canada.

Stern, Jessica. 2004. 'Beneath Bombast and Bombs, a Caldron of Humiliation', *Los Angeles Times*, 6 June, M1.

Stethem, Nicholas. 1977–8. 'Canada's Crisis (2): The Dangers', *Foreign Policy* 29 (Winter): 56–64.

Stidsen, Sille, and Jens Dahl. 2006. 'Editorial', in Sille Stidsen, ed., *The Indigenous World 2006*. Copenhagen: International Working Group for Indigenous Affairs, 10–13.

Stienstra, Deborah, Claire Turenne Sjolander, and Heather Smith. 2003. 'Taking Up and Throwing Down the Gauntlet: Feminists, Gender, and Canadian Foreign Policy', in Turenne Sjolander et al. (2003: 1–12).

Stockholm International Peace Research Institute (SIPRI). 2007. 'Recent Trends in Military Expenditure'. At: <www.sipri.org/contents/milap/milex/mex_trends.html>. (12 Nov. 2007)

Strategic Counsel. 2006. *A Report to the Globe and Mail and CTV: Perceptions and Views of Canadian Armed Forces Troops in Afghanistan*, 13 Mar. At: <www.thestrategiccounsel. com/our_news/polls/2006-03-13%20GMCTV%20Mar9-12%20(Mar13)%20 Afghanistan%20-%20Rev.pdf>.

————. 2007. *A Report to the Globe and Mail and CTV: The State of Canadian Public Opinion on Afghanistan, Conrad Black*, 16 July. At: <www.thestrategiccounsel.com/our_ news/polls/2007-07-16%20GMCTV%20July%2012-15.pdf>.

Summerfield, Derek. 2001. 'The Invention of Post-Traumatic Stress Disorder and the Social Usefulness of a Psychiatric Category', *British Medical Journal* 322: 95–8.

Sylvester, Christine. 1996. 'The Contributions of Feminist Theory to International Relations', in Steve Smith, Ken Booth, and Marysia Zalewski, eds, *International Theory: Positivism and Beyond*. Cambridge: Cambridge University Press, 254–78.

Taylor, Charles. 1974. *Snow Job: Canada, the United States and Vietnam (1954 to 1973)*. Toronto: Anansi.

Thomsen, Robert C., and Nikola Hynek. 2006. 'Keeping the Peace and National Unity: Canada's National and International Identity Nexus', *International Journal* 61: 845–58.

Tickner, J. Ann. 1997. 'You Just Don't Understand: Troubled Engagement between Feminist and IR Theorists', *International Studies Quarterly* 41, 4: 611–32.

Tiessen, Rebecca. 2003. 'Masculinities, Femininities, and Sustainable Development: A Gender Analysis of DFAIT's Sustainable Development Strategy', in Turenne Sjolander et al. (2003: 108–23).

———. 2004. 'NGO Strategies for Gender Mainstreaming in HIV/AIDS Programming', paper presented at the International Studies Association Conference, Montreal, 17–21 Mar.

Tilly, Charles. 1985. 'War Making and State Making as Organized Crime', in Peter Evans, Dietrich Rueschemeyer, and Theda Skocpol, eds, *Bringing the State Back In*. Cambridge: Cambridge University Press, 169–91.

Trudeau, Pierre. 1963. 'Pearson où l'abdication de l'esprit', *Cité libre* (avril): 7.

Truman, Harry S., Clement Attlee, and William Lyon Mackenzie King. 1945. 'Declaration on Atomic Bomb by President Truman and Prime Ministers Attlee and King, Washington, 15 November 1945', archived by NuclearFiles.org: A Project of the Nuclear Age Peace Foundation. At: <www.nuclearfiles.org/menu/key-issues/nuclear-energy/history/dec-truma-atlee-king_1945-11-15.htm>. (7 Nov. 2008)

Tuch, Hans N. 1990. *Communicating with the World*. New York: St Martin's Press.

Turenne Sjolander, Claire. 2005. 'Canadian Foreign Policy: Does Gender Matter?', *Canadian Foreign Policy* 12, 1: 19–31.

———. 2007. 'Two Solitudes? Canadian Foreign Policy/Politique Etrangere du Canada', *Canadian Foreign Policy* 14, 1: 101–8.

———, Heather A. Smith, and Deborah Stienstra, eds. 2003. *Feminist Perspectives on Canadian Foreign Policy*. Toronto: Oxford University Press.

UNEVOC-Canada. 2002. 'Youth International Internship Program: Creating Overseas Opportunities for Young Canadians', Canadian Centre for UNESCO's International Project on Technical and Vocational Education and Training. At: <www.umanitoba.ca/unevoc/yiip/english/obj.shtml>. (27 Nov. 2008)

United Nations Association in Canada. 2007. 'Canadian Participation in UN Peacekeeping: Chronology'. At: <www.unac.org/peacekeeping/en/un-peacekeeping/fact-sheets/canadian-participation-in-un-peacekeepinga-chro/>.

United Nations Committee on Economic, Social, and Cultural Rights. 2006. *Consideration of the Reports Submitted by States Parties Under Articles 16 and 17 of the Covenant: Concluding Observations of the Committee on Economic, Social, and Cultural Rights (Canada)*. New York: UN.

United Nations Development Programme (UNDP). 1995. 'Redefining Security: The Human Dimension', *Current History* 94, 592: 229–36.

United Nations Sub-Commission on the Promotion and Protection of Human Rights. 2002. *Final Report of the Panel of Experts on the Illegal Exploitation of Natural Resources and Other Wealth in the Democratic Republic of the Congo*. New York: UN.

United States Department of Defence. 2004. *Fact Sheet: Provincial Reconstruction Teams*. Washington, 27 Sept.

United States Department of Justice, Inspector General. 2002. 'The INS Contacts with Two September 11 Terrorists: A Review of the INS's Admissions of Atta and Shehhi, Its Processing of Their Change of Status Applications, and Its Efforts to Track Foreign Students in the United States'.

United States Department of State. 2005. Remarks of Secretary of State Condoleezza Rice, 'Announcement of Nominations of Karen P. Hughes as Under Secretary of State for Public Diplomacy and Public Affairs and Dina Powell as Assistant Secretary of State for Educational and Cultural Affairs', 14 Mar. At: <www.state.gov/secretary/rm/2005/43385. htm>. (16 Nov. 2008)

———. 2006. *Fact Sheet: Provincial Reconstruction Teams*. Washington: Office of the Spokesman, 31 Jan.

Valpy, Michael. 2007. 'This is Stephen Harper's war', *Globe and Mail*, 18 Aug.

van Ham, Peter. 2001. 'The Rise of the Brand State', *Foreign Affairs* 80, 5: 2–6.

Van Rooy, Alison. 1998. 'A New Diplomacy? How Ambassadors (Should) Deal with Civil Society Organizations', in Robert Wolfe, ed., *Diplomatic Missions: The Ambassador in Canadian Foreign Policy*. Kingston, Ont.: School of Policy Studies, Queen's University, 145–61.

———. 2002. 'Branding Territory: Inside the Wonderful Worlds of PR and IR Theory', *Millennium* 31, 2: 249–69.

———. 2008. 'Place Branding: The State of the Art', *Annals, American Academy of Political and Social Science* 616, 1: 126–49.

Vengroff, Richard, and Jason Rich. 2006. 'Foreign Policy by Other Means: Paradiplomacy and the Canadian Provinces', in James et al. (2006: 105–30).

Verner, Josée. 2007. 'Notes for a speech by the Honourable Josée Verner, Minister of International Cooperation, at the breakfast at the Board of Trade of Metropolitan Montreal, International Development Week 2007, Montreal, Quebec', 6 Feb. At: <www. acdi-cida.gc.ca/cidaweb/acdicida.nsf/En/RAC-2511126-LSX?OpenDocument>.

Vickers, R. 2004. 'The New Public Diplomacy: Britain and Canada Compared', *British Journal of Politics and International Relations* 6, 2: 182–94.

Wæver, O. 1995. 'Securitization and Desecuritization', in R. Lipschutz, ed., *On Security*. New York: Columbia University Press, 46–86.

———, B. Buzan, M. Kelstrup, and P. Lemaitre. 1993. *Identity, Migration and the New Security Order in Europe*. London: Pinter.

Walker, R.B.J. 1984. 'The Territorial State and the Theme of Gulliver', *International Journal* 39, 3: 529–52.

———. 1993. *Inside/Outside: International Relations as Political Theory*. Cambridge: Cambridge University Press.

———. 2002. 'After the Future: Enclosures, Connections, Politics', in Richard Falk, Lester Edwin Ruiz, and R.B.J. Walker, eds, *Reframing the International: Law, Culture, Politics*. New York and London: Routledge, 3–25.

Walters, W. 2006. 'Border/Control', *European Journal of Social Theory* 9, 2: 187–203.

———. 2008. 'Putting the Migration-Security Complex in its Place', in L. Amoore and M. de Goede, eds, *Risk and the War on Terror*. London: Routledge, 158–77.

Weber, Cynthia. 1999. *Faking It: US Hegemony in a 'Post-Phallic' Era*. Minneapolis: University of Minnesota Press.

———. 2005. *International Relations Theory: A Critical Introduction*. London: Routledge.

Weber, Max. 1958. *The Protestant Ethic and the Spirit of Capitalism*, trans. Talcott Parsons, Introduction by Anthony Giddens. New York: Charles Scribner's Sons.

Welsh, Jennifer. 2005. *At Home in the World: Canada's Global Vision for the 21st Century*. Toronto: HarperCollins.

Wendt, Alexander. 1994. 'Collective Identity Formation and the International State', *American Political Science Review* 88, 2: 384–96.

West, D.A. 1991. 'Re-searching the North in Canada: An Introduction to the Canadian Northern Discourse', *Journal of Canadian Studies* 26, 2: 108–19.

Whitaker, R. 2004–5. 'Securing the "Ontario–Vermont Border": Myths and Realities in Post-9/11 Canadian–American Security Relations', *International Journal* 60, 1: 53–70.

———. 2005. 'The Investment Climate in Afghanistan: Exploiting Opportunities in an Uncertain Environment', World Bank Finance and Private Sector Development Unit, South Asia Region, Dec.

Whitworth, Sandra. 1998. 'Gender, Race, and the Politics of Peacekeeping', in Edward Moxton-Brown, ed., *A Future for Peacekeeping?* Basingstoke: Palgrave Macmillan, 176–91.

———. 2003. 'Militarized Masculinities and the Politics of Peacekeeping: The Canadian Case', in Turenne Sjolander et al. (2003: 76–89).

———. 2004. *Men, Militarism, and UN Peacekeeping: A Gendered Analysis*. Boulder, Colo.: Lynne Rienner.

Wibben, Annick. 2008. 'Human Security: Toward an Opening', *Security Dialogue* 39, 4: 455–62.

Wilkinson, Paul. 2007. *International Relations: A Very Short Introduction*. Oxford: Oxford University Press.

Wilmer, Franke. 1993. *The Indigenous Voice in World Politics: Since Time Immemorial*. Newbury Park, Calif.: Sage.

Wolfe, Robert. 1998. 'The Many Diplomatic Missions of Canada's Ambassadors', in Robert Wolfe, ed., *Diplomatic Missions: The Ambassador in Canadian Foreign Policy*. Kingston, Ont.: School of Policy Studies, Queen's University, 1–27.

World Bank. 2008. 'Canada and the World Bank: Working towards a Better Future for Afghanistan', 16 Jan. At: <web.worldbank.org/WBSITE/EXTERNAL/TOPICS/EXTSOCIALPROTECTION/0,,contentMDK:21615898~menuPK:282642~pagePK:64020865~piPK:149114~theSitePK:282637,00.html>. (25 Jan. 2008)

Young, Allan. 1997. *The Harmony of Illusions: Inventing Post-Traumatic Stress Disorder*. Princeton, NJ: Princeton University Press.

Zalewski, Marysia. 2006. 'Distracted Reflections on the Production, Narration, and Refusal of Feminist Knowledge in International Relations', in Brooke A. Ackerly, Maria Stern, and Jacquie True, eds, *Feminist Methodologies for International Relations*. Cambridge: Cambridge University Press, 42–61.

Index